ISRAELI
PREOCCUPATIONS

Israeli Preoccupations

DUALITIES OF A CONFESSIONAL CITIZEN

HAIM CHERTOK

FORDHAM
UNIVERSITY
PRESS
NEW YORK
1994

Library of Congress Cataloging-in-Publication Data

Chertok, Haim
    Israeli preoccupations: dualities of a confessional citizen / by Haim Chertok.
    p.   cm.
        ISBN 0-8232-1546-6 (cloth) : $25.00 — ISBN 0-8232-1547-4 (pbk.) :
    $16.95
    1. Chertok, Haim.   2. Jews, American—Israel—Biography. 3. Yeroham
(Israel)—Biography.   4. Israel—Social life and customs.   5. Women—
Israel—Social conditions.   I. Title.
DS113.8A4C46   1994
956.9405'4'092—dc20
[B]   93-45638
                                                                                                        CIP

PUBLICATION OF THIS BOOK
WAS AIDED BY A GRANT FROM
THE HENRY AND IDA WISSMANN FUND

Printed in the United States of America

To Jen, Ted, Shai, and Miri,
residents of so many of these pages

CONTENTS

ACKNOWLEDGMENTS

In different form, portions of *Israeli Preoccupations* first appeared in a varicty of journals including *Challenge, Congress Monthly, Hadassah, The Jerusalem Post, Jewish Frontier, The Jewish Review, Midstream, The Nation, The New York Times*, and *Tikkun*. I also wish to thank Harrison [Hon] Lee, an old and good friend, for his generosity, and present and past editors at Fordham University Press.

ISRAELI PREOCCUPATIONS

INTRODUCTION.

WITNESSING IN THE NEGEV

THE SEVENTEENTH of Tammuz of the Jewish calendar year is a long, hot midsummer day of fasting and mourning. Unlike the fast day named for obscure Gedaliah or the fast of the first-born that precedes Passover, seventeen Tammuz invariably sneaks up unawares. From year to year it slips my mind whether it commemorates the destruction of the outer walls of Jerusalem preliminary to the destruction of the First Temple, of the Second Temple, or of them both. Whatever the disaster, generally by midafternoon I have succumbed to torpor and headache: fasting strikes me not in the gut but in the shallow sockets behind each eye. Such is my eyewitness to our twin destructions.

In 1976 my family and I passed our first summer as new immigrants to Israel at Moshav Masuot Yitzhak, a religiously observant, communal farming settlement on the road to Ashkelon comprising mainly Ashkenazi Jews of European background. I was surprised to discover that, unlike for the stricter, longer, more generally observed summertime fast of Tisha B'Av, most of the moshav's members, in particular the younger ones, ignored the Spartan fast of Tammuz. For them it is just another day of work in the fields, the chicken coops, or the greenhouses. It was much the same with most of the traditional Sephardic Jews in predominantly Moroccan Yeroham, the Negev town where we live: only relatively few congregants in our synagogue bother observing this abstemious day of summer.

Until what follows, my most memorable fast of Tammuz occurred during my fourth summer in Israel: I was in the midst of my second tour of basic training (at least one too many for any lifetime). The seventeenth of Tammuz, the day when our company was scheduled to make the final and longest of our three cross-country marches, was exceptionally hot. The small group of fasters was assigned to guard

1

the barracks, i.e., to pass the day on our butts. Rafi, a sometime yarmulke-wearer, had surprised the lieutenant with the news that he too usually observed the fast of the seventeenth. Sporting a wry smile, he joined the rest of us at the barracks. By sheerest chance, at noontime three of us spotted Rafi darting from the back door of the dining hall. Though he insisted that feeling faint he had only drunk a glass of water, none of us was persuaded. Particularly during basic training, one needs dollops of help from one's friends to get by. Rafi's breach had effectively severed his connection to the rest of us: both the observant and the nonobservant shunned him for the remaining two weeks of training.

Nearly a decade later the fast of the seventeenth fell on the fourteenth of July, the commemoration of the crumbling of an anti-Temple in a worldlier capital. Both the fall of the Second Jewish Temple and of the Bastille mark historical watersheds. This year, however, nothing quite so earthshaking had been noted in our date-book; nevertheless, several unusual entries stood out. For that evening of July fourteenth—technically, of course, the eighteenth of Tammuz but appertaining to the rhythm of the fast day—my wife and I had been invited to celebrate the wedding of the daughter of one of her coworkers, a Russian immigrant.

Now, a wedding for such a date is highly irregular. (Traditionally, the middle of Tammuz embraces a three-week period during which weddings are not performed.) And on the evening following sundown of the seventeenth itself! Save out of ignorance or contempt, who would schedule a wedding for then? Further, what sort of rabbi would agree to officiate at such a wedding? The whole business was out-of-joint.

Marcia tried to beg off. She came home from work defeated. But there was nothing for it. Like American Jews, Russians tend barely to reproduce themselves. Angelica was the treasured, only child, and Larisa, the doting mother, would never truly forgive such an act of remission. This year, our family custom of breaking our fasts with waffles and coffee would need to be foregone in favor of *perushki* and vodka.

The other date-book notation for that day—Project Renewal—was crossed out, smudged, then rewritten sideways in the crowded square of space. Under the aegis of PR, for seven years mighty Montreal had been linked to the proletarian yeomanry of Yeroham. Groups of visiting Canadians had come again and again. Nearly the entire extensive public works program which has changed the face (if not the image) of our town—the jewel-like library, the repaved main street, the state-of-the-art sports center—has been funded by the good, generous Jews of Montreal. Unconscious as Larisa and Angelica of any Jewish import to the year's fourteenth of July, a delegation of forty Jews from Montreal would be spending much of the day in our Negev town. The director of our community center—the *matnas*—requested that I join them for a late-morning tour of Montreal-funded projects. It would be followed by a festive luncheon at Eli Cohen School.

We fifteen or so English-speaking families in Yeroham are regularly called upon for a variety of such civic chores. Just three weeks earlier, in fact, a dozen visiting Canadians had been apportioned to dine among four Anglo households. Ten days later we would absorb Sylvia, an effervescent nineteen-year-old volunteer, into our household for a week. (Supposedly South African, she turned out to be from Montevideo!)

Nearly always, our display of noblesse oblige turns out better than anticipated. Turning on the tap of hospitality as a hungry bystander at a multicourse Moroccan luncheon on a foodless, drinkless seventeen Tammuz, however, seemed a bit burdensome. I decided someone else could fill the breach while I pursued a less rigorous strategy for getting through to waffles at sunset.

On July twelfth a follow-up call came from the *matnas*. She had received a request from the head of the Montreal delegation that I attend the luncheon. The cause: my eyewitness account contrasting the visit to Yeroham of ultra-nationalist Meir Kahane with that of poet Yehuda Amichai had been featured in the June issue of *Hadassah*, the largest-circulation Jewish monthly in North America, and had been read by some of the visitors. In the end, succumbing to the call of duty and ego, my inner temple of resistance caved in.

As usual for the daytime fasts that punctuate the Jewish year, Marcia and I had set the alarm to go off before dawn so as to fortify ourselves in the waning moments of the Tammuz sixteen. With predawn omelettes under our pajamas' strings, we scarcely endure any duress at all—truth to tell—from this species of half-day fast. At his request, our ten-year-old son rose to join our repast. Determined to fast, this year he would match stomach pangs to clock beats. Since he consented to sip some water during the heat of the afternoon, we in turn consented.

That afternoon, the dining hall at the Eli Cohen School was bedecked with bunting and Maple Leaf flags. About a dozen round tables were laden with plates that the well-met guests were polishing off with gusto. On the makeshift platform, a woman in her late thirties gestured broadly. She was meeting with scant success trying to ride out the squeals of a stampeding microphone. I was beckoned to the central table by the smiling *matnas* director. I had arrived at the right moment.

The aroma of Moroccan grill still permeated the room. It elicited the day's first palpable pang of hunger. The buoyant Canadians wore benevolent smiles, stylish clothes, satisfied expressions. Six local women in aprons and kerchiefs—through an aperture at the far end of the dining hall they could be seen bustling over food and dishes— had produced this tasty feast. Moroccan is, after all, among the most distinguished of Jewish cuisines. At the center table sat a mixed delegation of Yeroham ward-healers and Montreal Jewish leadership major donors. With them sat my neighbor Mia Cohen, a UCLA-educated mathematics professor at Ben-Gurion University, who like me was drafted time and again for sundry chores with the visiting firemen. She threw me a look charged with *significance*—"Here we go again!"

"Haim, come right over here and meet . . ."

Unheard names, warm hands, vigorous grasps. Suntanned men in plaid shorts, women in colorful hats and smiles. Good will, cameras, exuberance. The microphone abated, and the meal clattered to a close of dirty plates. I turned away a waiter who balanced a tray of glazed pastries and dozens of small vessels of pungent Turkish coffee.

A couple in their fifties approached. She: "I am *so* pleased to meet you. We read your article. It was very sensitive." [Thank you.] He: "I had no idea that the politics in Yeroham were so complicated. Do you really like it here?"

"Yes, I suppose I must, but I don't think about that so often," I yelled over the renewed screech of the errant p.a. system. "I've been here ten years now. It's just . . . well . . . home." Before the nose of the overzealous, teenaged waiter who lowered a tempting tray of sticky, honeyed pastries and steamy brew before my own rebel nose, I drew a horizontal line in the air: my version of Israel's universal negative finger. "If I didn't like it, I wouldn't have stayed."

The leader of the Canadian party advanced. "Would you say just a few words to the delegation about Yeroham and what you're doing here, Haim? They would really appreciate an in-depth personal account . . . but you only have five minutes," he added with a significant glance at his watch. "As usual, we're behind schedule. You have no idea," he pursued, picking up his earlier theme, "how significant it is for members of the party and for the whole Montreal Jewish community to hear from someone who actually lives in Yeroham."

I understood. These brightly clad, effervescent visitors are of critical importance to long-time residents of a town so bypassed that except in the immediate environs, until four years ago no road sign signaling its existence could be found. Yeroham and a score of other Israeli towns and neighborhoods that it resembles genuinely need the support of the Jews of the Montreals, the Sydneys, and the Miamis to fund the amenities that make them feel they are making progress.

In contrast, even a cursory glance out of a bus window while riding through most of Israel's non-Jewish towns and villages, unsupported by Bedouin, Druze, or Circassian diasporas, offers a vision of barely relieved bleakness: missing schoolrooms, muddy streets, unrepaired sanitation facilities, poorly equipped recreation centers. The difference may be traced less to outright discrimination by Jerusalem—though there has been that—and more to the solid cash Project Renewal funnels from these philanthropist-tourists in their walking shorts and bright blouses.

I could easily appreciate that the ex-Bronxite who wrote for publications that arrived in their mailboxes would be perceived as a more credible witness, more like one of them, than the "natives"—their affable ex-Moroccan hosts. I could testify that they were not being taken for a ride, that the food, smiles, speeches did not mask some kind of con. The Montrealers did not want to admit that something in them craved such reassurance. But I wordlessly recognized their need and did not consider it either base or baseless. Rising to speak, empty stomach rumbling within, yet once again I rebuffed the darting waiter.

The delegation leader introduced me as though *I* were the visiting celebrity come to join *them*. There was a fine irony in this. In Yeroham, the swathe I cut with my nib is highly circumscribed. Though my Anglo-American friends know that I do not sit idly at home, when I finally sally forth most afternoons, I seem to melt comfortably into the ranks of Yeroham's unemployed. Most of my fellow townspeople have little conception of a "writer" who does not spend most of his time writing Torah scrolls and mezzuzahs. *Free lance* does not signify. How could one possibly fill one's table writing stories about happenings in a place many of them habitually denigrate? Now suddenly, before a generous slice of local officialdom, a lightning bolt of honor—*koved*—was being hurled by these much-valued visitors from afar. Puzzling for them, for me it tasted like unsought nectar on a day of fasting.

I decided to strike a mildly jarring theme in my five minutes of local fame. Yes, thanks to Montreal, Yeroham *looked* much nicer than formerly. Yes, the Montreal college students who came every summer as volunteers to work with youngsters in Yeroham's summer camps did wonderful work. Yes, thanks to the generosity of the Jews of Montreal, Yeroham could offer improved recreational and educational services. Still, the town's real need was not for further philanthropy. Yeroham was welfare-ridden, lacking a diversity of employment opportunities; yet surely, there were hundreds of successful Jewish entrepreneurs in Montreal. Could not a consortium of them investigate avenues for investment in new businesses or manufacturing that could provide employment opportunities in Yeroham, particularly for the young people just out of the army or completing their university studies?

My auditors were polite, but the questions that followed tacked a familiar course.

"How did you happen to come to Yeroham?"

"When will they finish paving the road over the hills from Beersheba?"

Seated, mildly disconsolate, again I waved off the smiling tempter who proffered his cursed tray of coffee and pastries. At the podium Mia offered her polished, five-minute account of Yeroham's serio-comic origins. Under my eyelids, my head began to thrum. Mia was followed by a woman speaking in French who announced that she had just been informed that the seventeenth of Tammuz was a day of fasting. Not only had they all enjoyed a delicious meal, but (pointing toward the perspiring mamas in the kitchen) it had been prepared by women who that day had not eaten! An appreciative round of applause broke out. It was scarcely my place to scotch the alleged virtue of my fellow townswomen. Still, I felt vaguely culpable. How could it be that my notions, so "sensitive" or "exciting" when perused in dens and parlors in Montreal, could be so readily discounted in person?

It was after three o'clock, time to depart at last. On their agenda still remained a quick look at Yeroham's artificial lake—the only one in the Negev—and then a return to their five-star Jerusalem domicile for dinner. Canadians began filing toward the door. Several noted my address and the title of a soon-to-be published book. A woman who owned a travel agency spoke of bringing people to Yeroham in the future. Could we make a video of a typical Moroccan repast? Might we investigate opening a tourist restaurant?

"Well, we don't get all that many overseas tourists . . ." I began to explain.

"Make me the video!" she ordered. "You'll get tourists. I'll see to it."

Outside, the red, pendulous sun glared down without pity. Within five minutes, most of the Montrealers had filed onto the waiting bus. Standing in the shadow cast by Eli Cohen School, I joined a group that included Mia Cohen, the deputy mayor, the *matnas* director, a Project Renewal functionary from Beersheba, and a Jewish Agency official. From inside the bus, several visitors were waving good-naturedly in our direction. Among the standing party, I alone ventured a modest flourish in return. The visitors had come to see how their generosity had been translated into good works. The officials had done their part to show them what they thought they wanted. The occasion had proceeded smoothly, professionally. Even I—rankest amateur in the company—basked for the moment in the warmth of having played my part passingly well.

Just then, IT happened. She was a doughy, heavy-limbed, sour-faced woman, probably in her early thirties but looking older by ten years. With one hand she pushed a bawling infant in a stroller; with the other she tugged at a three-year-old who looked quizzically at the bus. Had she materialized just two minutes later, she would have encountered no one. As it was, she trailed in her wake a gray, adventitious storm cloud that spread a menacing shadow over our picnic. The youngster was gnawing into a half-loaf of bread. The woman herself could have been the harridan from *Maggie, A Girl of the Streets*. (Why was the austere spirit of Stephen Crane dogging my day of fast? Was Yeroham Yellow Sky?) As if she naturally belonged, as if she fitted in, fulfilled our tableau, she took her place beside our little, waiting, curbside group.

"Who are they?" she demanded of no one in particular. No one replied. "Oh, *I* know who you are," she called out toward the mute tourist bus in Moroccan-syncopated Hebrew. "Did you have a good time in our beautiful Yeroham?" she caustically inquired. "I *bet* you did, and I bet they kept you from meeting any real people while you were here, didn't they?" Dropping her child's hand as if to puncture holes in the opaque, enveloping air, she raised her voice to a shriek. "LOOK AT ME! Just LOOK!" Her straining face had visibly purpled.

Matnas director Pini stared fixedly toward the dining hall, deputy mayor Mordi—as if checking for signs of precipitation—inspected the blank, neutral sky. The two Jewish Agency functionaries conversed with each other as if the woman were a wholly spectral visitation. Mia and I exchanged an incredulous glance. Was this daymare really happening? What dybbuk of the absurd had dispatched a wraith along this street at this very moment? Were the special effects that had been conspired in conjointly by hosts and visitors, was the whole shebang going to dissipate in the presence of this screaming woman and her two yowling kids? What could possibly appease the profundity of her wrath, her explosive compound of show biz and genuine misery?

As if triggered by the gesticulating figure, a current of renewed excitation seemed to flow from the somnolent bus. Misconstruing, the visitors raised hands again to signal cheerfully in our direction: they were waving at us, at the woman! If either of us had caught the other's eye, we would have broken into incoherent laughter. Trying to smother the comic incongruity, nervously stroking my beard, I raised my hand as if to acknowledge the final salutes of the exuberant visitors. *When would the bus start to move?*

"MY HUSBAND IS OUT OF WORK," the poor woman screeched in a pitch rivaling the microphone that earlier had poured decibels over us. "After ten years with the Border Patrol, they fired him. I have these two and three others at home. I CAN'T WORK. All we eat is BREAD." I looked at her buster of a boy-child. Sure enough, as if rehearsed on cue, he devoured a chunk of pasty dough.

The woman turned from the bus to confront Mordi and Pini. "We don't want your charity. We don't want welfare. WE WANT TO WORK. I don't have enough money to feed my family. GIVE US WORK. Why do you hire only the Arabs? What about us poor Jews?"

Mute spectators to her desperate testimony, not one of us replied, not one of us moved. We all could hear the revving of the bus's motor.

Pull out, damn it! we silently willed. The sad-faced woman looked at us with scorn and incomprehension, and then again turned toward the busload of sated, dozy, good Canadians in their air-conditioned, interior bullet. The pause was a prelude to a final eruption of dry rain and thunder.

"GO! GO! KEEP YOUR SHITTY MONEY! A lot of good shitty rich people like you do for the likes of me!"

Sure enough, as if triggered by her scatological outburst, the sleek vehicle began to pull away from the curb. A final flurry of waves was aimed in our direction. Pini, Mordi, all of us responded mechanically. Though I could not discern more than the bold outlines of the faces behind the green-tinted windows, I could imagine the fixed expressions, the twin moons of pleasure and satisfaction behind each thick, lime-hued rectangle of shatterproof glass. On an obscure fast day, no less, how good of the local people to have prepared such a fine meal to celebrate their visit from the New World!

The bus turned the corner and disappeared from view. The spokeswoman who had borne witness for *les miserables* of Yeroham retrieved her three-year-old's fingers and pushed up the mild incline of sun-splashed Eli Cohen Street. It was easy to imagine her encouraging the charge of the Bastille.

At a quicker pace, Mia and I walked toward our homes in our comfortable Ben-Gurion neighborhood. It was breathlessly hot, but I confess that all the way home we chuckled nervously. We had ad-libbed silent, featured parts in a bittersweet episode. Despite close acquaintance with the character type, in spite of her having plucked the very strings whose theme I myself had struck not thirty minutes earlier, the two of us were no better able than the local politicos or the innocents from Canada to respond to her pleas. Had hunger so addled my brains that I could feel little more than annoyance toward the woman who that day had come so perilously close to stealing the final scene of *A Midsummer Day's Fast?*

Since I first came to the Negev, hardly a day has passed when I have not been surprised, angered, bemused, startled, or otherwise deeply moved by an unexpected fusion of person and event. The years, in fact, have transformed me into something of a close observer of my local scene. Ruminating over larger episodes and personal transactions that have passed since the publication of *Stealing Home* in 1988—years of intifada and peace talks, of Russians and Ethiopians, of my own forward motion into my fifties and grandfatherhood—I realize that these compose the intellectual, political, and . . . yes . . . moral accounts of both a reluctant eyewitness and sometime participant in Israeli fasts and festivities, frustration and frivolity, remorseful days and material ways.

Ranging from the critical and adversarial to the credulous and celebratory, the following accounts trace a running tab of endemic irritations that persistently erupt from beneath the surface of the Israeli body politic—the Palestinian presence, the marginality of Jewish women, sores that refuse either to disappear or to heal of their own accord. No one, however, can fix too exclusively on abstract preoccupations without paying a grievous human toll. The longest section, therefore, narrows its focus to the daily quirks, vexations, and beguilements of seventeen years of awakening and lying down in a very particular locale in the Negev. Finally, unable to leave the past utterly to its own devices, like Lot's woeful spouse, I close with saline, backward glimpses of the American Jewish community I once thought to have left definitively behind.

Once more at home, I felt the onset of the inevitable headache that accompanies a day of fasting. No termagant, this was a familiar old demon whose arrival I anticipated. He was, in fact, a trifle late. Before getting ready to celebrate that evening's wedding, I lay down for an hour of rest. I could do worse than hope that, for readers, plaint, headache, and animadversion succumb in the end to waffles and ice cream or an evening celebration in a Beersheba of their own.

PART ONE.
PALESTINIAN WRONGS
AND RIGHTS

"What do Arabs dream about?" asks the painter, who as expected sat
himself down at my table. "What do they dream about?"

Anton Shamas
(*Arabesques*)

PALESTINIAN WRONGS
AND RIGHTS

A S THIS is being written, the peace process between Israel and Jordan, Lebanon, Syria, and the Palestinians is well into its second year. Surviving the temptations of pessimism and excessive optimism, it has now passed into the toddler stage. Press and politicians alike refer to its stages as "rounds," as though speaking not of peace talks but of a championship fight. However frustrating they are, these peace rounds have been infinitely preferable to armed hostilities. No, another round of war does not feel probable, but neither is it entirely inconceivable . . . yet. On the other hand, that a sunny peace of good feelings should soon break out with our neighbors, with the Palestinians, or even among ourselves does not feel imminent. Such has been the equivocal measure of our progress.

It was about four years ago when I became conscious of renewed intensification of peace activity at Israel's grass roots. I received a phone call to come to Beersheba to attend a planning meeting to establish a Negev chapter of Oz Veshalom (Strength and Peace), a dovish organization—more a club, actually—of observant Jews. Two weeks earlier an Oz Veshalom meeting at Jerusalem's Khan Theater had surprisingly attracted an overflow crowd, many of them turning out for the first time. Several weeks later came a second call, this one about a bus leaving Beersheba for a Tel Aviv rally of Shalom Achshuv (Peace Now), Israel's best-known peace organization.

The following week Shalom Achshuv sponsored its very first public meeting in Yeroham. Among the speakers was PLO-connected lawyer Ziad Abu Ziad, the first Palestinian in anyone's memory to address a gathering in any Negev development town. Although he didn't receive a rapturous welcome, nearly one hundred appeared and listened to him with respect and close attention.

After years of quiescence, there seemed to be movement, the fruit

13

of a general, almost visible striving among many Israelis for disengagement and peace with the Palestinians. It was distress in Kfar Saba, Haifa, and Ashkelon, not, after all, guilty consciences in Stockholm or manifestoes in Manhattan that had forced Yitzhak Rabin to desist from Arab-bashing when he served as defense minister under Yitzhak Shamir. It was not British or American but Israeli protest that had led a Likud justice minister to declare that Israeli soldiers should be explicitly informed that the exercise of force on prisoners for the purpose of punishment, for example, or humiliation was manifestly illegal.

The vast majority of Americans never attended even a single demonstration against the war in Vietnam. Nor could it honestly be claimed that anything close to a majority of Israelis was involved in this resurgence of peace activism. Nevertheless, like the comparable situation in America two decades ago, there have been enough of us to make *any* government take notice, to hold it accountable for its actions.

For Palestinians living under Israeli occupation in Judea, Samaria, and Gaza, the measure of success of five summers and winters of sticks, stones, tear gas, bullets, and strikes is not the degree of international attention to their plight and goals. It is the heightened attention of us Israelis. After decades of avoidance, machinists, students, bus drivers, dentists—*all of us*—cannot avoid thinking and talking about the lands we have occupied since 1967. Their residents have become our preoccupation.

All this may sound very strange. Have not Israelis all these years been debating the future borders of this country? Well, ideologues of the expansionist Gush Emunim, the Greater Israel settler movement, certainly are fixated on the subject. I have Jewish friends, both orthodox and secular, who feel that Judea and Samaria are their inviolable patrimony. I understand them. Oh, how well I understand them. Just as Palestinians have nurtured vain hopes that one morning they would awaken to find the offensive Jews had blown away like so much sand or dust, so I have friends who would wish away, bribe away, shoo or shoot away those whom they consider 750,000 interlopers.

Prophetic voices such as Professor Yeshayahu Leibowitz's and analytic ones such as Meron Benvenisti's have repeatedly issued dire warnings. But not until residents of Gaza, Daihaishe, Jenin, and, yes, Jerusalem forced the issue was the average Israeli required to confront the day-to-day reality of the Palestinians. I speak not only of Palestinian nationalists but also of the largely apolitical center and of those labeled "collaborators," almost one thousand of whom have been executed, generally in barbaric fashion, by masked patriotic thugs who parade under names like Eagles of the Intifada.

For beyond barbarity and disgust is the hopeful thing—in the end, the really important thing. After years of averting our gaze, we are at last confronting difficult choices and are engaged in a process that takes fuller account of Palestinian inhabitants of the territories. Yet most private encounters with Palestinians still entail silent pain. Even after the "closure" of the territories, the "black work" in the Israeli economy—agriculture and construction—remains dominated by Arabs. But though they may spend weeks working on a construction project in, say, downtown Beersheba, eye contact is rare and dangerous. The unspoken rules of the New York subways hold sway.

In my English class at Ben-Gurion University last semester sat a small cluster of Arab students. At least to my immigrant eyes and ears, their jeans, swarthiness, and accent did not readily betray their origins. Were it not from their names—Fuad, Suliman, Moen—and youth (since they don't serve in the army, three years younger than Jewish coevals), one would not readily identify them as Arabs. I discovered myself subtly favoring these vulnerable Arab young men and women, markedly encouraging them.

English does not always proceed without false starts or doublethink. "Migration," a new word for some. Birds do it. Bees do it. People . . . uh . . . sometimes. "Nomads" is as close as I veer toward reality. "Exploitation," as in Marxist theory, as in South Africa. Eyes avert. I equivocate. The classroom is simply the wrong forum. Moen and Fuad do not seek gratuitous grief from a well-intentioned American transplant.

My son, home for Shabbat from his army *hesder* yeshiva, described an assembly of eleventh-grade girls he had that week been asked to address at a religious high school. Invited in order to describe what it was like to be on patrol in Gaza, he shared the platform with another, more hawkish *hesdernik* soldier who described *his* experiences in Nablus. It was a "balanced program." The surprising thing, my son reported, was that the audience expressed not only sympathy for Israeli soldiers but also measured comprehension of the position of the Palestinians.

Censors of Jordan's foreign-language television station are sometimes comically inattentive. Ammon would have it that Israel enjoys no weather at all, that its athletes never participate in international sporting events, that its songs are never performed at the Eurovision Song Contest. Yet often enough, their American-made sit-coms incongruously feature Jewish characters or situations. They recently ran a documentary about the condition of the blind in England. One elderly woman was shown being assisted. The commentator identified her as Jewish, and noted that "Jews take especially good care of their elderly."

On the other hand, during the early stages of the intifada, Jordan TV broadcast a miniseries on the life of Martin Luther King, Jr. Week after week it presented its audience with clips of civil rights marches and demonstrations. How, I wondered, could Palestinians watching this footage not recoil at the contrast between what had been their own supine dependence on other Arab countries or the extraterritorial PLO and the self-reliance of African Americans who made themselves into such adept practitioners of auto-emancipation? Indeed, during the week of King's birthday, Israel TV itself ran a program featuring much of the same material.

Now, of course, neither rock-throwing nor ax murders are nonviolent; nor are gasoline bombs the weapons of peaceful resistance. Nevertheless, only the blind could have missed the pivotal point: whether African Americans or women, Palestinians or Jews, the oppressed must liberate themselves. No one can do it for them.

Admittedly, I am not exactly made rapturous by this Palestinian coming-of-age. After all, one target of the teenaged rock-throwers has been my older son, Ted, who faces yet another month's reserve duty this coming year. Still, even when the human spirit is fueled by fanaticism, one is bound to acknowledge and . . . yes . . . to admire the resilience of a spirit that refuses to be cowed by superior force. A sine qua non for the resolution of the situation is now occurring: Palestinians on the ground have been asserting themselves; Israelis now take them seriously.

Only through resistance have they validated themselves as potential partners for negotiations. Would that it had been more in the spirit of Martin Luther King, Jr. Perhaps Israel could have done better than to expel nonviolent advocate Muburak Awak back in 1987. It was just weeks later that another Palestinian on a hang glider wafted into Israel from Lebanon. Before *he* could be dispatched, six Israeli soldiers were dead.

No Israeli government can ever restore the West Bank situation to what it was in the days preceding intifada. Aside from the border patrol, which is heavily composed of members of the Druse community, the army is composed of the general Jewish population, most of whom have little or only moderate sympathy with the larger aspirations of the Jewish settlers in the territories and little heart for extended conflict that inevitably pits them against teenagers and women. Precisely because most of us sense that the display of excessive force against civilians is demeaning, degrading, dehumanizing—that it draws a curtain on the Zionist dream of creating a just society—the Palestinians have indeed had some success in wearing us down.

With less and less reserve, do Israeli Arabs label themselves "Palestinian citizens of Israel." It is, however, extremely unlikely that any sizable number of them would prefer to live in an entity called Palestine that would largely overlap territory occupied by Israel since 1967. What Israelis and Palestinians must resolve is how Jews may continue to live in territory self-administered by Palestinians, perhaps in some mutually agreeable ratio to the number of Arabs residing within Israel.

Without question, such a path entails grievous dangers, but I believe that the status quo, wherein most babies born under Israeli authority are not Jewish, bodes the greater long-term peril. I also recognize that my reading of things may, of course, be egregiously mistaken. Nevertheless, any Israeli government had better comprehend that most Israelis would prefer to bet on the army's ability to deal with a Palestinian entity—attached, semidetached to Jordan, or free-floating—to an indeterminate extension of unrest and turmoil.

I have no illusions about the nature of any Palestine. The rise of Islamic fundamentalism has scotched what had at best been a meager possibility that such a Palestinian entity might adopt genuinely democratic forms in the foreseeable future. Even if effectively demilitarized, this totalitarian parody of Zionism will almost surely inflict brutality on its own citizenry. And it will pose a constant threat to Israel. I grant it all. Nevertheless, the Palestinians cannot forever be denied their greater share of self-government and sovereignty, limited or otherwise. As with much else, we Israelis will make our painful adjustments and learn to live with it.

In the end, the easy part is admitting that the Palestinian case and cause, albeit characteristically buttressed by massive historical distortion, advanced by irresponsible leadership and frequently by barbarous means, at the human level is grounded in a substantial measure of legitimacy. The harder part, especially for an American Jew whose definitive life-choice has been to leave America in order to raise his family in Israel, for whom the continuing existence of Israel, however imperfect, as a democratic Jewish state is his bedrock historical insight and commitment, is what to make of it.

Since the founding of the State of Israel, Palestinian Arabs have suffered the indignity of two occupations: a score of years at the hands of their fellow Arabs from Jordan and thereafter Israel. It bears stating and restating that Palestinian pain has been very largely self-inflicted: Israel accepted the two-state solution proposed by the United Nations in 1947; surrounding Arab nations and the Arabs then residing in pre-state Israel rejected it. Violence and distrust preceded this rejection, to be sure; war, occupation, humiliation, invisibility have been its consequence.

Erupting two generations later, intifada boils down to a Palestinian demand for a recount, for a re-accounting. The Labor Party's victory in the election of 1992 argued that a narrow but clear majority of Israelis (though not necessarily Israeli Jews) are willing to consider the matter very, very seriously. The final outcome of this fresh taking-of-stock is not yet known.

Intifada's greatest success has not been to forge or to legitimize a Palestinian people, and surely not to humanize or to ingratiate themselves in the eyes of very many Israelis. It has simply been to render heretofore invisible men, women, and children visible. Everything, including and especially the stagy Rabin–Arafat handshake and the mutual recognition of the Palestinian Liberation Organization and the State of Israel in September 1993, springs from that.

What follows reflects cross-currents and anxieties, the ambiguities, hopes, apprehensions, and doubts of an American-Israeli Jew struggling to reconcile ideals and personal experience with history and conscience. Do not expect to encounter "a solution," "solutions," or even a totally unified perspective. The unfolding historical situation is too complex, the human reality simply too intractable, for that.

Raised Jewish and "liberal" in America, however, I am blessed and cursed with a double dose of pragmatic optimism. Some would label this stance an unfortunate bias, a symptomatic malady, an incurable syndrome. Nevertheless, after all the bloodshed and pain, I believe that recent fitful approaches toward human amelioration are not an illusion. They are, rather, merely essential. Indeed, I would even argue their inevitability. At bottom, an ancient narrative is being re-played on a wrinkled landscape: sooner or later, after taking prudent measures to ensure survival in case of miscalculation, the children of Jacob have had to cross the Jabbok. Old accounts with Esau have had to be squared. And sooner than many believed possible, Esau, in turn, is coming to acknowledge, accept, and come to terms with Israel. My calculation. My belief.

URI

MEGIDISH, ז"ל *

NO; we were not close friends, merely friendly acquaintances. Curly-haired, gregarious Uri Megidish was more than a decade my junior, but in the way of families in our small North Negev town, our families and lives overlapped. Year after year, the oldest of his four kids occupied the same classroom as Miri, youngest of my four. Looking back, I remember that our most sustained conversations occurred on the two or three evenings a year when we awaited our respective turns outside the classroom door to partake in those ritualized parent–teacher meetings. Some parents would remain inside for twenty or more minutes. Uri and I both knew in advance that our session within would be brief: neither of our children was a "troublemaker."

For a time Uri served as assistant principal at Kol Ya'akov Elementary School. Later, he took over a tougher job: principal of Yeroham's school for disruptive children who could not function in regular classrooms. It was a role for which he was both popular and notably effective. Although his background was Iranian, Uri generally prayed with us at the town's "American congregation." It was much closer to his home than Yeroham's Persian synagogue. Since he had an agreeable voice, especially for Shabbat afternoon *mincha* services, we regulars looked to him to lead the prayers as *hazan*. In short, the Uri I knew was an unusually fine, thoroughly decent person. A good man.

Sometime in 1985 or '86 our paths crossed at Soroka Hospital in Beersheba where my wife and, for a much longer time, his son were both hospitalized. I recall accompanying Miri to visit her sick classmate. It was on that occasion that I first heard from Esther Megidish that she and Uri soon planned to move their family from Yeroham

---

*Zichrono l'vraha, or "May his memory be a blessing."

to start new lives in Gush Katif, a cluster of small Jewish settlements—mainly Orthodox—in the Gaza Strip. I sensed that my jaw fell momentarily open, but I camouflaged my dismay as best I could, ascribing it to regret that Yeroham would lose such a fine family. I wished them much luck.

Would it have served any purpose to disclose what really passed through my mind? Or, perhaps in the light of subsequent events, what purpose was served in smothering it?

Even while still in America, before we made our aliya to Israel, Marcia and I had become members of a group called Garin Neot Midbar—Oasis in the Desert. It was a gathering of twenty or more presumably like-minded American and Canadian families who intended to initiate a communal settlement together "Somewhere in the Negev." Vague and romantic, yes, but it seemed to suit us . . . until three weeks after our arrival in Israel in June 1976. "Somewhere" turned out to be the Gaza Strip, where a string of new Jewish agricultural settlements was being planned. The rationale we were offered was that these settlements would serve as a buffer between two vastly larger Arab urban centers: Khan Yunis and Gaza. Detailed maps and a master plan gave it all an air of tangibility, of reasonableness, indeed, of inevitability.

Increasingly apprehensive, I tried to remain dispassionate. What, really, did I, a raw newcomer to Israel, know about "the situation"? Supported by the Labor government—then, as now, the prime minister was Yitzhak Rabin—the plan perhaps made more sense than I properly understood. One evening I attended a meeting where a Jewish Agency economics expert explained how we new immigrants would manage. He praised the virtues of hothouse tomatoes and flowers, spoke about a new regional school for our children, a new road that would bypass Arab settlements, subsidized villas, a tourism center, access to a virgin beach.

At the close of his presentation, the questions from this audience of potential settlers dealt exclusively with technical matters. Save for one. "Knowing all that you know, would you consider moving your family to live in the Gaza Strip?" I politely ventured.

The speaker's response was instantaneous and, to my ears, patently honest. "Speaking as an economist, I believe that from the national perspective the project isn't viable. Profits will never pay off the highly subsidized initial cost of the hothouses. Speaking personally, I mean as a husband and father of three—do I look crazy to you? Not in a thousand years would I plant myself and my family between Gaza and Khan Yunis."

I was dumbfounded. Here was the *expert* himself. *This* was the Jewish Agency's man's honest opinion. Yet more astonishing, only one or two others of my fellow *gariniks* seemed to pay his reply to my query the slightest mind.

"Just politics," I was later told. "What can you expect from a leftist?"

Yet the longer I considered the whole idea, the nuttier it sounded. How could a few hundred Jewish families possibly serve as a "buffer" between heavy urban concentrations of Arabs, most of them refugees or their offspring? What, really, was the point of setting up agricultural settlements in an area already densely populated and suffering from a chronic shortage of water? In such circumstances, how could the government or the army possibly ensure the safety of our children? Yet ground had already been broken, subsidized hothouses were being imported from Holland, "villas" were being built, and Garin Neot Midbar (later renamed Garin Katif) was already chalked onto planners' flow charts.

A year later, we and several other "leftist" families came to live in Yeroham. By another route, so did Uri and Esther Megidish. A decade after, Uri and Esther bought the hothouse, the virgin beach, the Gaza dream that Marcia and I had rejected, and for six years we lost touch with them . . . until the day after the festival of Purim in March 1993. The lead item on the morning news broadcast was the shocking news that Uri Megidish, father of four, resident of a moshav in the Gaza Strip, had been axed and knifed to death in his van, close by his greenhouse. The brutal murder was committed by two teenaged Arab workers who had worked for him for three weeks.

As in an old, resilient script, immediate repercussions followed a well-worn pattern: Gaza Strip settlers violently protested a lack of adequate protection; government spokesman Mota Gur elucidated how terrorism would never deter Israel from seeking a political solution; the PLO's Fatah claimed "responsibility." The BBC reported the murder of Uri Megidish in its usual taciturn fashion: a sixteen-year-old Arab in Tulkarm and another in the Gaza Strip were killed by Israelis following "the funeral of a Jewish settler." Details about just how that Jewish settler came to be butchered did not merit mention.

A succession of Israeli governments—Labor-led in 1976, the subse-

quent Likud hegemony under Begin and Shamir, the brief Peres–
Shamir coalition, and now Labor once more—has exercised
consistent bad faith with the Israeli people. No, for the most part they
are not guilty of promulgating blatant lies . . . not exactly. But just
days after the murder of Uri Megidish, Housing Minister Ben-Elazar,
yielding to public pressure, agreed to accelerate construction of new
houses in Katzrin, the major Israeli center on the Golan, *just as
though there was little question that the Golan Heights would forever
remain under Israeli jurisdiction.*

No, no arms were ever twisted to force anyone to move to Yamit. Or
to the Golan. Or to the West Bank. And no one forced Uri Megidish to
move his family from Yeroham to the Gaza Strip. Nevertheless, over
the years Israeli governments have fostered conditions that have made
options that should have been nonstarters sound tantalizing to some
of our finest young people. For this, for the consequent agonizing loss
of a growing congregation of Megidishes, it seems to me that they
cannot escape a considerable degree of culpability. It makes me very,
very angry.

As for combating random terror emanating from any of the Pales
tinian organizations is concerned, this is one Israeli leftist who con-
fesses the sad necessity of countenancing most of the protective
countermeasures for which the State of Israel is ritualistically con-
demned by human rights organizations (such as Amnesty International), organizations which implicitly subsume and justify such
heinous acts as the murder of Uri Megidish under the head "national
self-determination."

Only late in the spring of 1993 did the Rabin led Labor government
begin to speak with more clarity and frankness to the electorate: yes,
part or all of the Golan Heights would be expendable in return for a
"real peace" with Syria. Yes, not all the West Bank would necessarily
remain forever under Israeli control. No, no more settlements would
be approved in the Occupied Areas.

I approve of this policy, but the fact remains that since 1967 many
thousands of Israeli families have purchased subsidized dreams based
upon illusions, upon implicit lies, upon unasked and unanswered
questions, and upon a silent collusion of a succession of ideologically
rigid or cynical governments. Of late, a number of them have been
new immigrants from the former Soviet Union for whom not "politics"
but good mortgage terms were paramount. Back in 1976, most of us

new American immigrant members of Garin Neot Midbar were much the same. Because the subtext of Gush Katif was that the government of Israel considered the Gaza Strip kosher, Uri Megidish, father of four, could have been any of my erstwhile comrades . . . yes . . . could conceivably have been the father of Jen, of Ted, of Shai, and of Miri. Almost as much as the killing itself, this realization embitters and angers me in equal measure.

. . . AND LEAVE
THE DRIVING
TO US

THE RABIN government's response to the surge of random murders of Jewish civilians early in 1993, mainly by Hamas terrorists aiming to throttle the peace talks (secondarily by Fatah terrorists striving to maintain credibility), was the temporary deportation of 415 Hamas and Islamic Jihad activists, principally from the Gaza Strip—an action that Arab publicists exploited ad nauseam in the international media. This was followed in March 1993 by the closure of pre-'67 Israel to all but a relatively small fraction of Arab day-workers. At least in its first months this effective reification of the former Green Line severely damaged the economic well-being of much of the Arab populace in the Occupied Areas and caused heavy strain on the construction and agricultural sectors of the Israeli economy.

Oddly unaffected by this closure, *as if nothing unusual had happened*, the largely empty #440 bus out of Beersheba still continued to wend its shockingly ordinary, north-northeast way toward Jerusalem via Hebron. Shaving about a half-hour off the roundabout, alternative #446 route, the #440 flies like a crow along the "scenic," ridge-line route through . . . a conundrum for the congenitally conflicted: (a) Judea, (b) the territories, (c) the West Bank, (d) Occupied Jordo-Palestine, (e) b, c, and d (f) All of the Above. The best answer of the moment often seems to hinge on the headlines of the morning.

One morning in April of 1993, preferring to wait thirty minutes to board the crowded #446 and to take its swooping, crescent path to Jerusalem via Kiryat Gat, two women in line in front of me declined the #440. Five years ago a ride through (f) was never exactly routine, but by April of '93 it could serve as a viable, ever-accessible alternative

25

to mountain-climbing in Nepal. I have one friend who refuses to travel to Jerusalem via Hebron on grounds of principle. I know others who make a particular point to take *this* route to Jerusalem. Out of tune with both positions, when I want to go to Jerusalem, I simply take the first available bus. In fact, the odds against encountering trouble along the way are long; but, politics and principles aside, what I could be sure of from past experience was that the #440 would harum-scarum through the streets and the hairpin twists along Derech Hevron less sedately than I would prefer.

Most of my fellow passengers, young men and women clasping rifles across their laps or between their knees, wore army fatigues. Two swarthy young men in jeans seated across from each other near the back door were probably Arabs. Directly to my front sat a pudgy, bearded man in his thirties, dark, curly hair tufting out from under a black, crocheted *kippa*. Next to him, her hair concealed by a flowery, blue kerchief, sat a young, prim-smocked woman. On their laps perched two little girls in matching dresses. Pale blue.

"Esti, sit still," the woman murmured in Hebrew tinged by distinctly American vowels.

Before we had even cleared Beersheba's industrial zone, several of the soldiers had slumped in their seats. Minutes later the two young women soldiers in khaki slacks, knees pressed against the backs of the seat in front, dozed upright. The driver was also in his twenties. If you're over forty on the #440, you may as well be 140.

Through the rearview mirror my eyes met those of the driver surveying his morning load. These drivers don't normally carry weapons; but the #440 isn't any old run, and he seemed alert to sudden eventualities. For practitioners of intifaddish pastimes, automobiles and buses may serve the same lethal purpose as boulders or bullets. Across from me the lower window had imploded into a beautiful, nearly symmetrical asterisk. It looked like a crippled snowflake or perhaps an Eliot-esque crustacean clawing around the bottom of the sea. The poet-artist? Probably some Mustapha or Mohammed who, had his parents moved a decade ago to Los Angeles, might have been a star Little League hurler. With uncanny aptness, the bus radio blared "Rock Around the Clock."

At Omer, last regular pickup before the #440 abandoned cozy, pre-'67 Israel, three gangly, high-school–aged yeshiva students, ritual fringes dangling from the shirtwaists, boarded our lithe, red submarine. (*Their* buses are green and clunky.) Three intrusive beeps on the bus radio. The driver automatically raised the volume ever louder so that everyone, even the sleepers, could attend to the hourly news. The faces of my fellow passengers disclosed not a flicker of interest.

Then something new: on a gentle slope to the left of the highway, at the point topography proclaimed the old border, an impromptu, higgledy-piggledy parking lot loomed. Here is where Arabs with permission to work in Israel leave their vehicles early in the morning and proceed to working places in special buses. Late in the afternoon, buses transport them back to this checkpoint, their private cars, their private lives. As if zigzagging an Alpine slalom course in slow motion, the #440 glided through one, two, three figure eights around the oil drums that now blocked the center of the highway. Private vehicles bearing plates of black on orange, telltale Israeli escutcheon, were lined ten or twelve deep in both directions. Their documents were checked, questions perfunctorily asked, and momentary eye contact effected. At military road blocks, however, the #440 is privileged. Motioned to keep moving by a smiling teenaged soldier, our driver navigated one-armed, in second gear all the way.

With a series of twists and curves the bus careened up, up, and around. Here, undulating hills are ochre and light brown. Were this California, them thar hills would be "golden."

My eye gladdened to sheaves standing neatly in patterns to the left of the road. In the far distance, several tiny figures—children, I thought—bounced along on the back of a donkey. Through the fractured pane, I stared fixedly at a flock of black goats. Closer to the road, a shepherd leaning his weight against a stick, his head covered with a flowing white cloth, glanced blankly toward the bus. Framed by my shattered glass, he could have been a dwarfish figure in a Flemish landscape—one in need of restoration.

Just around a bend, a stone quarry. Several workers operated a crane; others seemed to move pointlessly around two great piles of rock, crushed into gravel, a.k.a. stones. A dirt road wriggled up the hillside to the right. A sign identified its destination as TENE, an army settlement, or *nachal*.

Like a toy on the landscape, the #440 held to the center of the road as it twisted and rose. Both to the left and to the right, minute agricultural, flattened, terraced patches flowed past. Vegetables. Olive trees. These farmers still rode donkeys; but then, the hillsides really are not much suited for mechanized agriculture. The governing Israeli myth still holds that only Jews are capable of greening the land: "Read Mark Twain! Read how barren it was when Melville visited." But *these* native agriculturalists—mostly women—seemed to be doing very well at making every square inch count. Almost surely some of the lettuce, peppers, and onions sold at my local *shuk* had been picked not far from here.

The highway narrowed into the main street of Dhaririya. Square buildings, each framed by a bit of land, perched over hillsides. The bus slowed and stopped, then disgorged two soldiers in front of the town's largest building. Topped by a blue-and-white flag, it was local Israeli military headquarters. On former occasions when I had ridden through Dhaririya on a market day, goats and sheep filled the highway and the #440 could little more than creep. Starting up again, it would slam-bang through town like a skier down a slope. The residents, long used to Israeli vehicles hurdling through their narrow streets, pointedly ignored us.

Now the bus slowed behind a truck delivering bread. Odd: to my fleeting glance, rather than flat, Arab-style loaves, these were torpedo-shaped, like Israeli bread. Like our bus. I gawked through my snow-flaked glass at the alien life to the left, then to the right. At the edge of the road an elderly woman, her heavy, cloth-covered load balanced on her head, tugged on a donkey. Long after she had dwindled in the rearview mirror to the dimensions of an ant, I could visualize her heavy gait, her stolid frame, her impassive face.

At the northern edge of town, where the houses were strung like beads along the highway, the #440 again slowed in traffic. Junior high school kids lined the side of the road. They were, of course, exquisitely aware of the transitory presence of the 7:45 out of Beer-sheba. It passed, at this place, at this time, six days a week. Most of the youngsters disdained looking in our direction, but one—suddenly turning—sought out passing eyes with which to connect if only through the thick, green-tinted glass. I alone obliged him and was instantaneously repaid by a cocked arm. My lips parted, but before I could squawk, the raised arm had relaxed and his face collapsed into a mocking grin.

The untossed, weightless missile reminded me of Marianne Moore's imaginary garden. Inhabited by real toads. The feeling of menace was heavy, not imaginary.

Out of town at last, our bus now labored behind a gravel truck that, like some great, defecating monster, deposited a thin, steady, turdy trickle in our path. What with the convolutions of the road, oncoming vehicles, and laden wagons, it took our driver several miles to lap the beast. Was the truck driver smiling? In the field, women and girls, heads covered, stooped at their work, a sight familiar to anyone used to driving in central California, say on Highway 99 from Fresno to Bakersfield.

There were fewer Israeli jeeps on the road, fewer Israeli flags mounting outposts than I had noticed on previous trips. I glanced over at the two Arabs on the bus. Like passengers on the D train to the Bronx, each stared blankly to his front, hands folded in his lap. On the outskirts of Hebron, one of the little girls to my front quietly, daintily vomited. Silently, deliberately, the driver drew a paper cup of water from the thermos tap mounted near the front door, filled it, and passed it back. The girl's father accepted it from the soldier to his front. As her mother cradled her head, the girl sipped.

With unconscionable speed we flew through Hebron, citadel of Moslem fundamentalism, infamous for the uprising of 1929 during which sixty-seven Jews were massacred, another sixty injured, and every synagogue razed. Between the buildings stood either olive trees or, supported on stakes high off the ground, rows of grapes. They look like scores of parodic crucifixions.

As usual, Hebron's large glass factory was closed. Our bus bore to the left to avoid the center of the city, and my eye anticipated something even before it registered from memory. Like the field of ashes in *The Great Gatsby*, a schoolyard transformed into a vision of desolation: the centerpiece of its decrepit playground was a rusted metal slide splotchily painted purple, blue, and red. It could masquerade as a piece of junk sculpture. Years have passed since I have spotted a child at play there.

The #440 slowed at a road block; a baby-faced soldier waved us through, but at the cutoff for Kiryat Arba to the right, a "settler" stronghold of around five thousand Jews, predominantly Orthodox, a Jewish couple boarded and one of the Arabs got off. From here on, the "settler" presence in Judea starts to thicken. A bit further north we passed the turnoff left of the highway to Gush Etzion, twenty-two kilometers south of the capital. My older son lived and studied at a yeshiva here for the better part of eight years. The five adjacent settlements of Gush Etzion were overrun during the War of Independence by the Jordanian army after a valiant defense, which gave the Jews of Jerusalem some breathing space. Its defenders were taken into captivity. After 1967, Gush Etzion was re-established.

A thick-thighed, Jewish jogger in satin green shorts—surely American—bob, bob, bobbed down the highway in our direction. He probably had set out from booming Efrat, just a few kilometers up the road.

A sign proclaimed ELAZAR. When I first arrived in Israel, this had been a communal settlement . . . a "problematic" one. Later I read it had been "privatized." Communal or not, Elazar was still surrounded by the same depressing wire fence at whose entrance a bored soldier, automatic rifle across his knees, sat cross-legged. A roadside sign at this point once had beckoned the wayfarer to a restaurant. It now declared BAKERY.

Traffic congealed near Daheyshe, the Palestinian refugee camp, which for several years has been obscured from the road by a high, corrugated metal fence. It was near here that several years earlier my bus had been bonged: a stone had clanged harmlessly off the roof of the passing vehicle. There was no sound of splintering glass. Nevertheless, we startled; hushed, anxious passengers looked around, then at each other. The driver floored the accelerator and sped us out of danger. For the remainder of that journey, each of his passengers had converted to fanaticism.

I looked twice at a yellow Volkswagen Beetle heading south. Its replica is driven by Mordecai, an American friend in Yeroham. This one bore a blue-colored license, identifying its driver as an Arab resident of the territories. Weird, the driver of the passing bug even *looked* very much like Mordecai. We entered central Bethlehem. Most stores were open—no strike today—but business was very spotty. In the distance to the right, a glowing apparition: the sun gleaming off the white, curved, modernesque roofs of Gilo, one of Jewish Jerusalem's "new" (i.e., post-'67) neighborhoods.

As the bus passed the tomb of Rachel, our driver—wizard of the sharp-twisting highway—caused Gilo momentarily to disappear. Three uniformed, armed descendants of Jacob's grandsons sat on duty in front of the entrance to the tomb. Evidently, two busloads of tourists were then within: one had arrived in an Israeli tour bus; the other, in an Arab.

Once again the radio beeped the hour; once again the driver automatically raised the volume. The bulletin was unchanged from the 8:00 a.m. report. Before the volume faded, we were flooded by a chorus of Art Garfunkel crooning "Bridge Over Troubled Waters." Sunlight burnished rows of yellow grapefruits, yellow lemons, stacks of copper oranges at fruit stands lining both sides of the road. Like extras in a travelogue, raffish, boyish storekeepers looked wistful as we passed.

Just before the #440 swerved left at the sharp turnoff for Gilo, at the turnoff to ecumenical Tantur Institute, the road widened. I recalled a trip north six months earlier, before the closure of the territories, when my bus had halted here for what seemed an interminable time. The intersection was being widened, and some ungainly, saurian road equipment was painfully striving to pivot and turn. Like extras in an epic from the era of Soviet Realism, Arab workers exercised their picks and poured tar with slow rhythm. I had gazed at one wizened ancient in a red and white kaffiyeh. He looked as though he could barely lift his shovel. Though he stood not ten feet from my window, I realized he could have been a thousand miles away. After perhaps ten frozen minutes, our vehicle had resumed its laborious progress from red light to red light, through familiar streets of Jerusalem.

A half-year later that ragtag construction crew, its light and heavy equipment, had vanished. Instead, occupying the newly widened zone of highway, there was another, somewhat more elaborate military checkpoint than the one we had navigated through farther south. This was a veritable gauntlet of sand-filled oil drums. Off to the left of the road, glistening beneath the broiling sun, yet another improvised Arab car lot. An Israeli jeep rolled slowly in the dirt to the right of the highway. The line-up here, in sight of Jerusalem, was considerably longer than the one we had cleared an hour before. Once again Israeli autos and drivers halted to be checked and cleared by efficient young soldiers. All except the empowered, specially privileged #440. Waved on through, it once again negotiated the obstacles with impressive finesse until it crossed the line. The finish line.

A buzz: a woman passenger signaled she wanted to get off at the next stop—sprawling Gilo. I breathed an involuntary sigh of relief. Cheap, amusement park thrills were over for another ride, another day. Was it not shocking that behind my extra-thick, green-glazed, firmly closed pane, the passing, curious scene had affected me, had actually *moved* me so little? I could not deny it. Once again I had passed safely through "All of the Above." It was all so familiar, so ordinary, so much like a roller coaster ride through Outer Mongolia.

For me, as I think for most Israelis, the closure of the territories had altered little or nothing. In spite of myself, could I honestly claim that my essential relation to the reality of the Palestinians I had viewed from my catbird seat on the #440 was even as comprehending, as intimate, or as natural as that of visiting delegations of Montreal Jews to the inhabitants of Yeroham? Probably not. The only consolation I can salvage is a consciousness of the magnitude of the deficiency.

BETWEEN RAHAT
AND A HARD PLACE

SHORTLY after dawn on the morning of March 4, 1991, jeeps and trucks carrying a detachment of three hundred men arrived at the compound of the families of Mitab Al-Qsasa and Salman Mohammed Abu Kaf. Their objective? To raze the buildings to the ground. This operation was carried out neither on the West Bank nor in the Gaza Strip. Nor was either Al-Qsasa or Abu Kaf accused of terrorist activity or incitement to violence, charges that frequently lead in those areas to the homes of the accused being sealed with concrete blocks. No, this yet more drastic consequence was meted out five kilometers from Hura, one of seven government-planned Bedouin townships in Israel's Negev. It passed unreported by the scores of Jerusalem's internationally based journalists and rated only meager coverage in the Israeli press.

What offense could have merited such severity? According to Eli Izhayig, spokesman for the Israel Lands Administration, "the Al-Qsasa and Abu Kaf families inhabited houses that had been constructed without proper license" (*Ha'aretz*, March 8, 1991). *They had built without a license!* And suppose the two Bedouin heads of households had applied for proper licenses? Why, then they would have snagged themselves fast on the Catch-22 that ensnares the Bedouin of the Negev. Building licenses are issued only for government-approved Bedouin townships. All other Bedouin structures in the Negev are ineligible.

The official Israeli government policy since the 1950s has been "to encourage" Bedouin to concentrate themselves in selected locations. The objective, of course, is to remove them from the open desertscape so that military, agricultural, and industrial development of the Negev can proceed unimpeded. For several decades this policy was rarely enforced. The situation altered drastically in the wake of the Camp

33

David Accords of 1979, which forced the Israeli Army and Air Force to evacuate their bases in the Sinai. A pressing need to locate training bases and to construct three new airfields within the narrow confines of the Negev made an unmonitored, uncontrolled Bedouin presence more than merely inexpedient.

Like the military, expanding townships regard the Bedouin as an impediment. Omer is an up-scale suburb of Beersheba. Its residents—overwhelmingly Ashkenazi and secular—are mainly professionals, many of them employed at nearby Ben-Gurion University. In general elections, a relatively high proportion vote for the left-leaning Meretz Party, which proclaims itself particularly concerned with the civil rights of Israeli citizens.

Adjacent to Omer may be found a fenced-in village of several hundred Bedouin who, after they were forced more than thirty years ago to evacuate traditional lands closer to Beersheba, resettled at the site. Officially, of course, their settlement is illegal. Fields on the south side of the highway, which the Bedouin had once dry-farmed, were expropriated and reassigned to a nearby kibbutz more than a decade ago.

Seeking expansion, Omer's city fathers have for some time been casting eyes on the "illegal" settlement of their most immediate neighbors: they have petitioned the Israeli courts to evict the Omer-abutting Bedouins. Neither the Meretz professionals of affluent Omer nor the leftists of the kibbutz have shed noticeable tears at the prospect of trespassing the civil liberties of these, their fellow Israeli citizens.

For millennia, tribespeople have roamed the Negev in search of water and vegetation for their flocks. Over the generations they became skilled as herdsmen and at survival under semiarid conditions. Traditionally maintaining a symbiotic relationship with the farmers of the Galilee, the Bedouin drove their flocks to forage over already harvested fields, clearing them of stubble in the process. As long as the Bedouin population was relatively low, and empty land abundant, their shepherd economy functioned smoothly.

The founding of the State of Israel marked the beginning of the end for both these conditions. The Bedouin infant mortality rate, which once had run to nearly 50 per cent, has been so reduced by the introduction of modern medical practices that today's Negev Bedouin population is around 70,000, a high for modern times. At the same time, since all land in the Negev is under the legal jurisdiction of the state, even Bedouin tribes who have lived in the region for many generations exercise no legal right over their traditional lands.

Unable to carry on with their traditional economy, encouraged to abandon their nomadic way of life, large numbers of Bedouin over the past decade have sought employment in factories or on agricultural settlements. And yet, like Al-Qsasa and Abu Kaf, like the villagers adjacent to Omer, about half the Bedouin stubbornly hang on to their traditional way of life.

Khalil Al-Okhbi, married, father of five, was born in 1956 in Al-Okhbi, a village of around one hundred dwellings just off the highway between Beersheba and Arad. Like Bedouin closer to Omer, the Al-Okhbi tribe had moved in 1951 after being expelled from its lands near Beersheba. Like twenty or more other good-sized Bedouin villages in the northern Negev, Al-Okhbi is not recognized by the Israeli authorities. Officially, it simply does not exist; its residents are "squatters."

Under Israeli statutes, construction of buildings without a permit is a criminal offense carrying penalties of heavy fines and imprisonment for up to two years. In 1982 Khalil Al-Okhbi was served with a court order to destroy his own house. He complied. Subsequently, Al-Okhbi explained, his wife built another home for the family on the same site. The Negev Regional Planning Authority then claimed that Al-Okhbi had circumvented the original court order. On the face of it, a reasonable deduction, and a new case has been brought against him. Prior to the case's coming to the court, however, the house accidentally burned to the ground. Despite the nullity of the house, the state insisted upon arguing the case. For his offense, Al-Okhbi was sentenced to a year in prison (seven months of it suspended) and a fine of three thousand shekels (about $1,000). The prosecutor has appealed this decision. He wants Al-Okbhi to serve a longer sentence and to pay a fine of one hundred thousand shekels.

One should not be startled to learn that though Israeli courts view noncompliance with the planning and building law with gravity, enforcement of these regulations is pursued with far greater vigor in the Arab than in the Jewish sector. In fact, as any close observer of the Israeli scene could verify, infringements of planning code regulations by Jewish homeowners are far from uncommon. Yet rarely indeed does it transpire that an Israeli judge issues an order for the demolition of a house belonging to a Jew.

Unlike other Israeli Arabs, significant numbers of young Bedouin over the years have volunteered to serve in the Israeli army, frequently performing an invaluable service as trackers along the borders. When, during the Gulf War, missiles rained down on Tel Aviv, several Bedouin settlements opened their doors to house Jewish families who fled for safety. In truth, the problem is not that most Israelis harbor a deep-seated bias against the Bedouin; it's simply that they are unmoved by their plight. For most Israeli Jews, their fellow Bedouin citizens amount to little more than a picturesque nuisance.

Efforts to concentrate all Negev Bedouin into seven large townships (only three of which have had *their* building plans approved) move apace. By judicial means, the lands which approximately thirty thousand Bedouin had occupied have been confiscated. Upon accepting compensation, their former inhabitants have moved to sprawling, urban conglomerations such as Rahat, north of Beersheba. Like Khalil Al-Okhbi, the overwhelming majority of the remaining forty thousand Negev Bedouin live precarious lives in homes that the state considers illegal. Any sunrise may disclose their homes ringed by the distinctive, olive-colored jeeps of the so-called Green Patrol. Every one of these homes is subject to legal demolition.

Realistically, would it not truly be wiser for the Bedouin to give up their unequal struggle, to surrender to superior power, to relinquish their lands and move to the relative safety and security of Bedouin townships such as Rahat? One morning in 1992, I decided to visit the place.

As things turned out, the ordeal of merely getting to the Bedouin metropolis of the Negev provided an instantaneous, total immersion into the Israeli underclass. At Beersheba's central bus station, here's how matters proceeded.

"Here's your ticket . . . one-way to Shoval," the station clerk said.

Odd. Shoval is a kibbutz on a secondary highway to Tel Aviv. Perhaps there had been a misunderstanding, so I once again requested a ticket . . . to Rahat.

"Sorry, Egged buses don't service Rahat. Just get off at Shoval, and the driver will point the way."

Elusive Rahat is no small, minor encampment. Its population happens to exceed that of Kibbutz Shoval by a factor of at least twenty! Yet even though most of Rahat's pita-winners commute daily to construction, factory, or agricultural work in Beersheba, Kiryat Gat, Tel Aviv, or neighboring kibbutzim—Egged buses neither enter nor make a circuit of its streets as they do in other towns as a matter of course. It would seem the sovereignty of the Egged Bus Cooperative does not extend service or recognition to what is supposed to be the urban cornerstone of the government's longstanding policy to concentrate the Bedouin of the Negev in urban enclaves.

At its inception in 1972, Rahat was considered a model of municipal planning. Its residents had received compensation for leaving their desert holdings. Each neighborhood of the new municipality was divided into units and apportioned according to extended families, or *hamulot*. Each *hamula* was granted a *dunam* (quarter of an acre) on which to build. Riding north out of Beersheba, however, I searched for a road sign validating the existence of Rahat. It was futile. In short, although from the principal highway from Tel Aviv to Beersheba, houses and minarets of spectral Rahat may be seen stretching for miles on the western horizon, for most Negevites the very quiddity of the fourth largest urban center in the north Negev is problematic.

Eventually, just as the ticket seller had indicated, my bus stopped on the highway just across from the kibbutz, and the driver did indeed steer me toward a narrow road that trailed off to the right. After about two dusty kilometers, the first buildings materialized, and, surprisingly, Rahat offered an initial impression of a thriving enterprise.

Scattered about—something like houses and hotels in a game of Monopoly after the board as been jarred by an elbow—were a considerable number of large homes, many quite attractive. Near the municipal offices, Bedouin men, the majority in everyday Israeli garb but admixed with many in traditional robes, entered and left Barclay's Discount Bank. Construction was under way on what looked to be terrain that had been chiseled out with an ice cream scoop; it would evidently serve for outdoor musical programs. Nearby stood a large structure that, upon completion, will function as a mini-mall. Several groups of school-aged kids loitered about, but not more than one might encounter on a Tuesday morning in Netivot, Yeroham, or other Jewish towns of the Negev. In contrast, not many women were in evidence and those who were wore traditional dress.

Rahat's mayor, Gomah Al-Kasasy, seated at his desk in his office, displayed a severe mien and looked imperious in traditional dark robe and kaffiyeh. A photo of then-President Chaim Herzog hung reassuringly if somewhat incongruously on the wall. Al-Kasasy replaced a functionary from the Ministry of Construction and Housing who from 1980 had served as Rahat's unelected mayor for nine years.

"Yes, until 1989 our mayor was a Jewish appointee," Al-Kasasy explained. "The government claimed that we Bedouin were not capable of conducting a fair, democratic election. We insisted that we could, which," he added with a wry smile, "is exactly what we did."

Al-Kasasy and two other representatives of the eleven-member city council are members of the Islamic Party, which is traditionalist, some would say fundamentalist, in outlook. Two council members, including amiable deputy Moussa Abu-Sehban (attired in Western clothing), adhered to the nationalist Democratic Arab Party of Abdul Wahab Darawshe. The remaining representatives included two Labor Party men and four independents.

"I will tell you something of Rahat's history," the mayor said. "This city was begun by the government in 1970 after the failure of Tel Sheva to properly develop as a Bedouin center. Because we have lots of buildings and a far greater population than Tel Sheva, Rahat is widely considered to be a great success. And it is true that, little by little, in some areas we do think we are beginning to make some progress. Our thirty-three neighborhoods now have a population greater than twenty-three thousand, not to mention another six thousand Bedouin in the immediate area whom we also service. But what you cannot observe simply by walking about is that many families are crammed into their houses like chickens inside coops. In this matter we have not begun to get the cooperation we would like from the government agencies or officials."

Rahat also contains seven elementary schools, one vocational school, one junior high, and one high school, all of which look much like standard Israeli school buildings.

"Yes," commented Abu-Sehban, "the buildings themselves are okay, but today we are at least fifty classrooms short. So, like our homes, our schools are terrifically overcrowded. Our birth rate, as you probably know, is one of the highest in the world: Rahat grows by around one thousand children every year, and more than three-fourths of the Bedouin are under the age of twenty. That translates into a need for an additional twenty to thirty schoolrooms every single year; we actually get six or seven, which means that the overcrowding in our schools worsens every September. Is it any wonder so many of our young people despair and do not finish school?"

"A similar situation," Abu-Sehban claimed, his Hebrew more demotic than the mayor's, "prevails in Rahat's medical facilities. We have plenty of doctors, some of them Arabs who were trained in former Soviet countries. But our clinic is ridiculously small for a place of our size."

Rahat's unemployment rate is supposed to be around 20 per cent. "It's actually higher," the mayor remarked. "Look at our city plan. These two areas in purple are zoned for industry, but these industrial zones have become a very bad joke: there is no industry in Rahat. *Nothing*. Why? Do our workers demand high salaries? Are they less skilled than other factory workers? Hardly. It is because the government refuses to designate us a 'development town,' with the result that, unlike all the other Negev towns—I mean places like Dimona or Kiryat Gat—we cannot offer potential investors or industrialists any tax incentives. Naturally, no one comes.

"Moreover, unlike other municipalities, we receive no help at all from the Jewish Agency. Nevertheless, when I spent three weeks in the United States last fall, I had meetings with successful Palestinian-American businessmen, also Saudis and Kuwaitis, who expressed willingness, even eagerness to invest in Rahat. The trouble is that they are forbidden to deal with us directly. The law requires them to work through the overseas agencies of the State of Israel, which naturally they are reluctant to do."

What about the promise made five years earlier by Amos Gilboa, aide to Professor Moshe Arens when he was Israel's minister in charge of minority affairs, that "there will be industrial building in Rahat within one month. . . . half [of the industrial zone] will be used for a textile plant that will employ five hundred people"?

"Later we will together inspect this beautiful-sounding, invisible 'industrial zone' of Rahat," Abu-Sehban interjected, a bitter grin at the corner of his mouth. "Year after year," he continued, "we dutifully update our five-year development plan and submit it to the Ministry of Interior. Year after year, nothing happens."

Rahat's total lack of industry has several unpleasant spin-offs. With so many of its citizens having to commute to work car-pooled into old, poorly repaired vehicles, the number of Bedouin killed or seriously injured in road accidents is far disproportionate to their numbers. As for the chronically unemployed, they tend, of course, to graduate into antisocial behaviorial problems, but Rahat's department of welfare consists of fourteen-and-a-half workers, or one for every fifteen hundred citizens!

Rahat lacks a municipal sewage system. Its streets lack sidewalks. "We need so very much," Al-Kasasy added with a hint of a smile, "but what do we get? After twenty-two years the Histadrut Labor Federation has recently built for us a new cultural palace . . . a place where nothing cultural happens."

But still Rahat attracts new residents. It grows annually. Houses are spacious.

"If newcomers still gravitate to Rahat, which is so overcrowded and offers no employment prospects, that merely shows how bad conditions are for Bedouin elsewhere," the mayor responded. "Our total budget for 1992 was 17 million shekels of which 6 million was a grant. In comparison, Ofakim, with thirteen thousand people, receives a budget of 35 million shekels. Where is the justice in that? I would settle for 80 per cent of Ofakim's allotment.

"You know, the government promised us Bedouin a Garden of Eden. Go and look around. Rahat may superficially look like a success, but the fact is that we are falling further and further behind. You want to know the irony of it all? Only about half of Israel's eighty thousand Bedouin live in Rahat and the smaller government-sponsored settlements like Lejya, Kuseifa, and Tel Sheva. The main reason most of the other half do not move is that those Bedouin see and understand that Rahat is failing. Most will continue to refuse to come because they can see how bleak their future would be here. And so by treating us as poorly as it does, the State of Israel works against itself."

What do Al-Kasasy and Abu-Sehban really want? "Just equality. Simple equality. Look at this," the mayor declared as he dramatically drew his monthly pay statement from the top drawer of his desk. "I pay 45 per cent of my salary in taxes. My full share. What I want and what Rahat wants is our fair share back."

I was guided around Rahat by Moussa Abu-Sehban who moved here in 1974 from nearby Revivim.

"Everyone today speaks about peace," he began. "I say peace begins at home. When I travel to a town like Arad and see the sorts of public facilities available there, things taken for granted, how do you think I feel? Rahat still doesn't have its own cultural center; I'm not referring to the center built by the Histadrut. Our football team does not perform in a stadium. For half the school year our children must try to learn while shivering in their coats because, with the exception of several kindergartens, none of schoolrooms is equipped with heaters. We are not demanding luxuries, but it seems that what the State of Israel thinks essential for many Jewish communities does not extend to us.

"Fate has decreed that our two peoples should live together. All we Bedouin want from the government is what rightly should come to us. We want to be treated as equals. Just look around. Do you think we get the same treatment as a Jewish town?"

A suggestion that there might be signs of improvement under a Labor-led government drew a scoffing rebuff.

"This new government has given us nothing," Abu-Sehban retorted. "In some ways it is even more right-wing than was the Likud. Let me tell you, events like the expulsion of the 415 Palestinians to Lebanon affects us here directly. First of all, it must never be forgotten that all Arabs belong to one people. But even closer than that, every one of us has relatives in Gaza or the West Bank. One of my nephews has been killed. We are greatly pained by these deaths; they influence our feelings. People are too used to referring to Bedouin as a natural bridge to the Arab world, a bridge of coexistence and peace. But the years of intifada have intensified our dilemma. That bridge is capable of bearing less and less weight."

What about the Bedouin who serve in the army?

"The number of Bedouin who volunteer nowadays is insignificant," he replied dismissively, "Maybe 100 to 150 a year."

The imposing Histadrut cultural facility is directed by Abu-Hani, a gregarious Labor Party man. He was very proud of it, especially its small but versatile theater, with a capacity of 161. The center offered literacy classes for adults, help for students after school, classes in knitting and sewing.

"At present, Rahat has no public library, but we are planning one," Abu-Hani added. "We have three soccer teams. Also, we operate a small-scale employment service from here. In the planning stage is a center for elderly Bedouin."

What about the mayor's animosity?

"Look, we've only recently opened. Some people are very impatient. There are also some who feel that public performances—theater or dance on a stage—are not part of Bedouin culture. I feel differently.

I think we can and should leap over a transitional generation and reach the young people. I think it can be done. There are always those who look to the negative side of the balance, at what we don't have. But the truth is that life in Rahat is better than it was for us in the past. For example, every house has a bathroom. We certainly do not lack problems, but improvements are possible. They take time, of course. Unfortunately, it is true that the state doesn't realize that Bedouin are less patient than we used to be. In my opinion, however, the threat or exertion of physical force is a sign not of strength but of weakness."

Near Rahat's health clinic, Abu-Sebhan was accosted by man in his fifties. It was easy to read the disappointment on the man's face when he heard the response.

"He was asking about his application for permission to acquire a plot of land upon which to build a house," Abu-Sebhan later explained. "That man has six children. He's been awaiting permission to build from the housing authority since 1988. All his papers are filed and in order. But he simply must wait.

"You see those large houses over there. I know that they look like homes of prosperous families. In fact, each room of each structure houses four or five persons. Each room! Can you imagine what living conditions are like, what sort of problems such overcrowding breeds! This was to be our 'Garden of Eden.' Can you conceive how we Bedouin, who love a feeling of space and freedom, feel? Some applications to build go back five or six years. I know of over 120 outstanding applications. Look around at those fields, those empty spaces. Is there a shortage of land upon which to build? Nonsense. All of it is properly zoned. Now perhaps you can better understand how frustrated and angry this pointless delay makes us."

Another suppliant approached the deputy mayor.

"He says, 'When it rains, his family has no place to go. They sit in the rain and get wet.'"

What does the Housing Ministry respond?

Abu-Sebhan replied with a caustic laugh. "Next month. Next month. Always, next month."

If for typical Israelis the various governmental agencies often seem like a dense tangle of overlapping bureaucracies, for Bedouin, who operate simultaneously under Israeli legislation and their own tribal laws and folkways, the situation can be hopelessly bewildering.

Outside the municipality offices, we were approached by a man named Abu Talib wearing a long Bedouin gown. Abu-Sebhan whispered to me that Talib was a successful man whose grown children were studying in schools outside of Rahat and doing very well. Histrionically turning to me and the deputy mayor, then to a small crowd of hangers-on, Abu Talib had something to vent: "Why does Rahat have no sidewalks? Whenever it rains," he complained, pointing to his thigh, "we must walk through mud up to here. I pay municipal taxes. What are you doing about this?"

Abu-Sebhan first addressed his constituent, thereafter he turned to me: "It's the same story. We get promises from Jerusalem for the municipality to build sidewalks . . . but no money. Perhaps they think Bedouin swim through mud like fish through the sea?"

When I reached the Spokesman for the Housing Ministry, he declared that "building permits in Rahat, as in every other place in Israel, are granted by regional councils, not by the Ministry of Housing," a piece of intelligence which drew a snicker from Abu-Sebhan.

"He's not telling the truth. If it were up to the regional council, new buildings would start going up tomorrow."

In his way, however, the Spokesman had spoken with sufficient clarity. For an ordinary, mud-footed Bedouin suppliant from the Garden of Eden, with his growing family stuffed into a single room, it is not difficult to imagine how, one month at a time, five years might pass. Much harder to figure is the rationale that lies behind a close-lipped policy which seems primarily designed to alienate the Bedouin of Rahat and to increase the power of their fundamentalist politicians.

SOBER AFTERTHOUGHTS UPON BEING STONED

ONE MAN'S history lesson is another's anachronism. This is nowhere more the case than in the Middle East, where the year or epoch to which one hearkens as "the beginning"—2,000 B.C.E., 1917, 1937, 1948, 1967, 1973, or the day-before-yesterday—can serve as an emblem. Of contention between Jews and Arabs, Israelis and Palestinians, does there remain unsaid anything new or newly significant? For the present, *what* is said is often less crucial than who says it, with what degree of passion or conviction, and to whom.

Gush Emunim—the Greater Israel settler movement—includes secular Jews, but from the start its motive force and philosophic basis have been drawn from among us observant Jews. From the "miraculous" deliverance into Israeli hands of all Jerusalem along with the Golan Heights, Gaza, and historic Judea and Samaria in 1967 until the national election of 1992, political momentum resided with those who viewed the times as divinely favored, with the coming of the messiah or messianic times as a salient political factor. This has placed a heightened burden of responsibility on Israel's more prominent religious peace advocates, academicians like Uriel Simon, Michael Rosenack, Uriel Tal, and Avi Ravitsky who roost in the organizational dovecotes of Oz Veshalom and Netivot Shalom. Indeed, they have exhaustively analyzed the religious dimensions of the issue. Nevertheless, efforts to spread their point of view have borne little fruit.

In fact, Israel's religious center has virtually disintegrated as a moderate political force. With notable exceptions, even those yeshiva-based rabbinic voices who have from time to time dissented have been reserved. Of late, muted as well has been the proto-messianic line issuing from Mercaz Harav, the Jerusalem yeshiva which has served as the philosophic font of Gush Emunim, a posture reflecting both traditional rabbinic temperament and the dangers inherent in the situation.

Not so every quarter. I vividly recall my astonishment while serving with a security unit in 1982 at Beirut Airport. Rather than an Israeli counterpart to a Bob Hope-Dorothy Lamour troupe, a contingent of Lubavitchers landed to serve up a Jewish brand of good cheer: "The Messiah is coming. What need does Israel have for a peace treaty with Egypt or with any Arab country? Jews don't have to compromise with goyim. The *moshiach* is coming and very soon." If such a reading were indeed correct, anyone who countenanced the return to Arab control of even parts of Judea and Samaria would be either a ninny or a traitor.

In separate enclaves of Judea and Samaria—the ancient Jewish heartland—around 110,000 Jews reside among 750,000 Palestinian Arabs. Well and good, argue hard-liners; that's 110,000 settlers more than there were twenty-six years ago. Nevertheless, everyone knows the pace of settlement has slackened to a crawl, which really means that the implicit question the West Bank settlers pose to the national conscience devolves to why should not 110,000 Jews rule over twelve times their number? If for two decades, why not for three . . . or indefinitely? With the army at their backs, with determination and guns, *something* will happen. More Russian settlers will come. The Arabs will be induced to leave "voluntarily." In a pinch, the *moshiach* surely will come!

This position is rooted in an interpretation of recent historical events that exercises a particular attraction for many religious Jews. One major prop is the writings of Abraham Isaac Kook, revered Chief Rabbi of Israel in the period of the British Mandate. Although Professor Zvi Yaron, Rav Kook's major expositor, argued that Gush Emunim theorists have distorted Kook's teaching, it is unquestionable that a strong messianic element may be mined from his thought. Hence, a train of repercussions. If messianic times are indeed upon us, then the view of Nachmanides, a prominent thirteenth-century biblical exegete, that ". . . we are commanded to take possession of the land . . . [and] we should not leave it in the hands of any other people" has assumed for many the force of religious mandate. Indeed, in 1979 this very position was officially endorsed by the Council of the Chief Rabbinate under the authority of Rabbi Shlomo Goren.

Now, if only the messiah had appeared in 1968 or '69 or even '79 to confirm the miracle of '67 . . . well . . . it all would have been so reasonable. After all, can Zvi Yaron, can I—can anyone—be so indelibly certain that we are *not* living in a time of messianic redemption? Am I, other religious "leftists," or the vast majority of Israelis wholly immune to nationalist exultation? Are we so repelled by the notion of an Israel that stretches from the Mediterranean Sea to the River Jordan, its undeniably "natural" boundary? Quite to the contrary!

To be honest, had events made it feasible for Israel to embrace organically a closer approximation of its maximal historical borders, little could have pleased me better. Together, the Holocaust and the pallid response in the West to the destruction of European Jewry definitively resolved the question of the vital necessity of a Jewish state. As for its dimensions, I would have taken any miracle I could get. But for an approximation of peace, by reason of the land's indigenous Arab population, most Israelis and I would settle for considerably less.

For over six years a group of English-speaking observant Jews in Yeroham conducted a study session based upon the weekly Torah portion. Before it expired, our final leader was a learned man with a wide-ranging knowledge of rabbinic commentaries and with strong political views. Although he knew full well that most of us were not especially sympathetic to his nationalist stance, every so often he would lead the discussion toward some putative parallel, some contemporary political lesson for the Jews to absorb in order to deal firmly, if not ruthlessly, with the non-Jewish inhabitants of the land of Israel.

Some of us would retort with contrary injunctions (say, Deut. 23:17), but he would counter with what seemed endless biblical warrant for harsh treatment of non-Jews in the land. My friend's fundamentalist, near-obsessive view was that now that we Jews are reestablished on our own soil, we don't have any further need to explain or to apologize to anyone for our actions vis-à-vis the Arabs inhabiting our land. All such defensive tendencies he ascribed to residual "diaspora mentality" of which, he remains convinced, we should now divest ourselves.

I recognize that he, like a Jerusalem friend of mine whose idée fixe is that Jordan is Palestine, is not entirely wrongheaded or even inconsistent. Yet he is incapable of deriving any wisdom from the formulations of Torah authorities such as Ovadiah Yosef, former Chief

Sephardi Rabbi, who has written that "if the responsible military and governmental authorities determine that if parts of the land of Israel are not returned there will be danger of an immediate war from the side of the Arab neighbors . . . and if the territories are returned to them the danger of war will recede, and there are chances for a viable peace . . . [then] it is permissible to return territories from the land of Israel in order to achieve this goal, since nothing overrides saving lives."

Rabbi Yosef here expresses what has been the dominant tendency of rabbinic commentary on relations between Jews and non-Jews down through the ages. As interpreted by Rashi in his Commentary on the Babylonian Talmud, *Tractate Arakhin,* Jews are commanded by the Torah to live in peace with the non-Jewish inhabitants, the *gerei toshav* of this land: "He shall dwell with you, among you, in that place where he shall choose within one of your gates, where it suits him best; you shall not oppress him" (Deut. 23:17). Maimonides' comment on Deut. 14:21—"You shall give it to the stranger who is within your gates, that he may eat it"—was that "one behaves toward *gerei toshav* with civility and kindness, as one would toward a Jew. . . ." In our times a similar position has been endorsed by Rabbi Joseph B. Soloveitchik, until his recent passing the most respected voice in the American rabbinate. Nevertheless, the Mercaz Harav position now predominates at most yeshivas throughout Israel.

Reinforcing the messianic triumphalism of Mercaz Harav theorists has been the situation on the ground since 1967. Even with the best of intentions, by its very nature, military occupation is oppressive. In such circumstances, although the need for the application of Jewish ethics is all the greater, the views of Rashi and Maimonides have been treated by West Bank settlers as increasingly irrelevant. Largely for this reason when my son Ted was finishing his army service, he and three of his *yeshivat hesder* soldier comrades heeded a request to volunteer for an additional four months of military duty beyond their normal term. They felt that it was important for soldiers who felt some empathy for the feelings of the non-Jewish inhabitants of the territories to be on the scene.

One riot-torn December in the early days of the intifada, for nearly two weeks, Ted led his platoon on patrols down the alleyways of Gaza and nearby Khan Yunis. Later he described the pain of engagements with ten- and twelve-year-olds in street demonstrations, the inner agony of being under orders to refuse water to the family members of Arabs he had rousted out of their homes in order to sweep up debris from the streets. "Keeping" the whole land of Israel has exacted an excruciating price which neither the young Lubavitchers at the Beirut airport in '82 nor Israel's current crop of nearly eighteen thousand draft-deferred yeshiva students need pay close-up: it cheapens our values and ourselves; it demoralizes our sons and daughters.

The irony is that for normative Judaism the sanctity of life has always exercised priority over preciseness over borders or the "wholeness" of the land. A governing paradigm for the primacy of ethical behavior entailing territorial compromise for the sake of avoiding violence occurs, it seems to me, in Genesis when Abraham compromises with Lot over borders: "Abram said to Lot, 'Let there be no strife between you and me, between my herdsman and yours, for we are kinsmen. Is not the whole land before you? Let us separate: if you go north, I will go south; and if you go south, I will go north'" (Gen. 13:8–9). As if signaling an "amen" from on high, God immediately reconfirms His promise of the land to Abram.

All observant Jews know that they are forbidden to use stolen materials when fulfilling the commandment to build a *sukkah*, a temporary dwelling, for use during the week-long holiday of Sukkot, that doing so abrogates the point and substance of fulfilling the obligation. Similarly, I would argue, it is illegitimate to fulfill what could be honorably understood as a mitvah, the commandment to possess Judea and Samaria. Not only because Judaism insists that peace is the supreme gift of mankind (indeed, Maimonides declared that the very purpose of the giving of Torah to the Jewish people in the first place was to promote peace [Gittin 59b; *Megilah ve-Chanukkah*]), but also because it entails *continual ethical transgression.*

The forty-sixth year of Israeli independence is also the twenty-sixth year of Israeli military occupation of these problematic territories. If the messiah has tarried, immigration has quickened. (The irony, of course, is that the overwhelming majority of Russian Jews have shown a singular lack of interest in settling the Greater Land of Israel.) It is also the seventh year of intifada. After a score of years without hope, Arab youngsters in Gaza, Dahaishe, and Ramallah took to the streets against our Jewish sons in uniform. Some would argue that they are being shamelessly exploited—and there is a measure of truth in this— but who is incapable of responding to their courage? At bottom, the

Palestinians cannot "win" in the streets, but they have prevented Israel from maintaining an occupation that most of us can pursue with easy conscience. This is no small victory.

Of course, I recognize all too well that many young Palestinian stalwarts in Gaza and the West Bank camps have been raised to believe that their true homes are the ones in Jaffa, Lod, and Ramle that their parents and grandparents abandoned in 1948. I know that many dream, indeed fervently believe, that one day they will return to them. Little does it matter now that the PLO policy of refusing to cooperate with repeated Israeli efforts to ameliorate living conditions of Palestinian refugees was cynical. It worked: enforced misery has helped to fashion a people. If they were not even thinking primarily about peoplehood or nationhood in 1948, after their own forty years in the desert, Palestinians today give every indication of being a national entity. Looking to the future, it seems to me largely to lie in Israel's hands and self-interest to make it worth the while of Palestinians to cease their violent struggle for recognition and dignity.

My aim is neither to whitewash the PLO's bloody record nor to minimize potential dangers to Israel. There is, however, a positive precedent to recall. In the eighteen months before June 1982, when the PLO had firmly established themselves as oppressors of the Shiites and Christians in southern Lebanon (then "Fatahland"), they collected taxes, organized economic enterprises, and ran militias that abutted Israel's northern border. Having something precious to hold, something vulnerable to lose, for one-and-a-half years they fired no *katyushas* into the panhandle of Galilee. Indeed, much to the chagrin of those such as Ariel Sharon, they painstakingly avoided provocation and maintained a quiet border.

In this period before Operation Peace in Galilee, there actually *was* relative peace in Galilee, and Begin and Sharon had to use the wounding of Israel's ambassador in London as a distant pretext for sending Israeli troops north of the border. The result was the destabilizing of southern Lebanon, an unpleasant situation which we must suffer to this day. Totally obscured was the real lesson of those months before June '82: provided with appropriate incentive, PLO terrorists can keep the peace and their word as well as, say, the Egyptians, the Syrians, or the British.

The Likud government's policy of refusing to talk with representatives of the PLO, which was equivalent to not recognizing their humanity, placed Israel in an indefensible moral posture. In a world where even Ronald Reagan negotiated with the head of the Evil Empire, Israel's fixed posture lost whatever tactical advantage it once may have held. Especially when it was well known that the Israeli government had already held numerous secret meetings with representatives of the PLO in the past, this policy became *stupid* for the obvious reason that we and they had vital matters to discuss—for example, Israeli POWs still somewhere in Lebanon (or Syria, or Iran). I believe most Israelis were relieved when in 1992 the Labor-led government repealed the law that made speaking with PLO representatives a criminal offense. The time was long overdue for an end to speciousness and hypocrisy.

For decades Israel acted as though peace and security could be secured best through a relatively benign occupation, quick retaliations to infractions, imprisonments, and deportations. Events proved this to be questionable, if not demonstrably fallacious. The countercourse prescribed by Abraham-the-Patriarch was suggested in 1948. Its timing was premature. More than forty years later the Israeli people elected a government committed to pursuing the Abrahamic solution once again, a government which recognizes that, notwithstanding 1948, the Palestinians of 1993 are a people, and the world recognizes that peoples are endowed with national rights. In return, the PLO seems prepared to recognize Jewish national rights *in principle*, and to commit itself over a period of years to demonstrate convincingly that their own nationhood does not endanger and is not irreconcilable with Jewish national rights.

Far more than the precise contours of predominantly Jewish Israel and/or of a predominantly Arab Palestine, our mutual well-being depends upon the hard-won recognition of our co-mutual dependency and legitimacy. Such is both the precondition to serious negotiations and its most critical desideratum. What Jews, in particular observant Jews, must finally, painfully come to understand and declare is that neither our biblical deed to the whole land of Israel nor special warrant by virtue of the Holocaust can permanently fully eclipse Palestinian national rights. Entitled to self-determination, we must not deny to others what we have wrested for ourselves. Our security, our moral standing, and our self-respect ultimately rest upon establishing and maintaining this balance.

In the end, the State of Israel could, I think, do far, far worse than to emulate the policy of Abraham-the-Patriarch. Not, I hasten to add, because we love Hebron, Bethel, or justice less than the followers of Gush Eminum or the hard-liners of Likud but because we value peace as the highest gift of all.

A DAWNING OF
AQUARIUS?

NTIL a recent rising of a tide of Mitsubishis, for no readily discernible cause beyond alliterative aptness, whereas most Palestinians preferred Peugeots, most Sabras sallied forth in Subarus. The week that Israel was supposed to begin withdrawal from Gaza (but because of unforeseen complications relating to security arrangements did not) my wife reported that her coworker at the Desert Research Institute in Sede Boker had decided, after much vacillation, to purchase a new Peugeot. At once a South African–born microbiologist rejoined, "Hah! Hah! Getting ready for when Arafat takes over Israel?"

This mild witticism evoked an inordinate flutter of nervous laughter in the lab. One of the departmental secretaries whose sister lives in a West Bank settlement, however, was visibly unamused. Naturally, both scientists vocally support the Rabin government, the forward movement of the peace process, and the Gaza–Jericho First interim accords of September 13. Despite the avalanche of works of peace— or, because of it—the contemporary Israeli style of joking remains edgier, more self-ironic than ever. The scent of shalom may be wafting in the wind, but not yet, not yet for us, the self-confident humor of heartiness, jolliness, or exuberance. The truth is that many of us Israelis feel more like bit players in one of Shakespeare's darker, more problematic comedies than members of the supporting cast joining together for a finale of matrimonial reconciliation in one of his romantic comedies.

The fact is, of course, that ever since President Clinton artfully choreographed the unequal squeezing of palms, things hereabouts have not been quite the same. True, Israelis of various ethnic shades and a surprisingly broad range of political complexions have permitted themselves to dream a Levantine version of the impossible dream.

52

The thing is, although quite a good number of us can hit the higher, more quixotic notes, after each new bloodletting fewer of us can sustain them for very long without a dying fall. Nevertheless, for the time being, a majority of us seem willing to hum along with the "Peace Process Serenade" in the lower octaves.

Likud leader Bibi Netanyahu's instinctive revulsion to *Sleeping with the Enemy*—revisionism's primal nightmare—led him at first to demand loudly a national referendum on the accords. Yet, the turnouts at largely Chabad-financed demonstrations against the Rabin–Arafat uncordial entente were surprisingly paltry. Even more significant than their low numbers was the composition of the demonstrators: overwhelmingly religiously observant, almost exclusively settler families from the territories and students from B'nei Akiva yeshivas. In other words, except for the settlers from the Golan Heights and the lower Jordan Valley, only Israel's intractable, hard-core, maximalist right-wing. In other words, the 20 per cent of the Jewish population that Rabin has already discounted.

Yet more to the point, the swing constituency of prototypical center-right supporters of the Likud, Tsomet, and even Shas parties has not demonstrated opposition. And that makes all the difference. As long as it continues to enjoy the acquiescence of a far larger Jewish majority of the general population to proceed with negotiations, the Israeli government led by Rabin requires only a parliamentary 50 per cent plus 1 in order to sign whatever future accords with the Palestinians and surrounding Arab countries they judge useful.

In November 1993 Ephraim Ayoubi, chauffeur to the prominent nationalist Rabbi Haim Druckman, was shot to death in Kiryat Arba, an ultra-nationalist Jewish stronghold outside of Hebron. (The perpetrators were probably from the Hawatmeh faction of the PLO.) On the evening after the murder, I attended an *azkara* of the fifth anniversary of the death of Esther Biton, my Yeroham neighbor, commemorated with prayer, study, and food. Seated apart from the women, about twenty of us men sat around the table presided over by old, nearly blind Ma'asud Biton. Aside from one other guest and me, all were Moroccans.

A passage of commentary on the Cabala led one participant to remark, "Every day another killing. The Arabs don't really want peace. What they still want is Jewish blood . . . without the risks."

Before the leader had returned to his text, nearly everyone around the table had murmured a few assenting words. Among Israel's large and volatile Moroccan population, suspicion of Arab motives and intentions obviously has not abated. On the other hand, no one gave voice to the notion that the Israeli government should abrogate its interim accords with the PLO. However reluctantly, for the time being these Likud and Shas voters seemed willing to let Rabin steer Israel's dangerous course toward . . . not quite peace but some sort of improved accommodation with the Palestinians.

Why haven't the right-of-center cab drivers, small shop owners, and bank clerks voiced public dissent? Surely not because of any change of heart. The reaction of North African Jews to Arabs—Sephardim will be the last to call them "Palestinians"—has always been more visceral than ideological. In this instance, while remaining instinctively wary, so far they have not been antipathetic to peace overtures. Ear to the pavement, the Likud's own mayoral candidates Roni Milo (Tel Aviv) and Ehud Olmert (Jerusalem), both of whom were successful in the November 1993 election, quickly distanced themselves from Netanyahu. Within ten days after eager Arafatian fingers had clasped our own P.M.'s drier digits, the Likud leader ceased bugling for a national referendum: he realized that he would lose disastrously.

Our left-leaning artists and professionals, however, as well our internationalist business community—Israel's Establishment, conservative, but with its traditionally leftist spin—have been bullish on peace prospects from the start. This had been reflected most readily in the steady rise at the *bursa*, Israel's stock market. For many of them, the prospect of lucrative deals, joint ventures, new projects, cultural exchanges, and breaching Israel's regional isolation has been wellnigh intoxicating. Habituated to blaming Jewish settlers for being where (and who) they are, many seem incapable of rousing sympathy for yet another Jew killed for living in the wrong place at the wrong time.

In recent months the Israeli press has accurately reflected our national schizophrenia. Its front pages, naturally enough, headline every Hamas-inspired bloodletting or abducted soldier, every demonstration and counterdemonstration; editorial pages have been variously cheerfully or cautiously ambivalent; feature pages have been garnished with euphoric visions of the dawn of a Middle Eastern Age of Aquarius. Who in Israel by now has not read two or ten times about how, with the coming of peace, a new highway will stretch, via the Trans-Israel Highway Number Six, from Alexandria to Aleppo? Of how, with the coming of peace, tens of thousands of chronically ill patients from Kuwait, Egypt, and Saudi Arabia will avail themselves of Israel's state-of-the-art medical care and facilities (in the bargain enabling unemployed Russian immigrant physicians to work)?

Or how about, with the dawning of shalom, the pipeline that will funnel natural gas from Egypt to Israel? Or when peace is established, the desalination plants enabled by the newly dusted-off plans (from a decade ago) for a canal from the Mediterranean to the Dead Sea? Or, in the peaceful era, about the Red Sea Riviera to encompass white sands, casinos, and the free ports of Eilat, Taba, and Aqaba? Or, with peace in our time, of regional tourism for visitors from the West, and the manifold joint projects in agricultural technology, aviation, and communications equipment?

How sweet, how profitable peace would be! Then, with the next morning's or following week's headlines, the photos of the bereaved and the funerals, seductive visions blur and dissipate . . . for a while.

What the pragmatic, politically vital Israeli center has not yet decided is whether it can truly credit these visions. The truth is that only a decided minority of Israelis are actually talking about reconciliation, let alone genuine shalom with the Palestinians—a designation that so ambivalently entails a place called Palestine. My dentist, a middle-of-the-road former American, may serve, I think fairly, as an Ashkenazi person-in-the-street. On a recent visit, an occasion which renders this *auditeur* supremely passive, I heard not a syllable either about peace or about retaining territories.

Yes, surely peace, security, and normalcy rather than ideologically fixed conflicts and borders are what a large majority of us deeply want. And yes, to be sure, Rabin is doing pretty much what those of us who voted him in had grounds to expect. At the same time, a decided minority of Israelis is feeling jubilant or even upbeat nowadays.

Early in January after the signing of the accords, soon after an Israeli had been murdered by Hamas, I encountered Esther Schvartz, a pensioner originally from Vilna, on a street in Yeroham. Innocently, I asked how she felt. Politics were not what I had in mind.

"How do I feel?" she repeated. "I feel as though things are falling apart, that we are losing our country. But," she added quickly "it may turn out for the best. Anyway, it's out of my hands."

Aware of their political isolation, somewhat belatedly some of the more sophisticated residents of the territories have been trying to gain support. Late in January, three English-speaking residents of the West Bank traveled to Yeroham to inform residents of the northern Negev towns of Yeroham, Dimona, and Sede Boker about the dangers of the peace process. One of the speakers turned out to be Chaim Makovsky who in 1975 and '76, when my family and I were making plans to move to Israel, had been the Israeli government's Los Angeles representative in charge of aliyah. We had not seen our *shaliach*, the man who had competently aided us in making arrangements to move from California to Israel, in many years.

It rained that evening, and the turnout for the three persons who had taken the trouble and braved the palpable dangers of driving the Hebron road by night was embarrassingly paltry. Nevertheless, in posing before us one disastrous possible scenario after another, Makovsky was informative, diplomatic, well spoken, nonprovocative. In the end, although his arguments are not implausible, although it is extremely difficult for us Israelis to conceive of a peace agreement with the PLO as something solid, substantial, or reliable, although a broad range of matters is not merely unresolved but seemingly beyond resolution, the three Israelis from the territories made no converts that evening to the settler cause.

And yet, almost surely, a decided majority of Israelis do not really believe, cannot yet believe that the PLO has genuinely abandoned terrorism. Hence, we are all too ready to credit accusations that Fatah and Hamas have worked up a good cop/bad cop routine for the edification of the Israeli public, Bill Clinton, and CNN. Nor do a great many Israelis, including many of us who enthusiastically or grudgingly lend support to the interim accords, yet believe that the Palestinians will forever be satisfied holding a cup that is two-fifths full rather than bewailing its being three-fifths empty.

Still, whatever the upshot, it is clear that the ice-jam of past decades of immobility is cracking at last and, with all its incumbent risks, most of us Israelis are willing to let it happen. With bewildering speed, we know the times truly are achangin' before our eyes. And while everyone would grant that it is indeed pleasant to bask in the glow of a moratorium on being castigated as racist torturers or neo-colonialists, that it is gratifying to host delegations from China, the foreign minister of Turkey, and King Juan Carlos of Spain, or even to be recognized by Zaire and Mozambique, no one truly knows what embracing peace with Palestinian neighbors will mean, what it will ultimately entail. So along with fitful exhilaration, most of us are apprehensive of awakening from our aquarian dream only to discover that we have been embracing damp phantoms.

In our heart of hearts, the great majority of Israelis, including a great many of us who willy-nilly support the course that Rabin's government had undertaken to pursue, continues to view the PLO as the enemy. Regardless of accords, notwithstanding the appearance or substance of "good behavior," I suspect that this will not change significantly until two events which are currently difficult to imagine take place: in either order, the removal of Yassir Arafat from leadership of the PLO and democratic elections among the Palestinians.

My hunch is that most Israelis are less enraptured by gaudier visions of the blessing of lions lying down with lambs—who are the lions? who are the lambs?—than are many American Jews. But, although we are predictably and increasingly restive in the aftermath of each new bloody "incident," at the same time we remain willing to go along for the ride . . . in the back of our Subarus. But if "Our Man in Jericho" cannot in the future muzzle the young lions of the intifada—both his own and the Hamas pack—Rabin, Peres, Beilin, and Company could find themselves trying out for *Love's Labor's Lost* sooner than they expect.

PART TWO.
DAUGHTERS OF ZELOPHEHAD

What is [King David] to do, now that he has heard that the son to whom he gave so much of himself at their last meeting has violated the daughter he has always adored? . . . He blames himself, of course. Amnon, as well. But he blames Tamar most of all.

Dan Jacobson
(*The Rape of Tamar*)

DAUGHTERS OF ZELOPHEHAD

W HEN Zelophehad, whom the Bible identifies simply as "a righteous man," died during the forty years of Jewish wandering in the desert, he left behind five unmarried daughters—Mahlah, Noah, Hoglah, Milcah, and Tirzah. Refusing to succumb to despair, victimhood, or the prospect of penury, the five women engineered a challenge to the all-male leadership of Israel that seemed to me to expand significantly the rights of women under Jewish law. Why, I wondered, especially in a time nascent with feminist stirrings, even triumphalism, have these heroines remained rela tively unheralded?

At center stage on two separate occasions in the Book of Numbers and yet again for a cameo reprise in the Book of Joshua, the five surely represent more than an incidental flourish. Might not their boldness cast, at the very least, a shadow on that chronic Jewish dilemma, the subservient status of women? About a decade ago I broached my notion, albeit in inchoate form, when my turn came one Shabbat afternoon to lead the Torah discussion group that held forth in Yeroham for five years.

"Shortly before the five daughters make their initial entrance," I reminded my listeners, "Phineas earned God's approbation by even-handedly dispatching both the Israelite Zimri and the Midianite Cozbi, a prostitute who had seduced Zimri into sacrificing to Ba'al-Peor. To undo Israel, Balaam had schemed to deploy brigades of Cozbis."

"Demonstrating," quipped Yapha, "how really treacherous we females can be."

"On the contrary," I rejoined. "It's of a piece with the earlier episodes of the ten spies sent by Moses to scout out the Golden Calf and to reconnoiter the Promised Land. On both occasions it was the Jewish

61

men who were notably susceptible to the allure of the alien. And this theme is echoed in the very next sequence, a second census evoking the earlier head count that was taken upon the departure of the Jews from Egypt. On that occasion it was not the women but the men who succumbed to doubt and despair, which, as we know, is the traditional reason women were exempted from God's fatal judgment of that first desert generation."

Leah's groan was audible. I had, I realized, invoked discredited nineteenth-century apologetics exemplified notably by Samson Raphael Hirsch in his *Commentary on the Torah*, which serves up such indigestible nuggets as "The Torah allows that women have a special love and great fervor in serving God through their unique calling in life. . . . In all the sins to which our nation has sunk, it has been the merit of the righteous women that has preserved us."

"So we Jewish women are more faithful than you Jewish men," Leah mimicked. "Terrific! Next you're going to tell us that Jewish tradition maintains that we women eat, drink, and screw on such a higher plane than you men that we have no need to engage in serious learning. Listen, that these or any other supposed virtues of Jewish women should exempt us from anything pertaining to humankind is simply unacceptable to any thinking person. I don't accept it."

Well, things were not going the way I wanted. I had expected the male participants to be taciturn, but I had not anticipated that Leah, Fern, or Yapha, not to mention Jennifer or Marcia, would discern not even a glimmer of pride, hope, or solace in the signal achievement of the five daughters.

"I'm *not* saying that . . . not exactly," I pleaded. "If you'll let me get on with it, you'll see." I had my leave and took a silent vow to exercise greater caution.

"Obtaining an audience before Moses, Eleazar, and the Great Assembly, the five sisters probably had no more than an evening to prepare their case. Whatever their differences, it was obvious that their only chance of success lay in speaking the next day with a single voice. If they failed, there would be no appeal. Imagine them in the darkness of their tent, distraught and anxious but eager, and excited that their case would get so prompt a hearing.

"One, probably Tirzah the youngest, likely still in her early teens, had to be the most impulsive: 'It's only right that whatever was our father's should belong to us. Urge them, Mahlah, convince them of the justice of it. Who was closer to him than his flesh and blood whom he loved? Moses will listen to you. He must.'

"Noah may well have echoed her younger sister: 'Without patrimony, what will be our chances for matrimony? Haven't you noticed that the men already look upon us rather differently? The nicer ones now stand more aloof. Impoverished, what will become of us? They will marry us off to ugly old widowers . . . if we're lucky.'

"Mahlah would have discounted this approach: 'Moses won't change a word of the law simply because our suitors now strike us as less than suitable. We have to exercise superior cunning.' She turned to Hoglah, the middle sister, the one with the greatest wit: 'You're right, Mahlah. We must be clever. It is not our standing that will alter our situation. Mahlah, you must remind Moses of the service our father rendered to him and to the Lord. Speak, as it were, in his stead, as if he were standing among us. Nothing else would avail.'

"Obdurately one sister, say Milcah, must have held back, skeptical about the whole business: 'We're wasting our time. Our father is dead. We have no standing before the Assembly, no rights. The men tomorrow will mock us. Even if Moses were to take pity on us, he would grant us nothing in the presence of the Assembly. Proceed if you will, but without me.'

"'You don't have to open your mouth tomorrow,' Mahlah declared, 'but you damned well better be there among us, Milcah. After all, you stand to benefit equally. Tomorrow Hoglah will stand at your right, and Noah at your left.' Each nodded. 'Tirzah, when I step forward, snuffle a bit—not excessively—then stand quietly at my side. Let's all get a good night's sleep. Tomorrow's going to be a big day.'

"The next morning, before Moses, Eleazar, and the Assembly, Tirzah at her side, Mahlah was the very picture of a bereft daughter: 'Our dead father refused to join the faction of Korah, which banded together against the Lord. He died for his own sins, leaving no sons. Let not our father's name be lost to the clan merely because he had no son! Give us a holding among our father's kinsmen!'

"This argument cut several ways. Although it urged what was, in effect, a radical extension of women's property rights, it did not insist upon full equality with men. Nevertheless, it would result in a breach in the heretofore absolute primacy of inheritance through and for men. The daughters' virtue was never at issue. Their righteous father had been no rebel; nor would his daughters be. Their argument was simply that their father's name should not disappear 'just because he had no son.'"

"That doesn't sound very revolutionary to me," Fern observed.

"True, but what a brilliant, disingenuous stroke!"

Had I done the daughters a disservice? Could their plea have been uttered in all innocence? I dared not breathe my suspicion aloud, but, as Hirsch had indeed maintained, the biblical view clearly held that in any given generation Jewish women were less likely to adhere to the contemporary fashion or faction of idolatry—the party of Korah. Hirsch's despised insight was securely allied to the tradition that permitted Sarah and Rebekah an understanding greater than their husbands' into God's intentions.

I could not deny that in the substrata of Jewish consciousness lurks an ingrained paradox. The metaphorical marriage of God to Israel has inevitably cast Israel in the distaff role. Infidelity, therefore, is inevitably imaged in feminine guise, and so the whole issue of Israel's unfaithfulness evokes the feminine principle. Hence, both for the daughters and for me, the need to exercise caution and good tactics.

"Asking nothing for themselves as women but everything as the daughters of a virtuous, departed father, the five achieved an instantaneous triumph! A new decree shot down from on high: 'The plea of Zelophehad's daughters is just: you should give them an hereditary holding among their father's kinsmen; transfer their father's share to them.' Followed by a general principle: 'If a man dies without leaving a son, you shall transfer his property to his daughter. If he had no daughter, you shall assign his property to his brothers.'"

After sons but ahead of brothers and uncles was the niche assigned to Jewish daughters. To be sure, these daughters are an exception to the rule, but was that not an improvement over penury for all? Furthermore (I argued), a symbolic action had been enacted, a breach whose larger significance has yet to be appreciated by Jewish feminists.

Silence!

To fill the void I invoked a final prop, an anguished essay by David Novak, an Orthodox rabbi, which I had accidentally stumbled upon in a back issue of *Judaism*, a Conservative movement journal. Novak had posed without mitigation the dilemma that traditional Judaism entails for Jewish women: ". . . if God can choose one small people— Israel—to be recipient of His Torah, then why cannot God choose men rather than women to be authorities in a society governed by

Torah? . . . Clearly, the inner meaning of Jewish particularism is not democratic."

Novak, however, could not rest easy with this formulation. "Jewish Feminism is not going to disappear or retreat into silence. . . . Judaism, it seems to me, can sustain a feminist revolution [only] if that revolution is a genuine development into a new historical situation. In such a revolution—actually evolution is the name for it—a new economy of relations is gradually worked out."

Well, what else were Mahlah, Noah, Hoglah, Milcah, and Tirzah all about? Yes, they could function as a palliative for exalted Jewish womanhood. Yes, they could even serve as a trope for the faithfulness of Israel to its covenant. But why not the more imaginative notion of the daughters as instigators of a "genuine development into a new historical situation," proto-(r)evolutionaries of a new economy of relations whose working out has been a vital undercurrent of Jewish history?

I looked up hesitantly. The jury was uncommittal, still apparently immune to my dialectic. Then Leah assumed the role of spokeswoman: "A story about five women who gain an inheritance merely because they have no brother doesn't have much to say to me. I think I would gladly relinquish any claim to whatever superiority that Novak, Hirsch, or you want to bestow for my mess of pottage—plain, old-fashioned equality. Are you finished?"

Well, no. In fact, the daughters reappear on the biblical scene, so I took Leah's question as my leave to proceed. Just before their second visitation, Numbers 31 dwells on the vast number of livestock captured by the Israelites from the Midianites (whose males and married women had been slaughtered but whose maidens were judiciously spared), a benefice that had itself been preceded by enumeration (in numbing detail) of how many hundreds of this and that kind of cattle to slaughter for the various sacrifices. From this juxtaposition, one might expect that the sudden acquisition of quantities of livestock—cattle . . . and maidens—would evoke the spiritual context of the sacrifices. Not a bit! Instead, the cowboy tribes of Reuben and Gad petitioned for permission to remain in the cattle-raising highlands east of the Jordan.

Moses was furious. He reminded those two tribes of their fathers' derelictions and of the ten tribes who turned "the minds of the Israelites from crossing into the land. . . ." Nevertheless, a workable compromise was attained almost at once: if first they would serve as the vanguard of the conquering army, Reubenites and Gaddites might settle east of the Jordan. And so the episodes close with a curious symmetry: two groups had approached Moses with parallel requests to emend the rights and obligations of inheritance. For the sake of justice, the petition of the five sisters was explicitly approved, whereas on grounds of expediency, that of the tribesmen was conditionally accepted.

I had arrived at my central notion: a structural model for ameliorating the status of women seemed to stare out from the pages of Torah. There it was, imbedded right in the very framework of normative Judaism. At last I seemed to have earned everyone's full attention. Risking anticlimax, I pushed on.

"Mahlah, Noah, Hoglah, Milcah, and Tirzah have a reprise at the very close of Numbers. The head of their clan of Manasseh complained of an inequity: the portion of land allotted to his tribe would diminish were the five daughters to marry out of the tribe. At once seeing the point, Moses declared that the daughters might marry whomever they pleased *as long as they choose from within their own clan.* 'No inheritance of the Israelites may pass over from one tribe to another. . . . The daughters of Zelophehad did as the Lord had commanded Moses.' Non-heiresses might marry into any tribe at all."

"Housewife revolutionaries!" interjected Jennifer.

I skipped the daughters' final walk-on in Joshua 17 which informs us that they were assigned lands not with the half-tribe of Manasseh (which had thrown their lot in with the Reubenites and the Gaddites) but rather among the Manassehites who had settled within the promised borders of the land of Israel. This further datum serving to associate the sisters with vessels of faithfulness would have been counterproductive rhetoric. Why did I not simply acknowledge Leah's cynical point: mainstream Judaism has always tended to view women as chattel whose chief value lay in their capacity for bringing forth sons.

The years have passed. My daughter Jennifer has married and is now the mother of three. Leah has attained international celebrity for her struggle with Israel's religious establishment. Former Shabbat afternoon discussion stalwarts Fern and Chaim have long moved to Jerusalem. As has Yapha. As at most stages of Jewish history, as in today's diaspora, there is in Israel an excess of available unmarried women and a corresponding dearth of eligible, unmarried men. Echoing the unmarried daughters of Zelophehad, Yapha is not the first young, single woman to have quit Israel's smaller towns for the better matrimonial prospects of its larger cities.

In *On Women and Judaism* Blu Greenberg, addressing the dilemma of unmarried Jewish women, casts a benign eye on those who choose to mother and raise children as single parents: "Thus, our best hope for an increased Jewish population, it seems, is to help cope with areas of conflict and tension, to blend the feminist and traditional models." My wife's response is more radical still. "Perhaps the time has come to reconsider Rabbi Gershom's thousand-year-old ban on polygamy. Is it really so obviously better for children to grow up in one-parent rather than in three-parent households? Why should expanding the options for Jewish women be 'antifeminist?'"

These days I am bound to admit that the impatience of Leah, Fern, Yapha, Jen, and Marcia was justified. For a distinction I had previously scanted now seems to me the most critical matter of all. When the sisters brought their case before Moses, it was God Himself who intervened to declare that "the plea of Zelophehad's daughters is just." I can't discern the smallest textual hint that Moses would have ventured to alter their condition on his own.

The contrast with when the Reubenites and the Gaddites brought forward *their* far more dubious request is sharp. Notwithstanding his animus, Moses soon devised an expedient on his own authority. Is it not clear that not the decision but *this*, its source, is the truly salient distinction to be drawn between the case of the five daughters vs. that of the two-and-a-half tribes? Looking to the justice of the contrasting claims, I had overlooked a critical difference and had drawn a grievously erroneous inference.

In matters pertaining to women, the prevailing judicial legacy bequeathed by Moses to succeeding generations of male authority is the claim of lack of competence to effect change! Unless God Himself were to intervene, amelioration of the status of Jewish women within traditional Judaism, no matter how just their case or oppressive their conditions, seems to be a virtual nonstarter.

But not quite! The parallel case of the herdsmen tribes, indeed, the very decree banning polygamy that was promulgated by Rabbi Gershom, points to the possibility of a different direction. Meanwhile, however, male self-interest and lack of will have garbed themselves in the iron suit of insufficient authority. Perhaps only when for the sake of justice—hence, for the sake of all—more and more observant women shrug off their passivity will a Novakesque stroke yet be pulled off. Looking at the scene around us, however, short of an epiphany, it's difficult to be optimistic. Today's Orthodoxy generally pays its more assertive faithful daughters no greater heed, repays them with no greater equity, than once it delivered to their foresisters in the desert: only what it absolutely must.

PRINCESSES
OF ZION

I N THE CORNER of an upstairs room in my house, a bulging, white nylon sack protrudes from under the dictionary stand. It looks something like the oversized parcels trans-Atlantic airline flight attendants cram with duty-free cartons of cigarettes, bottles of scotch, or perfume for bargain-seeking high flyers. This container, however, is innocent of designer lettering proclaiming WINSTONS, SEA-GRAMS, or CHANEL. Displaying four perfectly blank exterior walls, it stands squarely on the floor like a tombstone awaiting the engraver's chisel.

What that oversized parcel contains are four cube-shaped corrugated boxes, each a bit squatter than a shoebox and topped by a folded, black plastic handle. Four meticulously packed hampers containing sandwiches, pickles, cookies—portable homecookin'? Not quite. As if some spray-gun artist had gone berserk, cautionary red Hebrew letters have been spread over nearly every square inch of every side of the four cardboard containers. At the corner of each container a yellow-and-black decal flashes yet another warning, this time not alone in Hebrew but in English, Arabic, and Russian as well:

DO NOT OPEN! Opening this kit deffects [sic] its efficiency! Keep in a dry cool place protected from sun. Keep away from children. OPEN THIS KIT ONLY UNDER CLEAR INSTRUCTIONS FROM THE CIVIL DEFENCE HEADQUARTERS.

With a black grease pencil, my wife has added markings of her own: HAIM writ on one cube, MARCIA on a second, MIRIAM on a third, and SHAI on the last. Since two of our four children live away from home, we needed only four masks in all, the contents of that ample sack. But I sometimes wonder about the many Yeroham households that consist of eight or ten or more souls. How and where many of my Moroccan and Indian fellow townspeople can safely stow their three or more sacks so as to forestall their kids from innocently deffecting the efficiency of their contents—and themselves—is something of a mystery.

It seems like just yesterday afternoon that Marcia, Miriam, and I strolled the few blocks to Shoshana Sapir High School, one of two distribution points in town. Shai, already by then a teenager, disdained to accompany us: at school he'd already been instructed about what to do in case of attack, and since kids are not issued identity cards of their own until the age of sixteen, we could pick his mask up for him. Right? Right.

Besides, he explained, common sense dictated that the danger of Israel's being targeted for gas attack from Saddam Hussein was extremely remote. Further, the logical target would surely be Tel Aviv or some other population center, not a small dot in the Negev where, in any event, the desert breezes may be counted upon to waft away such gas that accident or weird design lobbed our way. Altogether, wasn't this whole business a waste of time and the government's money? So Shai stayed home. Notwithstanding my son's bravado, however, I have not encountered a single Israeli who disdained to pick up his or her gas mask, the cost of which, we were informed, had already been deducted from our income taxes.

Thursday was the final day for regular distribution, and together with the rest of the local citizenry whose last names crowd the end of the alphabet, we walked over to the high school for a free demonstration and to collect our merchandise. One of the unanticipated adjustments we were forced to accommodate ourselves to since moving to Israel has been alphabetical banishment from top-of-the-morning letter C to endgame Hebrew letter shin: Chertok to Shertok, Eden to Hades. In a land of forms and queues, it makes a palpable difference. This time the problem was more basic: as I had half anticipated, the only family member listed was my older son, Ted, who, since he had floated off to teach Jewish subjects at a high school near Philadelphia for the year, was the only family member to have no possible use for a mask.

During the late seventies I had taught English for two years at Shoshana Sapir. Or, rather, I "taught" English and resolved that my own kids would never suffer incarceration within its walls. Since that time it had been absorbed into the ORT school network and, word has it, improved markedly. Well, I had to admit that it did look more tidy.

I anticipated a problem because although we lived in Yeroham, our names were not inscribed on the official voting roster, the basis for gas mask distribution. And why not? Well, in order to qualify Shai and Miri for entrance into what we considered a significantly better school than Yeroham afforded—in this instance, a bus ride away in Beersheba—we had registered with the Ministry of Interior as residents of a flat in the latter city as well. It was dubious but probably legal. Having squared our ethical circle, we were still undeniably guilty of circumvention, ruse, and royal botheration.

We stood in line at a door marked Station One. Not finding us listed, the young woman soldier, or *hayelet*, looked up uncertainly from her registry. At her side stood tall, bearded Chaim, for over a decade our friendly mail deliverer. Dressed for this occasion in army fatigues, Chaim now delivered both us and the *hayelet* from ambivalence.

"It must be a computer snafu. I know they live at 1015. Why not sign them up on the sheet with the new Russian immigrants?" Chaim suggested to the green-eyed *hayelet* in charge of checking the roster. She hesitated briefly—could she read our minds?—before deciding to comply.

At Station Two, a classroom, about twenty housewives were already seated and watching a video that depicted how to prepare a room in the event of a gas attack. Only one other man sat in the room; others would appear in the evening after work. This was mainly a time for women and children. Each wore an impressively serious mien. One of the mothers—Irit, about thirty—imperceptibly nodded in my direction. She had at one time been my English student in this very building.

Together with the others, Marcia, Miri, and I focused on the voiceless little figures on the video screen. They were efficiently at work securing windows, doors, and light switches with insulation and sealing tape. Then they calmly covered them all with sheets of plastic nylon and plastic tape. We had entered the prophylactic realm of Practical Pig.

Next to the boxes of gas masks the camera focused a close-up on neatly stacked towers of canned corn and tuna, two glass bottles of water, a transistor radio, an emergency light, books and games "to help pass the time with the children" a video voice explained. (How many Israelis have that much extra room in their closets? How many have real *closets?*) This was followed by a woman demonstrating how to don a mask. (First under the chin, then secure the rest of the head with straps and snaps. Don't forget: first the chin. Roger.) Everyone in the room was admirably attentive: why couldn't English lessons that once had bounced off these very walls been nearly so well heeded?

The video show was over, and we were shepherded to Station Three, an adjoining classroom. Here a plump, jolly-looking *hayelet*, about nineteen, discoursed on how to prepare one room in the house for the remote eventuality of a gas attack. This was an exact repetition of what we had just viewed on the video screen, but, I mused, pedagogically sound. The young woman spoke rapidly, without notes. After ten minutes she was spelled by a second *hayelet* who, just as we had seen on the video screen, demonstrated each of the five pieces of protective equipment we would be receiving. It struck me that although these young women in uniform must have delivered their spiels dozens of times in the course of that week, they still managed to make their presentation lively.

I was conscious that our eleven-year-old daughter at my side was taking it all in. Both of the *hayelot* performed admirably; the second one, her dark ponytail animated by her perky demonstration, was exceptionally pretty. Both wore khaki slacks and blouses. Except on infrequent occasions, only the relatively rare, religiously observant woman soldier dons a skirt; as often as not, she comes from a religious kibbutz.

Earlier that week a moving poem called "Mobilization" had been awarded first prize in the BBC's International Poetry Contest for 1990. Written by Karen Alcalay-Gut, an acquaintance who teaches English at Tel Aviv University, it expressed her pride and her anxiety upon the imminent entrance of her daughter into the Israeli army. The award was quite a surprise: the BBC does not normally hand out prizes to Israelis.

Two years of national service is the norm for young Israeli women, a national rite of passage from home. The sight of groups of pretty eighteen- to twenty-year-olds bearing their dufflebags, Uzi or M-16 strapped over their shoulders, is perfectly common in Israel. For a number of easily comprehended reasons, *hayelot* are not assigned to serve with frontline combat units, but in a country of Israel's dimensions, the distinction between the front and the rear can be rather academic.

It happens, of course, that *hayelot* spend their years in uniform filling secondary, demeaning, "female" functions—like filling the coffee cup of a colonel. And it also still happens that *hayelot* are treated like morale boosters, cheerleaders for the frontline troops . . . but less frequently than formerly. *Hayelot* type letters but also work as airplane mechanics, intelligence analysts, and stunningly well as platoon sergeants in charge of getting raw male recruits shaped up in basic training.

For their infants, in place of gas masks parents received a box tent made of extra heavy plastic sheeting with a flap that sealed shut. Each of these contained an inside pocket capable of holding baby bottles upright and incorporating a plastic "window" through which a parent wearing a rubber glove might insert a hand to assist. The tent was supported by a collapsible aluminum frame. Altogether, an ingenious apparatus! Also bulky. Also not cheap. Since the inside of the tent gets very warm, the dark-haired *hayelet* advised parents to cover it with a damp towel and, if possible, even to direct a fan in its direction.

For children aged two to four, parents were bestowed a special plastic hood that covered the upper half of each child's body. Those from four to eight were provided with a small mask to which was attached a hood that fastened at the shoulders. Our instructress called a young boy forward to demonstrate. In short order she succeeded in getting him into the contraption. The apparatus includes a tube through which water may be sucked. The youngster—he was about six—was ordered to try it.

"Are you drinking?" the *hayelet* asked.

He nodded affirmatively.

Then, finally, there were the gas masks: "A small size to fit children from eight to fifteen," the uniformed teenager explained, "and a regular mask for those from fifteen . . . to one hundred and twenty." It was not a joke and no one smiled.

The masks came equipped with a motor ventilator which, once functioning, would render communication very difficult. Each kit contained a syringe filled with atropine, an antitoxin for use in case of exposure to nerve gas. As nonchalantly as if she were selling earrings, our *hayelet* explained, "The syringes come in three colors. Each contains different quantities of atropine suitable for different age groups."

I mentally instructed myself to forget colors two and three. "White. Everyone in my household would use the white. That's all I have to know."

"In addition," the two-striper proceeded, "the syringes are color-coded with green at one end, yellow at the other. The green end goes down, like grass; the yellow side, like the sun, goes up."

Green down. Yellow up. Gotchya.

Then, shockingly, the young woman lifted her left leg against a chair leg and, as if holding a needle, smashed the pulp of her hand against the flesh of her thigh, making a splatty sound.

"If there's exposure to gas, plunge the green side right through the material into the skin. Hold it for three seconds."

At my side, Miri involuntarily shuddered.

"Then release. For babies, jab into the thigh or right through the diaper into the tush. It can even be done inside the tent. Afterward, attach the empty syringe to the flap of the tent or to the lapel of your shirt so that anyone coming on the scene will know that you've already been jabbed. Getting two shots by mistake could be very dangerous."

Yes, that'd be one stupid way to get oneself deffected, wouldn't it?

"Any questions?"

A woman with a girl of six and an infant raised a hand: "In case of attack, who should put on the mask first?"

"Adults should don their own masks first; then, from the oldest to the youngest, attend to the children."

To my surprise, my Miri, touchingly grave: "How long do we have wear the masks?"

Hayelet: "Gas normally dissipates in about two hours, but you could wear them safely for up to six hours. Also, since gas is heavier than air, an upper story of a house is safer than ground level."

There were no further questions. In the hallway, we came to Station Four, for the actual distribution of masks. Directly in front of us a middle-aged Russian couple was fruitlessly trying to explain that they wanted an additional mask for their adult son.

"He's at work now," the man repeated in Russian to the frustrated soldiers. Buried nearly three decades, my rusted Russian—legacy of a year of training at the U.S. Army Language School—enabled me to make clear to the man that his son had until ten o'clock that night to pick up a mask, that he even could come during the following week. I had surpassed my woeful past inadequacy as a language instructor in these halls.

I was reasonably sure that weeks after the distribution of the masks the streets of Yeroham would resound with the shouts of kids wearing *deffected* masks playing war games. My apprehensions were entirely misplaced. Once the government's dither over whether and when to distribute gas masks had passed, several hundred chubby, slim, ponytailed, curly-haired, plain, pretty, resolute *hayelot*—flight attendants for a nation temporarily up in the air—distributed the 3.5 million gas masks with the calm, dispatch, and competence—indeed, éclat—which eased an anxious nation into a tone of self-confidence.

Station Five: 11:00 at night, four months later, the upstairs room across from my office—our family's "sealed room." Following instructions, its windows had been sealed with heavy sheets of plastic and tape. Boxes marked HAIM, MARCIA, SHAI, and MIRI in black grease pencil had been opened and had been pitched into a corner of the darkened room.

First the chin. Then the rest of the head. Each of us tested the air flow of our pig-snouted rubber faces. Thirty minutes earlier scuds had exploded in two other regions of the country. Silently, behind our masks, each of us impatiently awaited the calm voice on the transistor to announce All Clear for the regional code that designated the Negev.

In our time of peril, the only notable *deffections* from Zion had been hundreds of Jewish American scions and princesses on one-year university programs who, heeding the ignominious alarm of mothers in Minneapolis, of daddies in Westwood, had flown for safety. Their masquerade had abruptly ended. Meanwhile, behind our masks, apprehensive but buoyed by the example and by the grace of our own regal daughters in khaki, Israel knew what to do and how to comport itself. The country was headed for a safe landing.

THE WOMAN
NEXT DOOR

A DISPROPORTIONATE number of women active in the Israeli feminist movement are transplants from the United States, but in the avant-garde of those forcing the issue with Israel's vested religious authorities one encounters an outspoken native daughter—a *sabrait*. Leah Shakdiel, our Yeroham neighbor, "the woman next door," has become since 1986 one of Israel's best-known, most outspoken feminists. A glance at her career to date says much about where Israeli women of consciousness are coming from . . . and how far they have to go.

Even amateur semioticians hip to local headgear would at once identify Shakdiel—hair largely concealed by a telltale kerchief—as religiously observant, or *dosi*. Indeed, she is youngest of the four children of Rav Moshe Zvi Shakdiel, one-time director of religious education for Mizrachi, the World Religious Zionist Movement, who, a latter-day Zelophehad, had only daughters. Notwithstanding her laughing disclaimer, Leah is much in their mold. Married to an American-born psychologist who is as much a feminist as she, mother of three, the teacher of Jewish studies evades nearly all of Israel's more convenient pigeonholes.

In her late twenties when she moved to Yeroham from Jerusalem in 1978, she became a member of Mashmia Shalom, our predominantly American "intentional subcommunity" which chose to settle in Yeroham in large measure because of its location within the faded, jaded pre-'67 borders—the Green Line. Shakdiel has also associated herself with Netivot Shalom, sister organization to Oz Veshalom, and with the Association for Civil Rights. Locally she sparked a protest vigil on the town's central plaza when Rabbi Meir Kahane came to address a rally, and hers is the address where nearby Bedouin steer their Peugeot pickups for aid whenever they are hassled by the rough-riders of the paramilitary Green Patrol.

There was early warning that Shakdiel would clash with established religious norms and authority. Upon getting married, she decided to retain her maiden name. "You might say it began as a joke during our courtship," she explained, "but jokes are, of course, usually meaningful. It was important to me that Moshe left the matter of *my* name to *me*. The key thing is that people should control the fundamental decisions of their lives. In the end I had to file a special request with the Ministry of Interior because it automatically assumes that any woman would gladly change her name. So my legal name was changed twice: from Shakdiel to Landsman and then back to Shakdiel."

Elected a member of Yeroham's town council in 1984, Shakdiel was one of that rarest of all Israeli political types: a flourishing Ashkenazi–Labor Party bloom in the Likud-tinted, overwhelmingly Sephardi hinterland. She declared her major concern as a council member to be education—"nearly everyone thinks the schools are Yeroham's most critical problem"—but her preoccupation was administrative: "My chief success here," she once said, "would come if the town council were run more professionally, according to established procedures. Unfortunately, I cannot claim much success."

It was two years later that Shakdiel, then thirty-five, catapulted to national prominence. She was positioned at the vortex of a complex situation impinging on two interrelated, highly controversial areas of Israeli public life: the boundary between religious and secular authority and the repression of Israeli women. Fueled by her agile tongue and ready smile, the combination proved explosive.

During one week in September, photos of Leah Shakdiel graced every Israeli newspaper, and her "case" was cited repeatedly in editorials of every stripe. Thereafter, public demonstrations were organized on her behalf, she herself was featured on Israel's two prime-time interview programs, and her case was debated in the Knesset. On the larger scene, *The New York Times* found her story fit to print, American Jewish publications zeroed in like Pooh bears to honey, the American-based New Israel Fund flew her to New York and Washington to enable her to clarify the situation for their constituency. Finally, Israel's Supreme Court accepted her petition to adjudicate her case.

What was it all about? A retrospective of l'Affaire Shakdiel reveals a fascinating mixture of dedication to principle and eye on the main chance, of high competence, mixed motivation, and occasionally erratic judgment. It also touches on some of the grittier depths of Israeli politics.

In January 1986 Yeroham's town council elected its four members to serve on the local religious council: three men and a sole woman. Twice before, Israeli women had been elected to this post; twice before, pressure exerted by the forces of tradition had constrained them to withdraw their names from consideration. So Shakdiel's service would have been precedent-breaking; nevertheless, at the time it was barely noted. Early in February the four names were routinely dispatched for confirmation to the Ministry of Religious Affairs in Jerusalem. Then six months passed with nothing at all happening . . . until the eruption in September.

What underlay the hiatus was a labyrinthine interplay of politics and religion. Religious councils were initiated in 1936 when, in line with its centralizing policy for all public spheres of activity in Palestine, the Jewish Agency subordinated the various agencies that provided religious services such as burial, marriage, and ritual slaughtering of animals under a single administrative authority. Nominations to each council had to be submitted by the chief rabbi of each municipality. From their inception, then, religious councils were creatures less of religious than of Zionist impulse. They were not invested with powers to make religiously binding decisions.

In 1949 local religious councils were reorganized into a national system, but their scope of operation changed only in 1963 when the local rabbis were divested of control. At that time it was decided that the size of each local council should be determined by each town or city council and that only 10 per cent should be nominated by local rabbis. Half of the remaining 90 per cent were to be appointed by the municipal councils themselves; the other half, by the Ministry of Religious Affairs in Jerusalem.

For Yeroham's nine-person town council, this meant the town and Jerusalem should each nominate four members, the local chief rabbi just one. But Israeli ward politics can be as Byzantine as, say, Chicago's. Locally, the nonpaying position of chairman of the religious council had been held for as long as anyone could remember by a National Religious Party (NRP) stalwart, an ex-mayor then sitting in the opposition. Under him, the religious council had become a fief-dom of the local branch of NRP. It was never convened. Indeed, no one even knew the names of those who were supposed to constitute its membership.

Nevertheless, budget requests for maintaining Yeroham's ritual bath in reasonable repair got submitted, some funds did get allocated and, somehow or other, spent or misspent. For many years, all this was enacted out of the mysterious if ample yarmulke of the religious coun-cil chairman who knew full well that as soon a new slate of members to his body was confirmed, his reign as permanent chairman would draw swiftly to a close. He therefore pulled every string at his disposal to delay the issue from coming to a head.

No one dare complain that the political configuration of Yeroham is devoid of piquancy. Another colorful wrinkle: at that time the town council was run by a Labor–Likud majority coalition of five. The opposition consisted of two representatives from secularist Mapam (power-base of Yeroham's Indian community!) and two from the NRP. So when the council majority decided to exercise its prerogative of electing its quota of 45 per cent to serve on its religious council, Shakdiel suddenly realized that no one could be elected without her support. Seizing the moment, she forced the hand of her dumb-founded fellow council members.

"The opportunity arose," she later explained with a disingenuous smile, "and I realized that it could be an historical, even revolutionary moment. Still, I really thought that it would somehow be aborted at an early stage at some administrative level. Even after seven months of Jerusalem's stalling to my repeated inquiries, I still thought the whole business would blow over in a day or so. I never dreamed just how much interest my nomination would generate, how important the issue would be to so many people. I'm not so sure that this alto-gether benefits me, but, frankly, the high degree of public interest is pleasing. I think it's significant, a sign that the time was ripe for this particular battle to be waged."

Although Israeli women have long served as cabinet members, and, lest it slip anyone's mind, one notably functioned as prime minister, the innovative breeze out of the Negev was not exactly hailed at the Ministry of Religious Affairs, then headed by elderly Dr. Yosef Burg of the NRP. Oddly enough, however, the main reason pragmatist

Burg pointedly ignored the Shakdiel nomination for over six months lay in yet another behind-the-scene's struggle for spoils.

A patronage dispute between the NRP and the ultra-Orthodox Shas Party over representation on these local bodies had been raging for over a year. Although its constituency does not even recognize the authority of local religious councils, Shas nevertheless wanted their share of the 45 per cent of the appointments coming down from Jerusalem. To protect NRP incumbents throughout the country, Burg, therefore, was sitting on the nominations not only from Yeroham but from twenty-one other local religious council slates! For seven months, not one appointment had been confirmed.

Now, the Israeli system of administration is not entirely hostage to the weight of one minister's thumb on the scale of equity. Theoretically a higher body, in this case a three-person committee consisting of the Prime Minister, the Minister of Interior, and—yes—the Minister of Religious Affairs, a troika then consisting of Yitzhak Shamir (Likud), Yitzhak Peretz (Shas), and Zevulun Hammer (NRP) was empowered to intervene. With such a shining prospect, however, Shakdiel gave the nod to the Association for Civil Rights to take her case before the media.

"I realized that only public pressure would make a difference. Still," she continued, "the astonishing response has far exceeded my expectations. Schoolchildren who have seen me on television now stare at me in wonder. I've gotten a lot of support from the secular community. My fellow members of the town council have also been supportive. I hear from one of my sisters every day." She paused for a brief but painful moment. "On the other hand, one of my other sisters has not called even once."

If, as she repeatedly averred, Shakdiel's main concern was "to return religious Zionism to its proper moorings, to creatively meet the challenge of modernity," the highly visible support she garnered from the Association of Civil Rights, in the forefront of court battles against religious coercion, and from Na'amat, the women's organization of the Histadrut labor federation with a good record for raising the status of Israeli women, was probably counterproductive.

Still, Shakdiel could not afford to be choosy in her supporters. The only minister who came to her defense was Gad Ya'kobi (Labor), and he did not sit on the Knesset's Religious Affairs Committee. Endorsements came from Rabbi Menachem Ha-Cohen, the Laborite

Knesset member who was anathema to the religious establishment, and from militant secularists such as Mordechai Virshubski. Either one of these would be the kiss of death for more traditional religious elements, the people whose minds she was purportedly trying to change! The New Israel Fund, which financed Shakdiel's lecture trip to the States, also frequently supports causes that could fairly be labeled antireligious.

"You have no idea how hard it is to persuade more open-minded rabbis to speak on this kind of issue in public," Shakdiel complained. "Still," she noted with satisfaction, "several prominent religious personages have been supportive: Rabbi Safrai, Professor of Jewish History at Hebrew University and Rabbi Bar Mocha, the chief rabbi of a town near Haifa who is also deputy chairman of the Association of Religious Councils in Israel."

And what about the other religious women? "Emunah, the National Religious Women's organization," Shakdiel grimaced, "backed off from the issue. Although they claimed to be for me in principle, they could not support me supposedly because of 'the way I was proceeding.' But I did get invaluable help from Professor Alice Shalvi of Jerusalem, who has led an effort to focus public attention on the issue."

Shakdiel also cited support from an obscure group within the NRP that sought its renewal through restoration of its original principles, prominent among which, she pointed out, was improvement of the status of women! "It's astonishing to realize today that over eighty years ago the Mizrachi Movement was in the forefront of the suffragette movement in Eastern Europe. At one time the NRP even elected women to the Knesset, but after the Six-Day War, the party lost its open orientation toward the modern world."

"Did you know," Shakdiel mused, "that back in 1944 Rav Uziel, Chief Sephardi Rabbi of Jerusalem, wrote in a responsum that women can be nominated for and vote for any public office? But perhaps most meaningful of all for me," she concluded, "was hearing from Rabbi Moshe Stiglitz, an old, old friend of my father's, who reassured me that Judaism has always had its great women, and that he knew I was one of them. It was very touching."

But Shakdiel was too savvy to believe for even a minute that her battle would be fought on sentimental grounds or on theoretical terrain where one rabbinic opinion tends to cancel the other. Indeed, noting that Israel's chief rabbis avoided taking any public position on her election, Shakdiel thought them wise. "It goes, in a way, to the heart of the issue. The truth is that they really should not issue rulings for an area of public life that is fundamentally secular. I have never doubted," she added, "that a sizable body of quiet opinion within Orthodoxy was sympathetic to my viewpoint. My intent was to work to force recognized Jewish authority to address this issue because I firmly believe that the monopolistic claim of the ultra-Orthodox to speak for authentic Judaism must, in the end, be challenged."

In the end, however, it was thanks to the intervention of secular authority that Leah Shakdiel succeeded in taking her seat as the first woman member of an Israeli religious council. She served out her full term, but any objective observer would probably conclude that thus far she has not made much headway in fulfilling her larger aims.

Feminist, religiously observant, civil rights and peace activist, and development town resident by choice, in 1992 Shakdiel ran for the Knesset on a slate headed by ex-Communist Charlie Biton. It was a serious lapse in judgment. The results were disastrous. Thereafter she took a one-year "sabbatical" from Yeroham to serve as principal of a "progressive" Orthodox school in Jerusalem. Intelligent, photogenic, emblematic of a new generation of Israeli women, first Israeli public figure to leapfrog from election to a local religious council to national prominence, the woman next door will almost surely be a figure to reckon with for years to come.

AND THERE

WAS LEAH!

L ATE in the spring of 1990 a friend, who herself would be delivering a paper on a subject of mutual interest, invited me to attend a literary conference in Beersheba. Attending events of this sort is not generally among my favorite pastimes, and this one was forbiddingly labeled "Plot and Rhetoric." Nevertheless, turn up I did at Ben-Gurion University's Lecture Room 501, and, to my surprise, I found the room filled to overflowing with perhaps 150 registrants.

At least four-fifths of those present seemed to be secondary school teachers, nearly all of them women. Even more than in the States, in Israel the arts pitch their tents in the distaff provinces; the male roost securely remains science and technology. This was BGU's annual literary conclave in honor of the memory of an Eleanor Artzyeli, an English professor who died out of season. I never met her.

At the front of the room, five folding chairs had been positioned side by side in a straight line, as if arrayed as a stage set for a piece of minimalist theater by Beckett or Ionesco. Before the chairs a card table had been placed upon which sat a framed photograph of an attractive, intense-looking woman, surely the visage of Professor Artzyeli. Beside it was a small blue vase out of which protruded bulbous, purple blooms. Had a candle been lighted, or incense burnt, she could have been Evita or an iconic Madonna.

Suddenly, as if responding to an offstage cue, a procession of five men filed into Room 501 and seated themselves at the five empty places: an English department functionary, a dean, keynoter Professor Harold Fisch, and two unknown burlies. (Security?) Perhaps, as still happens even after seventeen years in Israel, I had overlooked or misconstrued something significant, but it seemed to me that the tab was daunting: males five, females zero. For a colloquium that purported to honor the memory of a woman, the ironic subtext was . . . well . . . delectable.

The first order of business was departmental: to award an annual prize for outstanding student achievement in English literature. Its recipient turned out to be a jeans-clad young woman seated directly to my front, one seat over. Upon accepting a sealed envelope, she shook each of the five outstretched male hands in turn. Unpasting the smile from her face, she then returned to her place.

Over her shoulder I watched as the young woman surreptitiously opened the envelope. She glanced at the amount typed on the check, then wriggled her nose. The year's Artzyeli Prizewinner then held the check before the eyes of her girlfriend seated by her side. The friend's nose also squinched. Then, smack in the middle of the dean's words of welcome, the two young women unceremoniously rose and made a fairly conspicuous exit out of 501.

Professor Harold Fisch is a well-known academic critic. He cut a tall, stooped figure; his gray hair was set off by a dark-blue crocheted yarmulke. After brief opening remarks, he switched from Hebrew to English, not inappropriate considering that his topic that day was "Shakespeare's Biblical Plots." Fisch's seeming argument was that in many of Shakespeare's plays the thematic disharmonies were structurally unresolvable. The reason? Because the different levels of plot played at authentic cross-purposes. In both *Hamlet* and *King Lear*, for example, an amalgam of classical and Christian elements inhabited the same plot and jostled uneasily.

In *Hamlet*, the introspective romantic hero was perennially at odds with the hero of a Roman tragedy of revenge. As for *King Lear*, although critics and even the play's own secondary characters make much of the parallel between the main plot and the subplots, Fisch underscored their intrinsic differences. Although these irreconcilable axes were a source of vital energy, both genetically and structurally, *King Lear* and *Hamlet*, he concluded, were dramas whose key elements were abrasively at war with themselves. Each consisted of bilateral plots that had been stuffed into a single bulging garment.

As a literary thesis, Fisch's presentation was stimulating; what I couldn't decide was whether the Hebrew University professor was operating on another level as well. Twoness, dialectic, doubleness, coexistence, and enrichment within a single structure that, notwithstanding the efforts of generations of critics, resisted being smoothed into seamless unity. Was I suffering from politics on the brain, or was Fisch not playing allegorical games with Israelis and Palestinians? Or perhaps, closer to Shakespeare's intentions, gender was his real issue.

Farfetched, I supposed, but for a symposiac daydreamer, it presented beguiling possibilities. Might not a day come when neoplatonic Jews and Arabs, not to mention men and women, would discover the means to break out of the bonds of their Aristotelian psychodrama? Perhaps had Fisch been more explicit, a brigade of nationalist-leaning high school teachers might have wriggled their noses and taken a collective powder.

At the 11 A.M., I was confronted by a pragmatic, Jamesian sort of conundrum: to choose one among the three simultaneously held workshops meant pragmatically unchoosing the other two. True to the spirit of my reverie, I opted for poet Karen Alkalay-Gut's session: "Order in Madness—Poems by Anne Sexton." Arriving at the indicated classroom, I counted only thirteen others attracted by the prospects of imposing order on bifurcating madness. Alcalay-Gut gamely handed out sheets of poems with which she aimed to demonstrate that Sexton's poems, far from constituting evidence of neurosis, were the strongest possible proof of her inner coherence.

> I have ridden in your cart, driver,
> waving my nude arms at villages going by
> learning the last bright routes, survivor,
> where your flames still bite my thigh
> and my ribs crack where your wheels wind.
> A woman like that is not ashamed to die.
> I have been her kind.

So ran the closing lines of Sexton's "Her Kind." Witchy poet, but like Hamlet temporarily sane, Sexton had at times been otherwise . . . and knew it. She had been "her kind." Alcalay-Gut then rendered another, similar awareness of Sexton's consciousness of otherness residing within: "A woman *is* her mother. That's the main thing." Yes, that was surely *some*thing. Two-in-one, unstable Sexton had contrived verses out of madness. In the end, however, in "real life," her center did not hold. Sexton did herself in.

The afternoon came and a workshop led by Shira Leibowitz, a friend since my first year in Israel. Its full title was "Rhetoric of Translation: A Comparison of Seven English Versions of the Story of Jacob, Rachel, and Leah." An entirely new cast of fifteen had gathered to witness Leibowitz's seven ways of looking at a blackbird.

Was it really likely, she posed at the outset, that Jacob would sleep with Leah and never realize she was not her sister Rachel? The answer with which we could rest, Leibowitz averred, was inherent in the translation we used *because translation is interpretation*. Her most extensive example relied on an examination of the reverent rendition of the text of Rabbi Moshe Weissman:

> Ya'akov, prepared for deceit, asked his bride for signs he had ar-
> ranged with her. She answered his questions, and he was sat-
> isfied. When Leah was about to be presented as the bride, Rachel
> thought, "Now my sister will be exposed to public shame. How
> terrible for her! If I have not been found worthy to build the Jew-
> ish nation, let my sister build it instead." She then revealed to
> her sister the secret signs. She even hid in the room where the
> couple were staying and answered Ya'akov's questions so that
> Leah's voice would not reveal the truth to him.

Was it plausible that Sexton's kind, unashamed to die, would be outstripped by Weissman's, unembarrassed to hide in her sister's nuptial closet? No, I decided, the strain on credibility was too great.

"Morning came," my friend concluded, "and there was Leah!" What a shocker! Or, just possibly, was it an example of mutual, implied duplicity by all three, even four parties? Shira's upshot? Rachel was . . . well . . . mainly Rachel, but Leah was at one and the same time both herself, her sister, and the embodiment of the Jewish people. More than sisters, Leah and Rachel were two faces, two stages of the one.

All right. By extension, was it not of a piece with Hamlet, who was both a Danish prince but also some other tragic bloke whose psyche, like that of Sexton's witch, ultimately eclipses, merges with, and destroys his own? It was just then that I was reminded of one of my most pleasant duties as a Jewish father. Upon my return home from synagogue on Friday evenings, my first duty is to bestow the traditional priestly benediction upon sons, daughters, whichsoever grandchildren are on hand. The text is identical for both genders except for the opening line. For boys it reads "May God make you as Ephraim and Manasseh"; for girls," . . . as Sarah, Rebekah, Rachel, and Leah."

The sequence of matriarchal names is patently generational, but a second glance reveals that it is not quite chronological. In the same way that favored, younger son Ephraim is given precedence, favored Rachel is invoked ahead of her older sister. A conventional inversion, it reflects not only the tradition as reflected in the body of extra-biblical folk material—the Midrashim—but also the dominant view of classical biblical commentators: priority properly adheres to Rachel. She is, after all, the irresistibly beautiful maiden, the beloved wife, and the mother of Joseph. Later, dying pathetically in childbirth, it is she who has long been popularly viewed as Jewish womankind's compassionate intercessor, later incorporated by Christianity into the character of Mary. Unloved, weak-eyed, Leah is . . . well . . . Leah.

To be sure, Nachmanides was assiduous in pointing out that Jacob did not *despise* his first wife; it was just that he, like the commentators themselves, loved her less. Propitiation of the younger and fairer is the constant, the general rule. Typical of the Midrashim is one that depicts God rebuking Jacob for the sole recorded instance when Jacob loses patience with Rachel's foolishness (Gen. 30:2). Consequently, at hundreds of thousands of ritually set, Jewish dinner tables on Friday nights, Leah gets supplanted by her younger sister. It is as if Rachel exacts perpetual retribution for that one night in particular when Leah supplanted her in Jacob's wedding bed, thereupon causing him to labor yet seven years more in order to earn her hand.

Yet, when viewed dispassionately, the biblical narrative crosshatch of incident and evidence lays a burden of error, divine disfavor, and punishment not on Leah but on her younger sister. It is Rachel who is haughty in disposition, long barren, a trickster, and a thief, in the end condemning herself to early death in childbirth. No, neither barrenness nor premature death is an unequivocal sign of God's displeasure; nor does the biblical imagination view them as merely adventitious. How has it come to pass that both popular and rabbinic Jewish traditions have perceived Rachel solely through the prism of the love of her husband and the merit of her son? Is this not perhaps just another egregious instance of the predominance of a sexist perspective?

When morning came, and there was Leah!

In separate ways Hamlet, Lear, and Sexton each succumbed to twoness as a curse; Jacob alone contrived to overcome it, to make of it a blessing. If Rachel could merge into Leah, if the young Eleanor Artzyeli winner could pull off what Hamlet, hero of a Roman tragedy of vengeance, could not, why, dammit it all, could not we? It seemed not impermissible to conceive that the fractured history, torn geography, and chronic madness of the land between the Jordan and the Great Sea might yet be healed.

Three years later, with the mutual recognition of the State of Israel and the Palestine Liberation Organization everything seemed possible. Part of the answer was that Jacob and Laban, Jacob and Esau could in time come to accord. As for Jacob recognizing, taking full account of Leah undisguised as Rachel, however, the problem seems more intractable. Except . . . except for a smile of hope at the recollection of the spirited young woman—winner of the year's prize for high achievement in English literature—who had stalked sanely, naughtily off the stage. After revealing a secret sign to her sister, before the eyes of five male co-directors, like an Ibseneseque heroine, she had translated herself out of a hackneyed, stale, male script into an unknown future.

I am sure both my daughters would recoil if one Friday evening, in the prologue to the priestly blessing, making private amends for Judaism's encrustation of sexism, I were to reverse the traditional sequence of the sisters. I confess, however, that for the past four years I have regularly been making a mental reservation on this occasion. Laban-like, mouthing "Rachel," I have been intending Leah in her stead. Sometimes I wonder whether, at the critical moment of bestowing his blessing upon his sons, ancient, purblind Isaac, not truly deceived, did not enact something of the sort himself.

No; the end is not given, and to dream that a polygamous plot might yet be played out in an Israeli comedy of harmony and reconciliation is not, I am at least sometimes persuaded, merely a sweet piece of midsummer symposium madness.

UP AGAINST
THE WALL, FLOWERS

IN THE HOUR before the sun fully emerges from the hills to the east, like some secret sect, ten to twelve Arab workers emerge to scrub the paving-stones, plaza, and even the mammoth stone blocks of the Western Wall, the *Kotel Hamaravi* itself. Bathed and groomed by this spectral crew, the Wall is daily readied to receive suppliants from far and near.

In 1989, the first of September coincided with the first day—*rosh hodesh*—of the month of Elul when, as on every new month at synagogues everywhere, psalms of Hallel are sung as part of morning prayer. Well . . . almost everywhere. Regarding one notable synagogue—the *Kotel* in Jerusalem—Israel's High Court has declared that the group of worshipers popularly known as the Women at the Wall (WAW) should heed the edict of Rabbi Meir Yehuda Getz, the officially appointed "Rabbi of the Wall," to pray in silence.

One of the WAW's guiding spirits is mild-mannered Judith Green. Mother of four, Harvard-educated, of non-Orthodox background, she may fairly serve as a representative WAW figure. She has resided in Jerusalem since 1973.

"Had anyone two decades ago in Cambridge said that scores of other women and I would regularly submit ourselves to revilement, to being spat upon, assaulted, and literally hauled over the stones at the *Kotel* for aberrant religious practices, I probably would have scoffed in disbelief or been struck dumb. That's still how many people in the States respond when I describe the brutality we've undergone: women in our group have been bitten and bruised. Our names and our eyes have been blackened. It's so outrageous that it sometimes seems as though every *rosh hodesh* is opening night for a new piece of theater of the absurd at the *Kotel*."

Green has served as co-president of Yedidya, a synagogue in Jerusalem's Ba'aka neighborhood where, within the boundaries of Jewish religious law, women play a more extensive role in ritual and prayer than is the norm at other Orthodox congregations. At Yedidya women may present a commentary on the Torah or wear prayer shawls. Sometimes women's Torah readings are conducted. Many ultra-Orthodox Jews view such aberrant behavior as a kind of desecration, and at the *Kotel* they reacted with ferocity.

"We believe," Green maintained, "that no single group of Jews has proprietary rights to the Western Wall. On the contrary, it should serve as common ground of all kinds of Jews and Jewish experience. The men's side of the *Kotel* offers a nonstop variety of *minyanim* [prayer groups]. Why must it be that for Jewish women alone prayer at the Wall should be a silent, solitary experience?"

Throughout their many months of undergoing abuse when trying to pray at the Wall, hasn't the WAW manifested just a patronizing trace, a bit of desire to *épater la bourgeoisie*? Have they never even been excessively loud or demonstrative? An unlikely stalwart at the barricades, Green was amused.

"Do I strike you as a rabble-rouser?" she laughed. "Believe me, our prayer has been decorous and subdued, but that has had no effect whatsoever in moderating the violence of the opposition to it. We've been saddened, distressed, angered and . . . yes . . . discouraged, but these past months have only strengthened our resolve to see this matter through to a successful conclusion. We're resolved to stay within the law and not to be intimidated."

In the first hour of dawn, the *Kotel*'s twenty-seven visible layers of flattened, massive stones appeared gray and purple in the thin light. They were like pages from a vast book that had lost its covers. On the mornings of *rosh hodesh*, as many as two hundred "Wall Regulars" had sometimes materialized on the scene. For Rosh Hodesh Elul, however, only about thirty-five of the regulars had gathered.

"Right-hand side for women, left for men" is how the guidebooks concisely put the matter. Between the genders stood a formidable barrier—a *mehitza*. The division was so clear-cut that even first-time visitors scarcely ever blunder. Although it was too early in the day to spot bright-foliaged tourists, on the women's side a dozen solitary figures were seated or standing in devotional attitudes close to the Wall itself. Others seemed just to loiter in the forecourt.

A short woman in her fifties slowly inched her way across the women's half of the *Kotel*, kissing the huge stones and muttering with every movement. For devotees like her, the *Kotel* is the very focus of their lives. They have come to feel so possessive about *their* wall that they feel fully justified to approach visitors with requests for donations or to reproach them for improprieties of dress or behavior.

By September 1989, the controversy at the Western Wall had shifted from the women's donning of prayer shawls and from women reading from a Torah scroll. The WAW had agreed to suspend both of these seemingly offensive activities. The newest problematic ground was the female voice itself. In accordance with the more puritanical strain of Jewish tradition, some ultra-Orthodox worshipers on the premises claimed that the mere sound of women's voices interfered with their own prayer. It was so distracting, in fact, that it drove them to fits of frenzy. Thereafter Rabbi Getz banned the singing aloud by women of the psalms of Hallel or anything else in his precincts by women.

The day before, yet another complication had arisen: the fanatical Kach Party, founded by Rabbi Meir Kahane (who a year later would be assassinated in New York) announced that *it* would send "enforcers" to protect the sanctity of the Wall from the infractions of the WAW. In fact, no Kach supporters turned up, but a score of extra police personnel were conspicuously distributed around the outer plaza.

At 7:30 the thirty-five women were joined by the four private security guards whom they had hired to protect themselves. In addition, two TV camera crews—one Israeli, the other Canadian—were readying themselves to film the day's imbroglio.

Virtually all its more vociferous opposition charge that the WAW's real aim is "to bring Reform to Israel." About 75 per cent of the WAW are of North American origin, a disproportion which has lent fuel to the oft-repeated ultra-Orthodox canard that WAW members themselves were Reform Jews. In fact, the overwhelming majority of the WAW women were active members of one of the several more liberal Orthodox congregations in Jerusalem's German Colony or Ba'aka neighborhoods. Only three identified themselves as Reform Jews.

The WAW started almost by happenstance. In November 1988 a conclave weightily labeled Conference for Empowerment of Jewish Women had convened in Jerusalem. At its climax, following the custom of the American Women's Tefila (Prayer) Network, participants gathered for prayer and celebration at the Western Wall. Why indeed at the *Kotel* goes to the nub of the conflict.

The *Kotel Hamaravi* is not only Judaism's most hallowed place; its open plaza is the natural focus for major national gatherings of celebration or protest, Israel's uniquely religio-national version of the Washington Monument and Tiananmen Square. In fact, without unduly arousing ultra-Orthodox hackles, the Western Wall is preeminently where Jewish pluralism reigns. All sorts of secular, musical, and even terpsichorean gatherings have taken place at the Wall without disturbances. Every four years, for example, the torch-lighted, ceremonial finale of the Jewish Olympics—the Maccabiah—is held here. One issue alone transforms the *Kotel* into a tinderbox: the public prayer of Jewish women.

That first women's prayer service, which followed the Empowerment Conference, passed without untoward incident. For its Israeli participants, it served as a galvanizing precedent. The following month, Rosh Hodesh Tevet, a group returned to pray at the Wall. Anat Hoffman, an articulate, UCLA-trained native Israeli, was there.

"Without fanfare, we quietly approached the *Kotel* carrying a Torah scroll. I myself brought the folding table. Some of us wore prayer shawls. Perhaps we were a bit overconfident, but we certainly were not loud or disorderly.

"Shortly after we started praying, *haredi* [ultra-Orthodox] women started to berate us. One called me a prostitute. Then one of their men tossed a metal chair at us from his side of the *mehitza*. That was followed by a dozen men who surged to our side of the *mehitza*. We could scarcely believe what was happening.

"Two of them grabbed me and started to drag me away from the Wall. I clung to another woman, but then we were both hauled across the ground like sacks of potatoes. My knees and elbows were skinned and bleeding; my dress was badly torn. They even tossed our *siddurim* [prayer books] to the ground and, if I hadn't clutched it to me for dear life, they would have thrown down our *sefer torah* as well. All the while, *haredi* women were cursing and spitting at us. If you can believe it, the police just sat in their cars and watched.

"We concluded morning prayers outside the Wall area, by the Dung Gate to the Old City. Yes, the *Dung Gate*. I was furious and humiliated, yet at the same time I felt a tremendous closeness to my sisters."

After this test of fire, as after each ensuing fracas, WAW members talked long and hard among themselves about what they had undergone. A majority decided that their praying as a group at the *Kotel* might not be such a capital idea. As they would after each ensuing fracas, they needed a detoxification session simply to exorcize their anger.

"But," Hoffman pursued, "I was simply overwhelmed by the good sense, the sensitivity, and the courage of my sisters in prayer. Bonna [Haberman], who holds a doctorate in moral philosophy, was a real inspiration. She has become our spiritual leader. For me personally there was another factor: as a Reform Jew myself, I resent being labeled 'not religious' while those people who manhandle us or their women who egg them on are the 'religious' ones.

"Why is it *their* Wall? By what right has it become private turf? As I see it, our larger aim is to reclaim the Wall as a symbol of Jewish unity. Dammit, we women are Jews as much as the people who violated us, and we have every right to be there. We'll be back again and again."

Hoffman's determination was echoed by Bonna Haberman, an intense-looking mother of three in her late twenties. For her, WAW represents "a whole new generation of sensitive Jewish women who have turned toward Torah. We study and we learn. This is part of an unprecedented movement of college-educated Jewish women of childbearing age."

The situation the WAW confronted was fraught with ironies. The religious issue had already been resolved in *their favor*. Albeit unenthusiastically, the universally respected Rabbi Moshe Feinstein had lent sanction to the women's prayer movement with one proviso: that a women's prayer group never recite certain prayers that may normally be said only by a duly constituted *minyan*. The WAW willingly agreed to Rav Feinstein's reservation.

Moreover, save for the venue, the women actually broke no new religious ground. Most of them have an opportunity to do whatever they have done—or tried to do—at the Western Wall within their own synagogues. Further, a smaller group of the WAW that continues—to this day—to gather to pray every Friday morning at the Wall usually remains unmolested. Yet, even despite the presence and support of a WAW male support group of husbands, month after month, *rosh hodesh* at the *Kotel* remained a battleground.

After curses and chairs flew in February, and police tear gas at the start of March finally dispersed both the WAW and their harassers, the WAW initiated nonviolent resistance training sessions on their living room floors. They practiced how to form clusters of five and how to cling to each other. They also demanded that women ushers be assigned to protect them from male harassment and from bodily injury.

When in July they were greeted by the sight of a contingent of young women in uniform, the WAW thought they had finally won one. Not for long. Soon these ushers were expeditiously ejecting the WAW members from the *Kotel* area. Nearly every one of the WAW was reduced to tears. Would it happen again in Elul?

An answer was immediately forthcoming. No sooner had they begun to pray *Ma tovu* . . . —"How goodly are your tents, O Jacob . . ."—when, as if spawning spontaneously, the vast *Kotel* plaza was bustling with scores of people. The WAW's lawyer Uri Ganor began to argue heatedly with Rav Getz.

"NO," yelled Rabbi Getz. "They may not. It is not and will not be the custom here. Those women are disturbing the men and the other women."

At that, the thirty-five "feminist radical reform Jews" adjourned to the Old City's archeological garden to continue their deviationist devotions. They recited the morning prayers, sang Hallel, and blew the ram's horn—the shofar—to herald in the Jewish month of soul-searching.

Bonna Haberman views WAW as the frontal wave of a larger movement. "Our real goal is to strengthen the bonds which support the Jewish people. The authorities—not we—are contributing to divisiveness in the Jewish people. For the first time in history," she averred, "growing numbers of Jewish women are ready, willing, and able to lead Jewish prayers. In the past year, I've taught about a dozen women to chant from the *sefer torah*. Workshops are held every Sunday night. More and more, our worship is no longer dependent upon men."

Once upon a time Chairman Mao decreed the blooming of a thousand flowers, then cut each of them off at the stem. To everyone's horror, Mao's fanaticism was resurrected in blood at Tiananmen Square. During the same period, month after month, the Women at the Wall—embodiment of the spirit of a thousand Jewish flowers—were taking some very hard lumps for us all. The WAW petitioned Israel's Supreme Court for permission to pray publicly together as an expression of their free exercise of religious conscience and civil liberties, and their right to be free from undue religious restraint. The issue, however, was far from entirely clear-cut. Unlike the United States, the State of Israel is, after all, not bound to avoid making laws that may favor one or another brand of Judaism.

Meanwhile, like Patience on a monument, our Violas awaited the verdict by praying together at the *Kotel* inconspicuously, as individuals. For four-and-a-half years, *rosh hodesh* passed into *rosh hodesh*. On January 26, 1994, the Supreme Court finally issued an opinion. Divided, the three justices directed Israel's Knesset to further study and debate the situation. For the time being, however, WAW's petition was rejected.

The resolution of these women to carry on may be a source of pride. At the same time, that they have had to struggle so long and so hard to achieve such relatively modest ends makes one almost want to weep for consternation and shame.

BEDSIDE
MANNERS

WHILE ROCKING Vered (Rose) asnooze one evening shortly before my favorite and only granddaughter would celebrate her second year of breath beneath our ozone-thin skies, I pondered what sort of gift might be especially appropriate to bestow upon L'il Charmer. Blue-eyed and flirty, smile asparkle, what tasteful enthusiasm she evinced for Grandpa's rock-us-both-to-sleep medley, most of which is traceable to *my* father's extended love affair with vaudeville: "Bye, Bye Blackbird," "I Wonder Who's Kissing Her Now," and "Me and My Shadow" on to "Who's Sorry Now?" and "Paper Doll."

If eyelids *still* flutter after all that, on to my irresistible pièces de resistance: "Carolina in the Mornin'" trumped by every last, glutinous verse of "The Ballad of Carolina Long-Grained Rice"—"I come from Carolinah, so pardon my drawwwl. . . ." By the end of *that*, my captive, tolerant audience, like similar audiences in years past, had succumbed to slumber and Mommy herself resurfaced.

"Do you remember," I asked, "where you were nearly two years ago?"

"Do I remember! Do you imagine," she responded far less tenderly than I had anticipated, "that I could ever forget? Don't expect *me* to get mawkish about the day I underwent the rottenest treatment I've ever suffered. Never have I been so furious."

Well, so much for my early evening dip into sentiment's tepid pool. Wrath unslaked by the passage of months, my usually even-tempered daughter turned positively bilious as she compulsively narrated the critical events of *her* daughter's birthnight at Beersheba's Soroka Medical Center, a hospital where more primal shrieks get addressed to heaven than at any other hospital in the country. It is also the home of Israel's only medical school whose founding raison d'être was "family care." Jen's rendition cut such a cathartic edge, I dared not interrupt.

Generational long division: unlike my son-in-law, unlike my son, I never felt constrained to accompany *my* wife to prenatal instruction or to assist her inhalations or exhalations. If marriage is participatory, I confess that in this matter I had voted absentee. Similarly, as for the more explicit or harrowing details of deliveries, I have never considered them to be . . . uh . . . my department.

As my daughter rendered her account, however, I recalled that in Soroka's new, commodious wing for new mothers, infant girl snug at her side, I had indeed heard snatches of Jen's litany of birthing botchery. Surely I had clucked sympathetically—how could I not?—but inwardly I must have discounted her tale of maltreatment because the important thing was that mother and baby had come through in fine shape, right? So now, two years later, having played dumb, having been dumb, still asking dumb male questions, I accepted my punishment: to hear it all over again from the beginning.

Months before her target date, acting on her intuitive version of the uncertainty principle, indifferent to the gender of the fetus, Jen had resisted submitting to an ultrasound test.

"Why?" she had inquired. This was an impertinence that elicited less an answer than a curious succession of retorts from attending physicians at Soroka.

Such as, "Don't you know you can drown in a glass of water? Trust me. It'd be much safer to have the ultrasound."

Such as, "There's more danger riding in a car than in taking an ultrasound."

"That may be true but what's the point of it?"

"The point is, it's harmless."

Next visit: "What! Still no ultrasound? Don't you realize we've been giving them for twenty years? They are perfectly safe."

Jen knew perfectly well that her doctor had invented instant history. Finally, a nurse, noting that Jen was not a nincompoop, spoke to her when the doctor was out of the room. "Look, the real point is that in many pregnant women there's a link between a high level of blood sugar and the weight of the fetus."

Ahh. The next day, my daughter submitted herself to the ultrasound test.

In her fortieth week of pregnancy, Jen checked into Soroka, and the doctors proceeded to induce labor. Aware that she was bleeding, after a few hours Jen informed an attendant midwife who at once loudly announced that Jen should immediately be sent upstairs to the ward. But no one heard or heeded, and no one checked her condition, so Jen waited where she lay . . . and bled . . . and bled. At the same time, her husband outside the door was being assured that nothing would happen before the following morning. He was sent home. Four hours later, following a perfunctory exam at 9 P.M., a doctor ordered my daughter upstairs to the contraction room!

At 10:30 a different doctor appeared with a long instrument in hand.

"What do you think you're going to do?" Jen asked innocently.

"What do you mean *think*?" he rejoined. "I know *exactly* what I'm doing."

A half-hour later a passing nurse remarked, "soon you'll be in the delivery room," but she too left my daughter unattended. At 11:55, in excruciating pain, aware of its import from the experience of birthing Vered's older brother, my demanding daughter began screaming at the top of her lungs. Someone wheeled her into the delivery room, where she had to move from one bed to another. Which she did . . . unassisted! Squalling, Vered premiered precisely at the stroke of midnight.

As she was being stitched, Jen lurched in pain.

"Stop jumping around," the doctor ordered. "You can damage yourself." Under his breath he muttered, "She should have had anesthesia."

Finally, this sorry sequence of male sensitivity unnerved even me: "You should have filed a complaint!"

My reward was a look that could wither an April of roses.

"Have you really forgotten? I *did* file a complaint! I recounted the whole business in a letter to the head of the delivery room at Soroka. Her response consisted of four points: it had been a particularly busy night; no one else had ever complained about that doctor; the baby and I are healthy, so what the hell were we complaining about?; and she didn't believe a word I wrote anyway."

I, of course, have little reason to doubt that events occurred just about the way my daughter recalled. Indeed, it is difficult to imagine why anyone would bother to make up such a fabrication. Still, perhaps Jen had merely been unlucky. Fairness mandated that I don the mantle of Investigative Journalist, simplicity itself since every kid's mommy within spittin' distance of Beersheba has been delivered at the same precincts.

Testimony of Tsipi, a young mother who gave birth nine months after Jennifer: during delivery she could hear her two doctors arguing about whether they should perform a Caesarean.

"Why?" inquired Tsipi, supine but not entirely disinterested in the outcome of the dispute.

"Because the fetus is in distress," came one doctor's peremptory reply.

"How do you know that?" she pressed.

"Then it's *you* who are in distress," he retorted.

Which, indeed, she instantly became.

On the following day, accompanied by five medical students, her doctor arrived in the ward and examined the new mother. Without a by-your-leave, he directed a student to perform the same procedure. When the student's report failed to satisfy, the doctor ordered him to do it again. With that Tsipi had the presence of mind to shoo the whole mindless crew from her bedside.

I turned to Leah right next door, a three-time victim of the joys of childbirth at Soroka.

"The last time, when actually in the process of giving birth, I had the ill grace to inquire 'What's happening?' My doctor's remarkable response was 'What do *you* care?' Then the second doctor recalled a joke he simply had to tell the first: 'Question: Why do you think there are so many gynecologists? Answer: Because just being a woman is an incurable disease.' I guess I should have been satisfied that he'd bothered to learn my name. It's just too irksome for our sensitive, well-educated doctors to read the names of the Bedouin women off the charts in the wards: every last one of them gets referred to as 'the Bedouin.'"

The only consolation I drew from these investigations came on my next visit to my eighty-nine-year–old father in North Miami Beach. I could report that vaudeville never died after all. Appallingly sick, it carried on still in the maternity wing at Soroka Medical Center in Beersheba.

Now, in fact, I myself am acquainted with several fine doctors who, doubling as sensitive human beings, wield their healing arts at Soroka, probably far from being the worst hospital in the land. Moreover, Jen acknowledged that the nurses upstairs afterward, in contrast to the delivery room doctors, were pleasant and considerate. And of course I am aware that doctors often work under conditions of extreme pressure and that in the end things usually turn out all right, right? Still, I am persuaded that the above account is far from atypical of how women undergoing childbirth get treated in Israel.

. . . If I had Aladdin's Lamp for only one day / I'd make a wish and here's what I'd say . . .

Well, I do know that this little gift will not quite make amends for my inattentive male lapses in the past. Nevertheless, since there's every likelihood that the paper doll herself will one night get wheeled into a Sorokesque delivery room, if my "Lament for Jen, Tsipi, Leah, the Bedouin, and All the Other Fair, Young Diseases" makes somebody sorrier, or increases the prospect that five minutes to zero someone just might assist her to move from one bed to another . . . why, then . . . Happy Second Birthday, Vered.

SOUL BIRD
OF THE NEGEV

ONDAY, the last week of June 1991, in the open-air courtyard
of the Be'eri Elementary School. It was a sultry evening in
Beersheba. I had arrived at dusk, right when the invitation
said the ceremony would start. Would I ever learn? After milling
among the several hundred other early arrivals—fellow parents, relatives, guests—I slumped into a folding chair, an aisle seat in the
courtyard. Of British Mandate or perhaps even Turkish vintage, the
ample, U-shaped, two-story school building looked as though it had
at one time been occupied by an army of coffee-sipping clerks and
functionaries as they manned their dozy battle stations. This evening,
it would be the scene of the graduation of around one hundred Anats,
Ronens, Gila'ads, Yitzhaks, and Tamars who composed Be'eri's
eighth-grade class together with Yishai, my thirteen-year-old son who
of late answered only to "Shai."

His school had been named in honor of Berl Katznelson, voice of
conscience of the secular Labor Zionist Movement of old. Shai and
his younger sister Miri attended Be'eri School because it accommo
dated classes sponsored by TALI, a parent-initiated educational movement designed to fill the gap between the dearth of Jewish content in
the secular curriculum in the country's public schools and the surfeit
provided by the religious schools. Because TALI is sponsored by Judaism's Conservative Movement, it bears a mild stigma in some Israeli
circles, but, amid the shoals of public education in this country, for
our part it offered something of a deep-water haven. What Katznelson
would have thought about us TALI schismatics, however, is not hard
to imagine.

During the year, both of our kids had achieved impressive grades
and had spoken well of their teachers, who struck me as diligent and
hard working. And yet . . . like many dedicated Israeli teachers, Ruti

101

and Eti suffered from the parochiality that comes of living on the outskirts of a small remote country. In unexpected ways, it got reflected in their teaching. Just a few weeks earlier Miri's reply to my routine dinnertime query—"Did you learn anything interesting in school today?"—perked my interest.

"We learned a lot in Geography about cities in Italy in the Valley of the Pooh."

I was conscious that my wife was also repressing a smile.

"The Valley of the Pooh? You mean the Po, like Edgar Allan, don't you?"

"Oh Daddy, don't be so picky. Eti said we could pronounce it anyway we wanted—Pooh, Poh, Fooh, or Foh. They're all okay in Hebrew."

The folding chairs in the school courtyard were now filling. Younger siblings of graduates raced about. The p.a. system Me-ooOOORRRED. Pshooooowed. Then once again emitted a chilling MeawhaEEEEEEEEE. Teachers grimaced and gesticulated. The centerpiece of the painted backdrop behind the platform depicted some kind of a large bird soaring in front of a wall. At home Miri had described having helped to paint it. The graduates, each holding a fluttering pennant, were collecting into pockets at the four corners of the second floor of the school building. Most of us guests waited submissively for noise and chaos to dissolve into Ceremony. I spotted Shai, laughing, talking with a classmate. He responded to my half-wave signal with a swift thumb's up sign of recognition, then returned to his friend.

The last time I had attended a school ceremony for Shai was the annual trip of his first-grade class—*kitah aleph*—when he was attending Yeroham's state religious school. On an excursion to Jerusalem, the proud first graders demonstrated their new prowess at reading by praying together at the Western Wall. Thereafter, parents and kids had visited the city's shabby biblical zoo where, parting ways with most of the others, Shai and I had taken off on a path of our own.

Could seven years really have passed since then? Indubitably. Yishai had grown into Shai, his own man, who two years before had chosen no longer to attend an Orthodox religious school.

Graduation ceremonies were already thirty minutes late when Debbi, originally from Wales, and her youngest daughter sat down next to me. Her oldest son was also a graduate, but not from a TALI class, so he was not one of Shai's special pals.

"When do you think this thing will begin?" I asked.

"Oh, whenever it does," Debbi replied. "It doesn't much matter, does it?"

Eti, my daughter's teacher, passed through the waiting audience distributing smiles and sparklers. I pushed mine into my breast pocket.

"When do we light these things?"

"Whenever everyone else does. You'll see," wise Debbi counseled.

Debbi's husband works in Jerusalem; he makes it home only for Shabbat weekends. In a small, somewhat chaotic household, she has raised their six well-mannered children and has remodeled their house largely by herself. She has learned, better than I, how to navigate Israel's less-charted waters. Two rows in front of us was seated a large family: a grandfather in a white shirt, a grandmother wearing a modish hat, the mother, a blonde-braided younger sister, and another woman, perhaps an aunt of the graduate. Obviously Russian. No father. Was she divorced? Was he at work? Still in Russia?

Suddenly a blast of martial music blared out of the p.a. system. Four columns of flag-bearers descended from the balcony exits, and scores of blue-and-white flags of the State of Israel rippled with the music's beat in the mild evening breeze. The Russian family exchanged gratified glances: graduation had begun with a Hebraized version of a Russian march! Teachers prodded the fourfold procession of thirteen and fourteen year olds to the front, and then, weaving them intricately back up the aisles and past the assembly, guided them back to the rear. Then once again the white-shirted, blue-trousered or -skirted aggregation marched, each one holding a flag aloft. To the front, the graduates who had been on the left now passed on the right. The intricate maneuver was clearly the result of hours of rehearsal (about which Shai had sorely complained: "We learned nothing today, just marching and more marching").

The much-respected woman principal of Be'eri rose to greet the restless audience and to praise her graduates, their teachers and parents. To progressively increasing noise and side-chatter, each of the three eighth-grade teachers and longest-winded of all, the TALI coordinator, did much the same. Finally, a blonde-haired girl with sharp features was called to the front: "I, Olga Rabinovitch, in the name of all the new *olim* [immigrants] in my class, want to thank our teachers, our principal, and all of our fellow students of Be'eri School for making our adjustment to school life in Israel so painless."

And then, music wheezing before turning ethereal, a spotlight shone on Soul Bird—*Tsipor ha-Nefesh*—a shapely graduate in blue tights and a gauzy gown who pirouetted onto the platform and prettily rose and fell to romantic strains, her face concealed by a bird-like mask. Evidently, *Tsipor ha-Nefesh* was intended to represent the inner spirit of striving and hope for the future of these youngsters, our sons and daughters who had just tipped into their teens. As the music dramatically rose and fell, Soul Bird fluttered across the stage. The assemblage in the courtyard was hushed, as if its collective heart had indeed stirred for a bird.

Afterward, a boy and two girls came to the microphone with some jokey repartee, followed by a flute and violin duet. Then three more students with a parody of school life followed by a troupe of student folk dancers. One attractive girl, Ayala, I was later informed, nearly lost her flowing headpiece during a sharp turn. The most ill-advised costume was a white miniskirt donned by a chunky girl. The poor thing was so self-conscious she could scarcely dance at all.

Shai was among the next three students who strode to the platform. Was that young fellow up there my son? He's taller, more muscular than I was at thirteen. Braces notwithstanding, he delivered his three lines loudly and clearly before darting offstage with alacrity. *Tsipor ha-Nefesh* then floated forth for what would be the first of three reprises. As the spotlight followed her movements, my own ninth-grade graduation from the all-boys Creston Junior High No. 79 in The Bronx bubbled up from deep recesses. (Girls attended Elizabeth Barrett Browning Junior High, across the Grand Concourse.) The year was 1951. In order to accommodate all the parents and other guests, the ceremony was held in the auditorium of William Howard Taft High School.

Jerry Atlas and I served as alternating narrators of "Vignettes of America." Two details: Miss MacMurray, our formidable music teacher, had rehearsed our rousing version of "Old Man River" to seeming perfection. (Did Eti teach her class about The Mississiffi?) As for a futurist skit, all I could recall was that I donned a plastic headpiece and a red bathrobe. The rest of that evening has blurred into blessed obscurity.

Off to my left I spied my son, the graduate, then spied upon him.

Obviously relieved at having polished off his part of the presentation, he was laughing with a boy and at the same time trying to impress what seemed to be a very pretty girl in the adjacent seat. She must be Tali, who he had from time to time referred to as "his girlfriend." Sweet Tali of TALI. Under that starry Negev, oh it almost made me weep to watch my son that evening, to weep for the tally of heart-breaking years that lay ahead before he would settle upon the final Tali of his heart.

Another trio of young comedians offered a skit that their classmates appreciated far more than their parents did; again some twirling folk dancers; again the flute and violin; and then the final, wrenching appearance of *Tsipor ha-Nefesh*. This time she took on a different coloration. No longer the embodiment of Negev Youth in general, the masked figure was transfigured into an incarnation of striving girlhood—of Olga Rabinovitch and Ayala and Tali and of my own sweet Miri who, in our sukkah one-and-a-half years later, would cele-brate her bat mitzvah, who six months thereafter would herself be a *Tsipor ha-Nefesh*, graduating into adolescence. Each, as gracefully as she might, was destined to trip toward womanhood on an unequal social stage rigged, here as elsewhere, against their completing their dance to the fullest.

Yet hints of change may be scented. In September 1993, at a general membership meeting of Yeroham's Congregation Afikim Banegev a protracted, heated discussion took place. In the end, the congregation voted to sanction the continuation of a women's prayer group some of its members (including, it needs be added, my own Marcia, Jen, and Miri) had organized to celebrate the arrival of each *rosh hodesh*, a service at which a quorum of ten women read from a Torah scroll.

The resurgence of women's prayer groups is a relatively new devel-opment in Orthodox Judaism and remains highly controversial. Its decision cost the withdrawal from the congregation of six or eight of its more traditional member families. However, it has positioned Afikim Banegev in the forefront of Orthodox congregations in Israel which encourage women not only to study but also to exercise their preroga-tives under religious law to the maximum.

Then, suddenly, the graduation ceremony was over. To the folky strains of campfire music, Debbi and I, with all the parents and other guests, lit our tapered sparklers and held them high against the night until they fizzled into stumps. For the moment, all our bright Soul Birds were extinguished, and darkness reigned. Then lights shone upon the audience, and Shai and I found each other. As we headed home for Yeroham, my son, unlike American kids of his age, was unembarrassed to take his father's hand. That too seemed a good sign.

PART THREE.
WHERE I LIVE
AND WHAT I LIVE FOR

The fields are organic of the whole, and of their own nature, and of the work that is poured into them: the spring, the garden, the outbuildings, are organic to the house itself.

James Agee
(*Let Us Now Praise Famous Men*)

WHERE I LIVE
AND WHAT I LIVE FOR

I T WAS largely by chance that a year after arriving in Israel my family and I settled in Yeroham, a raw, unplanned, oft-excoriated, dowdy map-dot thirty-five kilometers southeast of Beersheba. Yet it has turned out to be our unlikely first choice as well. For longer than we endured New York City, for more than double the years we stayed in California, it is in Yeroham where we have remained. Obviously, much about the place corresponds to our inner dispositions, our emotional needs, our psychic economy.

Yeroham's attraction lies not only in its relative isolation but also in its very problematic character, its against-the-grain roughness and the piquancy of daily interaction with Ruti at the post office, Maurice in front of the bank, Ninette at the clinic, or any other of my seven-to-eight-thousand fellow inhabitants. This is no metropole, no garden suburb, no bucolic retreat in the countryside. More, however, than in Tel Aviv, and more than in Jerusalem, here it is that I am at home in Israel.

For most of our first dozen years in Yeroham, summer was the cruelest season. Early most mornings during July and August rickety trucks rolled in from the north and parked in front of a house or apartment building. Another family was moving to Petach Tikva, to Ariel, or merely to Beersheba. Some of the departing families had long threatened to move. Most took us by surprise.

Close-up: a knot of curious kids watching movers tote a couch and beds by their legs. "How does that scrawny guy manage to move down a flight of stairs with a refrigerator on his back?" All the possessions of the family are uncovered, shamefully exposed to the eye of the sun.

For those of us who have not merely washed up here but had consciously chosen to come and remain, for whom Yeroham is Zionism, zionism, or even "Zionism," leaving town is not the same as shifting from one Tel Aviv suburb to another. It is more like abandoning a commitment, the cancellation of a vow. Each departure left in its wake a particular aura of desertion. Indeed, one family with whom we had been friendly did not inform us or anyone else of their intention until their very final day in town!

Those who left always contrived good and adequate-sounding reasons. Justifications. Few did not blame the patent, the myriad inadequacies of the place: the lack of discipline in the schools, the inefficient local administration, the dearth of culture. In truth, there was a good measure of truth in all this. Some of this summer's outflow had originally come to Yeroham to make a mark, to effect fundamental change: at the music conservatory, in the schools, in the mayor's office. In most cases, their efforts were blunted; nearly all suffered frustration. Yes, Yeroham needed talented, creative people, but my, oh my, how wondrously it seemed to undermine, to discourage them!

So, every summer since my arrival here in 1977, key—nay, absolutely essential—people have left the scene. Melancholy hovered over the place as another irreplaceable family skipped out. Someone again would remark how, like grains of sand through a sieve, tens of thousands of persons had "gone through" Yeroham, as if hundreds of thousands have not "gone through" New York or Jerusalem. It happened every summer.

From among our circle of friends, one of the first evacuees from Yeroham was Yapha, an American-born librarian, who purchased an apartment in one of Jerusalem's "new neighborhoods" in the northernmost part of the city. For many years we always thought of her whenever the morning news broadcast that the windshield of the #25 bus she took to commute had gotten stoned while passing through an Arab neighborhood. Occasionally, one or two passengers sustained what were usually described as "light injuries." Even though she now commutes by a different route to work, that news item has remained her signature tune in the ear of memory.

When I first moved to Israel's Sicily, the trip from Yeroham to Beersheba, a twenty-minute flipflap for a sober crow, took us groundlings longer than an hour. Worse still was the humiliation. We endured our portion like sullen hostages to hostile fortune. Hour after hour the bus shuttled Yerohamites through the heart of rival Dimona, a larger city twelve kilometers to the north.

The return leg home from Beersheba was particularly galling. Dimona, you see, enjoyed not only its own direct service on the #056, three times as frequent as Yeroham's #057, but it purloined our poor route as well! The sight of the #057 lumbering into the dock was the signal: over the metal railing from the adjacent queue hurdled open-shirted hairies, vigorous *hayelot*, mothers with pencil-sharp elbows, bratty darlings. Even toothless crones navigated the symbolic barrier to all but monopolize the front of our #057 queue. Only the laid-back Black Hebrews, an African-American subcommunity long-established in Dimona, refrained from the discourteous sport. Was it supportable that Dimonans should be seated while we Yerohamites had to stand on our own #057? Naturally, we did not passively abide being displaced from seats on what was, after all, *our* bus. Murmur, like as not, led to shove and shout. On occasion, to melee.

Then, less on account of Yeroham's nebulous political clout, but more because many new military bases began to dot the vicinity, a process leading to a righting of accounts was initiated. In 1980, workers started repairs on the so-called Oil Road, originally constructed by the British during the Mandate period. The name, a compound of hope, greed, and pathos, says it all. This scenic but long neglected passage bisected the hills from Yeroham to the Beersheba-to-Nizzana highway, hypothetical hypotenuse to the right triangle our #057 wrote hourly in the wind. Since the War of Independence it had been a preserve for the four-wheeled driven and traders in camels. Now bulldozers mutely testified that the status quo was not a mandate from heaven. We took heart. But, then came the Lebanese fiasco, labeled "Operation Peace in Galilee," and funds dried up. Just four loopy kilometers short of completion, the money and the roadwork gave out.

To the delight of local citizenry, Egged did not permit that roller coaster stretch to deter its rescheduling plans: the #058—a new, direct service from Beersheba to Yeroham along the Oil Road—was initiated. What exhilaration! No more rubbing carcasses with *that* supercilious crew or transecting *that* place. Moreover, fifteen minutes had been whittled from a typical trip. True, we now endured four kilometers of passive aerobics, but precious time had been netted, all of it in your basic flanks-down, upright position.

Six years later the reappearance of the 'dozers signaled a prospect of further amelioration. With the passing months, the mint-new strip of smooth, dark ribbon that paralleled our bumpy grind visibly unwound. One day it happened. Pennants unfurled, cameramen barked, politicians vacuously smiled, and the roof of the #058 within which I rode displayed a banner that stretched across the entry to the glory road. A cop handed a paper cup of something bubbly to our driver. All the passengers beamed. The final four kilometers of new road linking Yeroham with Beersheba had been completed.

What so recently had taken nearly an hour, ten minutes of which was akin to being strapped in the front car of the Wabash Cannonball, had been cut to a smooooth-'n'-easy thirty-five minutes. No longer at the final bend-bounce in the road do queasy-stomached toddlers deliver forth like clockwork. Never again need eyes squinch and wrinkles sprout north of the brow-line from trying to keep in focus the squiggly lines of an article. On the Egged Bus's #058 run, sacroiliacs formerly tensed for a jouncing are now loose as geese. It took time, yes, but today the trip from Yeroham to Beersheba exacts less time, less wear 'n' tear than it used to take me to get from The Bronx to midtown Manhattan. Yeroham's splendid "isolation," a liability in most people's accounts, one of the primary reasons its erstwhile citizens have moved along, had been mitigated.

These days, of course, many buses in Israel run far less smoothly than our #058 down the good ol' Oil Road, a sobriquet which seems less a misnomer than formerly. After all, in order to lubricate the normal friction of our poor human affairs, people must be offered more than promises or platitudes. There must be genuine grounds for hope. Surely that's largely why, at the same time taking the bus out of Yeroham has taken a benign turn, the municipal commute between Jerusalem's northern neighborhoods and downtown West Jerusalem continues to intrude on the morning news.

For many years I suppose I harbored a degree of resentment toward those who, for reasons good and sufficient according to their lights, had vanished from town . . . until I noticed that the sinking ship did not go down. For one thing, a preponderance of talented, effective people has always remained. Equally important, although the absence of those who have departed has always been a conspicuous presence, a silent, unheralded influx of revitalizing replacements has never ceased to arrive. And so, while for the past decade-and-a-half-going-on-two since my arrival here Yeroham *has* grown but not really all that much, while by some standards it has not been much of a success, Yeroham's sheets not only still billow smartly in the evening desert breeze. Better than many, they balance.

ECONOMY

H INDU philosopher Govinda Lal and crotchety émigré Artur
Sammler have the following exchange in Bellow's *Mr. Sammler's Planet*:

A. S.: "Margot can't drive. What will you do with the Hertz
car?"
G. L.: "Oh, damn! The car! Bloody machines!"
A. S.: "I regret I can't drive. . . . Not to drive is the latest snob-
bery, I've been told."

Over the years in America, I pushed around in a Pontiac, a Ford,
two VWs, and a Honda—five bloody machines in all—and even
manifested feelings of affection toward two of them. Moving to Israel,
however, has made an insufferable elitist of me. The impressive network of intercity bus transportation was one important contributing
factor; a 100 per cent import duty, doubling the price of all vehicles,
was another; but nothing was more decisive in effecting my transformation than witnessing the strength of those anarchic impulses that
merely being seated behind the wheel seemed to loose from the
chthonic hearts of many Israeli drivers. If this be ecology for the
chicken-hearted, make the most of it!

We spent our first months in Israel on a communal settlement.
Immaculate swards, graybeards in blue shorts striding purposefully,
youngsters and matrons peddling along the grassy paths, but for me
the main attraction of this insular enclave was not its egalitarianism,
its idealism, or the sense of inner security it nurtured. In practice,
behind the pastoral façade, these are mixed blessings. But one wholly
unalloyed benefit of rural communal life, and one usually not found
elsewhere in Israel, is that kibbitzim provide a bulwark of peace and
calm against the servile worship of a pantheon of exotic deities—
Suburu, Volvo, Citroën, Mazda, Opel, and a honking host of compet-

ing demigods. In Israel, each of these insatiable sovereigns daily exacts a remarkably heavy toll of human sacrifice. Vital statistics: Israel leads the world in the number of automobiles per kilometer of highway. It averages around a traffic fatality a day.

When I first moved to unpretentious Yeroham, the place was an asylum for cyclists, a paradise for pedestrians. It was sometime in the early eighties that the shrewd serpent first hissed, "Who said that you must walk about so awkwardly on your own two sandaled feet?" So our branch of Bank Hapoalim eased restrictions on car loans. Needless to report, it was an immensely popular maneuver. My fellow towns-people learned the pleasures of negative monthly balance, and the slick bank manager got himself elected mayor of the town.

It little matters that Israeli bus service is superior, that even its taxi fares are markedly lower than in the States. Autocracy decrees the fouling of air, the gawd-awful drivers, the dangerous roads, the pricey gas, highway carnage, the blasting horns, the outrageous car prices, the strangulated cities. But could Jews ever long resist the worship of foreign idols that, promising yet more freedom, deliver them and us into thralldom?

Nowadays I walk my local streets among the diminishing band of philosophers, inverse snobs, and Moroccans too elderly or "primitive" to change their ways—in truth, not all that bad company. I recognize, alas, that as recent arrivals from Moscow and Chelybinsk settle in, their long-suppressed desires to behave like Americans impacting upon us, a desperate situation is bound to worsen. Even my daughter and British-born son-in-law have chosen the broad Israeli way: indentured servitude to a driving school.

Still, Sammler and I are not entirely alone. During my first years in Yeroham, I arranged for poet Yehuda Amichai to come down to speak to students at the local high school. How delighted I was to perceive that Israel's premier poet is of similar disposition to Margot and Govinda Lal. He gets around by cab or bus. Yet, moreover, it strikes me that on my visits to his home, I don't recall seeing a trace of modem or computer cable.

I, on the other hand, have developed a suspicious dependency on my Apple computer—eight years old and already "classic." Like all word processors, it suffers from a grievous downside. In contrast to trusty old Underwood, Apple spews forth an exponentially heavy stream of refuse, fodder for our gluttonous landfills. Especially in a country that imports wood pulp, one-sided fields of print, like one-sided phonographs of yesteryear, seem to me an offense to economy, ecology, forestry, husbandry, health, and common sense.

Although I really do know better, although for most Israelis my eco-niggling serves as comic relief, from time to time I revert compulsively to the social activist wavelength I used to broadcast in California. Since I myself was a grad student before learning that *compost* was something more than a wiseass epithet Walter Winchell used to sling at "fellow travelers," having myself been fetched up in a citadel of urban consumerism, I instinctively comprehend my fellow townspeople's dogma that "new" is "better," ergo "desirable."

It was my good fortune, however, to have married into a family whose roots run deep into the rich mores of the Midwest where "new" may be okay, but until you show me otherwise, m'friend, tried-and-true is preferred, recycled better yet, and making-do-without-it best of all. Yes, I sometimes backslide, but over the years, I have changed in the bone. Eschewing paper-piggery, for years I have waged a quiet campaign for rectitude by submitting text to editors, even printing some correspondence, on the invitingly blank side of previously printed sheets.

My metamorphosis has been effected under the tutelage of my good wife, inobtrusive practitioner of an art that Claude Lévi-Strauss once labeled *bricolage*. The range of her activity never fails to amaze. When recently I inquired into the antecedents of a familiar, gray-and-black checkerboard skirt that Marcia was wearing: "Why it's practically new," she replied. "The gray squares are cut from a pants suit your mother gave me about twenty years ago. The black ones," she continued after a moment's deliberation, "why . . . they're from your wedding suit."

My wedding suit? From thirty years ago! I looked more closely. So it was. And what about her black sweater?

"Oh, I reknit this years ago from a long, flowing black scarf I made when I was still in high school. It's just like the one Ingrid Bergman wore in *Anastasia*. When we came east in '67, I unravelled the scarf and made it into a sweater."

In short, before ecology became our fashionable necessity, it was my Wife's Way. Everything salvageable takes on new life not only out of righteousness, but also because there lies the path of creativity. In fact, the fundamental ecological impulse has never been been merely one of economy: it is more a matter of inner, primal disposition—an aesthetic. Properly deconstructed, her daily apparel is a text interlarded with allusiveness in which the past seamlessly coexists with the present. Like master quilter Shakespeare taking hot pleasure in patching and repatterning Plutarch, Caxto, Lodge, natural-born *bricoleurs* like my wife take theirs in refashioning tired old garments into usable new plots.

In comparison, my own papery activism, not to mention creativity, is tamer stuff. On the wall to my back hangs a calendar of New York City views, which was issued by Chemical Bank. Its year is 1982 and the dates of each month happen to coincide with the same day of the week in the year of 1993. Nostalgia spices my pleasure in recycling old calendars and deciphering cryptic notations for appointments past. This private, self-reflective sphere usually yields far greater satisfaction than the upshot of lifting a halfhearted lance for causes good, just, or beautiful. Dutifully, I report the doleful upshot of a recent engagement on behalf of Lady Ecologia against the dragons of Israeli bureaucracy.

Browsing through a regional bulletin of the Association of Americans and Canadians in Israel (AACI), I noted that a major impediment to recycling soft-drink containers is their composition: whereas concoctions from Coca-Cola or Tempo, a local equivalent, do their sloshing and fizzing in bottles composed of two kinds of plastic, Crystal's soft drinks are peddled in containers made of one. It seems that two-plastic bottles are prohibitively expensive to recycle. Well, we almost never buy Crystal drinks, but I had observed that their colorful elixirs were encased in one-piece plasticized suits that stood on bulbous lobes looking something like Bart Simpson's cranium. The bulletin urged readers to lobby Coke and Tempo to follow Crystal's lead.

How many responded to this appeal, I cannot say, but since Tempo Bottling is a pillar of Yeroham's economy, this gave me pause. Conscience bestirred, I mailed an appeal to Tempo's national headquarters in Netanya. Its brief, pointed, Orwellian gist: One Plastic Good, Two Plastics Bad.

Not expecting an early response, I also took the path of direct action. That very evening I asked Miri, then thirteen, to pick up a bottle of Crystalline brew at the store.

"Why?" responded our temerarious throwback to her grandmother on *my* side of the family, champion of the newfangled. "I want Sprite."

"Okay," I replied, "get Sprite, but also get Crystal. I want to show you something at dinner."

Curiously, the bottle of Sprite stood erect in its green plastic base, but the clear plastic bottle of Cola à la Crystal wobbled precariously; it was, to my consternation, imperfectly imbedded in a base of black plastic! Ah ha! Crystal played its game both ways. Ecological sermon sticking in my throat, I reached to pour a glassful of lemony soda.

"So, why'd you make me buy this other stuff?" our little sprite persisted.

"Oh, I heard Crystal Cola was very good for upset stomachs . . . but I'm feeling better now."

Three nights later, once again during dinner, when most Israeli things come to pass, the doorbell rang. It was Chaim-the-Postman thrusting a telegram—in Israel, especially, a *welcome* form of communication—for me to sign for. Putting aside trepidation, I discovered it was from Tempo! Were I to call their Netanya office, "Aviva" or "Feldman" would be pleased to speak with me about my concern.

Now, is that impressive public relations . . . or what? The next afternoon, I gave it a shot. After three calls and ten minutes of an on-hold concert, a gruff voice informed me that Aviva was out. As was Feldman.

"Do they often go out together in the afternoons?" I undiplomatically ventured.

"Look, why don't you try tomorrow. In the morning."

On the morrow: "Aviva, this is Haim Chertok from Yeroham, Tempo's second home. I got your telegram. You must have something urgent to report?"

"Actually, it's not me. It's Mr. Feldman who wants to talk with you. Please hold."

Eventually . . . never mind how long . . . I heard friendly tones.

"Mr. Chertok, yes?"

"Mr. Feldman, yes. I got your wire. Long distance is getting expensive, so may I get right to the point? Is Tempo planning to change the composition of its bottles?"

"Ah, to change our bottles would be very expensive. But, Mr. Chertok, we do want you to know that Tempo is responsive to its customers. Especially to those from Yeroham."

"But you have plans," I persisted, "to switch to one-plastic containers?"

"Not exactly, but we're always ready to cooperate. Our bottles currently comply with government standards. I wired to tell you that if you would like the regulations to change, you should contact Uri Marinov, head of the environmental division at the Ministry of Interior. And rest assured that just as soon as the government requires bottles composed of one type of plastic, Tempo will comply with the law."

"Ah, Feldman, that's good, so good of you. And Tempo. And thank you for sending me a telegram."

Crumpling my communication from the rear guard of Israel's environmentally concerned bottlers, in my own halfhearted fashion I left it at that; I left it to others to take the field against Marinov, Feldman, and classic, two-plastic Coke. My expedition had come to little more than a Tempo in a teapot. The cause, I am obliged to admit, does not lie exclusively in the stars. Admittedly something of a crank, I lacked the purist's zest for extending the fray. Several times a year, in fact, I might be spied sidling up to the counter at Hertz's Joint, just opposite Beersheba's central palace of Egged. Yochi, who mixes a Bloody Mazda, presides.

"Fix us up with a mean machine, gal."

After the initial strangeness wears off, I confess to feeling empowered, seemingly reinvigorated seated once again behind the wheel. True, when I turn into traffic that darts and weaves in and out of the three lanes of Derech Hanissim, when I start at the first blare of a horn and recoil at the stench of fumes (here, still heavily leaded), the illusion that I'm somehow enjoying myself rapidly wears thin. Nevertheless, since I've paid so dearly for the privilege of operating the bloody thing, it's one that I try to husband.

A yet more grievous revelation: "Haim," croons an inner, serpentine voice, "cut the blarney. If for what you paid in Manhattan you could have your old Honda Civic sitting curbside by your house in Yeroham, wouldn't you smile? Think how happy your children would be."

Yes, I am not immune. Even though I know better, I am susceptible. Although I have breathed the smudge of Haifa, viewed the murk over Beersheba, squirmed in a vehicle that sat backed up thirty minutes at the entry to Jerusalem, in the end I am a sinner like the rest.

Yes, I would vote for an Israel governed by its poets and philosophers, but until that day, I too would probably bite.

> And we shall build
> Los An-ge-les
> Here in Jeru-salem's green
> And pleasant bowers.

SOUNDS

F OR BOTH good and ill, my little town in the Negev has altered much since I first arrived on the scene. When acquaintances inquire why I remain, the brew I usually serve forth is spiced with Smallness, Remoteness, and Tranquillity—qualities I find congenial. Since these usually suffice, there is little need to burden the recipe with equally relevant notions which might be viewed as eccentric, perhaps even threatening: namely, that where one chooses to reside and the nature of one's dwelling accurately reflect one's underlying values and commitments. Or that the greater one's radial distance from society's center, the greater the likelihood a person has of finding his own true center.

When we first moved into the newly built Ben-Gurion neighborhood, it stood at the very edge of town. Our house was separated from the Rubin Cultural Center by a gentle-sloping wadi, barren save for a single stand of tamarisks and three swaying eucalyptuses. Once or twice a month we would be startled by the apparition of a Bedouin leading goose-necked camels no more than ten meters from our front door. It was a nineteenth-century sepia print of the Holy Land walking off the page.

Over the years, Yeroham has not budged many inches in the direction of Tel Aviv; it retains enough of its aura of splendid isolation to safeguard the psychic distance I seem to require. In contrast to life in the city, it is still relatively quiet and tranquil. Nevertheless, boxed off from the desert by the newer Shaked neighborhood, we no longer are privileged to occupy the very rim of town. Courtesy of Project Renewal, our tamarisks and eucalyptuses have long been felled, our wadi leveled and replaced with tennis courts. To compound the tramp, tramp, tramp of Development, Amos-the-Prophet Street, our frontal road that once dead-ended into a pile of construction debris, has for some years served as an artery for buses and homegrown kamikazes. One of my sometime threnodies, overburdened by a surplus of matter, is "Serenity Lost."

On a somnolent Shabbat afternoon in 1992, shortly after the dining table had been cleared, a peaceful hummmmm seemed to float on air. Variously reading, playing cribbage, crawling after the cat, vaguely studying, or dozing, the family had composed itself into a tableau vivant of "Up a Lazy River." Itamar, my four-year-old grandson, plainly aiming to reach the ceiling—if not the sky—was meticulously layering plastic blocks into a tower.

Suddenly all of us drew up rigid at the rhythmic blasts of a horn, *many* horns. In a trice, Babel tumbled, and Itamar yowled his frustration. Was it a wedding party? On Shabbat! A charivari? Mardi gras? Whatever it was, one helluva tumult was sure drawing closer: a brassy chorus of four masculine, heart-shriveling spondees answered by feminine trochees and iambs: BEEP BEEP BEEP BEEP / BEEP-BEEP B' BEEP. Ooover and over. Signifying, "Come one. Come all. Join the jubilee."

Shabbat shalom annulled, thoughts turned transcendental. Had the End of Days arrived? Had Amos or Messiah descended upon Yeroham? Three of us dashed out the front door. Damned if the whole caravan wasn't turning at the corner right up our street. Yosi-the-Cop in his undershirt, Phoebe-the-Babyminder, Suzi and other Moroccan neighbors—observant, nonobservant alike—a dozen children, all agape, all peering toward the source of the commotion. No; it was not Donner and Blitzen in the lead but a bus crammed with young, shouting celebrants, mostly in tennis shorts. Behind trailed a string of twelve, maybe fifteen cars, each festooned with streamers and balloons, all horn-blasting away. Passing our door, the processionaires gesticulated toward us astonished bystanders, then a block ahead turned into the parking lot of the sports center.

Hah! Ha-AH! Shabbat soccer for the socceroos. Okay, but what ever happened to regnant status quo arrangements between the religiously observant and the secular? I looked quizzically toward Yosi, his yarmulke askew as if he'd been rudely awakened, but my back-fence neighbor was all smiles. Something special, he explained to me, as if to a child. After six years of striving, without funds, without a proper field, Yeroham's soccer squad had been elevated to a higher, more prestigious league.

"Biggest news in town . . ."

As indeed it was. Time for a petition or civil disobedience? No, but definitely time for a vacation. So, well you may imagine what we most craved when a week later we embarked on an excursion to the green, green hills of Galilee, a trip that in the eye of memory has assumed the shape of a transparent parable.

After busing to Haifa, we took possession of a rented Subaru for our northern peregrinations. Our first target was Kfar Clil, a tiny place I had never heard of before, one not even marked on roadmaps, but the home of Allen Afterman, an American-born poet of my vintage whose work I had read and much admired. Clil, he had explained by phone, consisted of around thirty Jewish families who over the years had purchased small farms from local Druze farmers. Since Afterman had chosen to reside in such splendid isolation, I fancied that he might share some of my own idiosyncrasies and enthusiasms.

Although the poet's village was unmarked from the highway, armed with his admirably clear directions, I never doubted the success of our mission. Rather than left to Acre, straight on at the intersection. Check. Highway 70 past Yagur Junction. Check. Forty-five minutes to go. Roger. Fifteen minutes north of the Haifa–Safed highway at Yasif intersection. Yep. Five minutes more. Now turn right at Jatt, and head down a country road for two kilometers. Item by item, it was much like following a new recipe for chocolate mango fritters. Curious, to be sure, but who could doubt the ultimately delectable result?

Two kilometers after the sign for Jatt, we turned the Subaru to the right onto a dirt road. Sure enough, after two more kilometers a twisting road rose up to the left—rose *very* precipitously.

"Let's . . . uh . . . drive on a little farther."

After one more kilometer, a dinky but somewhat more level road branched off sinisterly. Giving it a foolhardy shot, three minutes later the Subaru halted in a grove of olive trees. Like our frontal road in Yeroham of yore, this Galilee lane had dwindled into nothingness.

"Hmmm! It must have been the first road we passed a ways back."

"But, further on, the instructions read 'Don't climb.'"

"That's further on. Maybe as we get closer, the directions get more metaphorical. Afterman *is*, after all, a poet."

Looking about in vain for a passing cyclist, a leprechaun, *anyone* who might properly interpret our lovely little map, I felt a surge of sympathy for land surveyor K., ever on the lookout for clues, hospitable to any passerby who might help him breach the castle's outer walls, unable to distinguish helpers from distractors.

Slowly backtracking from the cul-de-sac down the dinky road to the dirt-packed biway, retracing our path a kilometer we nosed sharply to the right, shifted to second gear, then ground painfully forward into first . . . to the first switchback where the Subaru, losing traction, spun its wheels several inches into the loose dirt and flying sand. For that day, at least, we decided to abandon our mission to Clil, *kfar* distinguished by an absence of signs.

As I rocked our vehicle first forward, then backward, as in the rear seat our daughter rocked her head in her arms—refusing to look— my wife gently navigated us back down the hill. Later in the day, from a point farther north I phoned the poet and reached his wife instead.

"Ah," she declared, "the trouble is that the turn isn't at the *sign* for Jatt which only announces that it's coming up. You should turn only at Jatt itself."

Which, upon reflection, I didn't recall we ever had passed.

The next day Afterman himself came for us at our hostel in Shlomit, but at the time we were out hiking. Upon our return, we found a message he had left which thoughtfully included a neat, little, hand-drawn map replete with squiggling arrows that led right into the driveway of his homestead. Rededicated to our original purpose— after all, not every day of the week do we wheel around Galilee—the following day we headed south on Highway 70, this time surely a yellow brick road. A second shot at Clil. Two kilometers north of the earlier sign for Jatt, we Subaru intrepids spotted a left turnoff to the east. Yes, it was a town, but the sign read neither Jatt nor Clil, but Sheik Dannun.

"DON'T TURN IN THERE!" Miri fairly shrieked. Perhaps un- fairly—who knows? Anyway, heeding her urgent request not to ven- ture through a place called Sheik Dannun, not without regret, for that year we gave it up.

Driving south, it struck me that Christopher Columbus—his quincentennary now having sailed into history—without benefit of such clear instructions, once had headed west to get to the East Indies. Foiled by the Bahamas, he unfoiled his brilliant solution: the inven- tion of the Indies West. And now five hundred years later, 450,000 Russian Jews undertook an inverse journey: embarking for the West, they have ended up smack in the middle of the Middle East. Hence, exercising a massive preference for Labor in their first national franchise as Israelis, they chose the Party of the West over the Party of the East. Both Columbus and Israel's latest windfall of immigrant citizens demonstrate the potential triumph of imagination over mere geography.

Not for lack of effort or the intercession of genuine helpers, at the time neither I nor other Israelis succeeded in surpassing intervaling points or interim accords en route to Ultima Thule. What I have confirmed is that neither chuggin' along northerly nor rollin' southward was there any sign of the place. Still, I refuse seriously to doubt that Clil exists, that Shalom genuinely beckons. In fact, if recent history is any guide, it is almost surely closer at hand than I, than many of us often imagine. So I have not given up on arriving. And when I do arrive, as one day I believe we all indeed shall, I wanna warn ya all to be prepared for one helluva BEEP BEEP BEEP BEEP/ BEEP-BEEP B' BEEP.

What is so hard to accept is that, even with the best will, there are terrains and times when there truly seems to be no means at all with which to navigate past dead ends to where we want to go, to get from Here to There. Which does not mean that we may desist from trying. Perhaps next summer. If not sooner.

VISITORS

FOR REASONS obscure, the day following a holiday in this country rates an extra day off from school. This past year, however, the Wednesday following the festival of Shavuot was a regular schoolday down in my northern Negev hometown. Well, it wasn't exactly a "regular" schoolday; but, nevertheless, the most prominent traffic on Yeroham's Thursday 8:00 A.M. streets were mothers or fathers clasping the hands of five-year-olds en route to kindergarten, all dressed up in blue and white, Israel's national colors. Ambling like pubescent penguins toward the entrance to Sapir High School were the usual clusters of paddling, waddling, jabbing, joking, jabbering, poking, Hard Rock Cafe denizens and jeans-poured sexpots.

Had cheesecake—we're talking Shavuot, holiday-distinguished dairy delicacies—so addled local metabolisms that everyone had forgotten that the day-after was Whitmanesque, given over to loafing at one's ease? Not quite. The cause was special. Very special. The president himself was coming to Yeroham. Yessir, yes'm, Ezer Weizman, nephew of Chaim Weizmann, Israel's first president, he of the single, not the double n, had a month earlier been elected Israel's newly minted president-the-seventh by the Knesset, and President Ezer had designated Yeroham as the object of his first official excursion.

Visiting schools in this workingman-workingwoman's town—by ironic fiat, sister city to sybaritic Desert Hot Springs, California— would be a centerpiece of the itinerary of Mr. and Madame President. Consequently, principals, teachers, parents, and even kids conspired to get those classroom seats covered with blue-'n'-white bottoms. Truth to tell, school attendance was probably higher than usual.

The president is coming! Like stuff from the chemistry set I got for a birthday way back when, the phrase reacted on the invisible ink of recollection. Back in The Bronx there once lived a fourteen-year-old kid fascinated by politics. If asked . . . if not asked . . . he could rattle off, say, the four candidates who split the electoral vote in the election of 1824. The day that President-to-be Stevenson came to address an outdoor rally on Fordham Road, not ten blocks from his apartment house, you could not keep him away. "To talk sense to the American people," Adlai had come all the way to *The Bronx*, which he would of course handily carry anyway.

Mounted policemen diverted traffic from the Grand Concourse. From the rear of a throng that backed well south of 189th Street, the boy had difficulty hearing what the Democratic candidate actually said, but he could distinguish the lucid, seductively rational tones, and he did catch several glimpses of the bald pate of one of his authentic heroes-made-flesh. For weeks afterward, this youngster floated on a cloud of elation. It lasted until the first Tuesday . . . make that Wednesday . . . in November.

The first inkling I had of the impending state visit by President Weizman was in Beersheba when a university acquaintance asked how I felt about it all. "Dumb" would have been accurate enough, but, given the scene, my reply stuck to the mode of the glib, sardonic, would-be witty. It is worth observing that some of my fellow townspeople were considerably more reflective. The week before the big happening, *Tashkif*, our local weekly, pondered that very point. I loosely paraphrase:

"Look; we could easily be cynical about this presidential visit. We might conjecture that the new president just wanted some cheap, easy, good publicity. Or we might suspect that he chose to visit Yeroham because he considered it one of the most depressed or depressing places in Israel, the very end of the earth. But what gain is there in being cynical? Since we will never know what exactly lies behind this visit, why not simply take it at face value? Without question, it is intended as an honor. Good. That is exactly as Yeroham should view it. Unlike our past encounters with officialdom, we will ask nothing from the president other than that he enjoy his visit to the fullest. So let us all do our best to give him and his wife a welcome they will long remember."

Our town administration steadily worked to coordinate the details of the itinerary, from the traditional blessing for a Head of State at his arrival and speechifying in the cultural plaza to visits and meetings at schools, kindergartens, *ulpan* (Hebrew language centers for new immigrants), and factories. Although Chaim Herzog, Weizman's immediate predecessor as Israel's First Man, was surely the best-traveled president Israel had ever had, *he* had never set foot in Yeroham. In fact, to the best of my recollection Herzog never had organized a safari even to Beersheba, let alone to the terra incognita beyond. Weizman gave promise to be the Scott, the Amundsen of Israel's presidents.

As the big day drew near, the town wore an increasingly festive face. Flags were displayed; colorful buntings, draped along streetlights on the main street. Notices of the forthcoming appearance covered bulletin boards and kiosks. The ones in Russian were noteworthy, perhaps even collectors' items: "Everyone: Come to the Cultural Plaza at 10 A.M. on Thursday to see and hear President Chaim Weizmann." Now *that* rare opportunity should rouse the multitudes! So in the end the president's polar expedition was no small thing for us provincials. By the morning of the big day, I too was hyped on the potency of its symbolism. Perhaps Weizman's speech would strike a genuinely resonant chord.

At 10:05 Marcia and I walked past the emptied tennis courts, half of which were now regularly requisitioned by the local soccer league for something like a kicker's equivalent of half-court basketball. We exchanged a knowing look: one afternoon two months earlier this had been the skirmish zone of one of my wife's more heroic stands against the forces of anarchy. Noticing through our kitchen window that the cars of several players were parked haphazardly in a bus zone instead of an adjacent parking area, Marcia went out to complain. At first ignored, then patronized by the offenders, instinctively taking a cue from Martin Luther King, Jr., disciple of the hermit of *Walden*, she parked herself smack in the middle of the court, a Rosa Parks refusing to budge until all the cars had been moved.

At first nonplussed, then flummoxed, finally stymied by her simple tactic, the players soon realized they had but one recourse. It had worked! Although the following week demonstrated that the nature of her victory had been decidedly short-lived, perhaps it pointed toward the untapped potential of nonviolent resistance in the ongoing Kulturkampf among the rejoined tribes of Israel.

Exposed to the glare of the sun, rows of white chairs gleamed in the town's Cultural Plaza. Overhead, a cluster of helium-filled, blue and white balloons floated lazily in the sky. The town choir, both children and adults, ranged themselves in the shade of some palm trees. With his every motion, their Russian director sowed anxiety and tension. Led by teachers, one class of kindergarten moppets after another, waving their flags, trooped toward us. Small groups of townspeople clumped around benches on the periphery, *but not a single person was seated in the center.* It was already 10:15. Was a fiasco in the offing?

Among the choristers we spotted Tuti, a friend, who was sewing a last-minute button on her daughter's blouse. Looking up, she pleadingly motioned us, nay, she implored us, to move to the sizzling center of the plaza. Someone had to be first, right? Who should it be, if not reluctant, dutiful, Americans? 10:40. How long could—should—kindertots sit waiting in the sun? Was Weizman mushing a trail to Yeroham by dog sled?

Dennis and Danielle, Maurice and Myrna, some Russian friends, appeared. Would only the town's Americans together with new immigrants thinking they would see Ezer's Uncle Chaim, dead and gone these forty years, turn out for the president of Israel! The p.a. system shrieked wildly. Oblivious to why this day should be different from all other days, several pairs of soldiers from a nearby base scurried past peering at maps of the town. Weizman, Weizmann, Shmeizman, Shmeizmann—they had limited time to fulfill a map-reading exercise. Were Weizman and company now snowblinded, or were they gazing at maps of their own somewhere to the north?

Suddenly, the p.a. flooded the plaza with music. *Those were the days, my friend / We thought they'd never end* . . . followed by the hypnotic march Army Radio plays every morning at dawn after a buglely reveille. On the roof of the library, an armed figure, POLICE boldly, blackly etched on an orange sash across his chest, gazed down on us. Self-important figures with two-way radios prowled the fringes of the nearly empty plaza.

And then, *and then,* several cars appeared rolling up Zvi Bornestein Street. Historians note well, it was 11:06 when President and Mrs. Ezer Weizman arrived that day at Yeroham's Cultural Plaza and took their places on the platform. As if conjured from invisibility by some magic potion, scores of townspeople materialized in his wake and streamed into the aisles of the seats in the plaza, gradually settling into seats. Within five minutes, the center had filled in with housewives, new immigrants, teens, photographers, loafers, and just plain folks. Under a blaring sun, anticipation ran high.

After a fresh fanfare, then a flourish, the choir winged smoothly into a Moroccan ditty, followed by two well-worn songs about Jerusalem. On the platform, two schoolchildren then rhymed out a touching welcome to the president, and then . . . and then, everyone on the dias and in the audience together chimed: LONG LIVE THE PRESIDENT OF ISRAEL.

Our mayor, wisely restricting himself to four minutes of welcome, noted that the town's distinguished visitor and his wife had presented the library with three hundred books and our town's young people with ten scholarships. At last the president, somewhat stooped, formerly a fighter pilot and head of Israel's air force, formerly a minister under Menachem Begin, formerly a lady's man, of late an advocate for peace with the Arabs, rose. He too would be mercifully brief.

"Before Yeroham was founded," he began "before the founding of the state, I often came to the Negev." Coming now to Yeroham first among all other visits was intended as a reaffirmation of the relevance of Ben-Gurion's vision of the gathering together of the exiles and of the blooming of the Negev. "I look forward," he concluded, "to seeing 4 million additional Jews in Israel, 2 million of them living between Beersheba and Eilat."

The applause was enthusiastic and sustained. He had planted the flag of his disposition. Five minutes later President Weizman was off to meet with the children in their classrooms, Russian immigrants in their *ulpan*, shopkeepers in the town's commercial center, workers in their factories.

Like Adlai's old nemesis, Ezer exudes genuine warmth and charm, has the common touch, is a crowd-pleaser. Judging by his inauguratory official visit, he'll make a success of his tenure as president. Just one thought nagged: wouldn't it be refreshing for once to have a president who made it a point of honor to talk nothing but sense to the Israeli people? Two million Jews in the Negev would surely constitute a colossal victory of Technology over recalcitrant Nature. It would, however, probably compromise, if not destroy, many of the values some of us hold for choosing to live here in the first place. How many more pyrrhic victories can we sustain?

THE VILLAGE

A s on most mornings for the past seventeen years, by 7:00 I had returned from my foray to our corner store—Makolet Lalouche—bearing milk, cottage cheese, and freshly baked baguettes. Since Aharon Lalouche's death about six years ago, the store has been run by his son Haim, aided for the Friday rush by his brothers; but my wife and I still sometimes absentmindedly announce to each other that we're dashing out to "Aharon's" for some fresh *pittot* or an extra sack of sugar.

Since the morning pace at our place is sometimes frantic, I had had little time to examine an oddly shaped sign that, crammed with text, had been newly affixed to an upper corner of the building which houses Makolet Lalouche. It hung to the left of the familiar, overarching placard promoting Noga ice cream's smiling cow and high above the cartons of Carlsberg beer stacked in the front window. What principally registered, as I ran off, was that the new sign looked official, noncommercial, and permanent.

The low, concrete structure which houses "Aharon's" seems as discordant as ever in our neighborhood of adjoining, one-story houses. It predates the construction of our Ben-Gurion Quarter by nearly two decades. For a number of years, in fact, Makolet Lalouche had stood like an abandoned fortress attended by its nearly forgotten ranger. The Ben-Gurion neighborhood, you see, had been erected over a ramshackle *ma'abara*: transit housing for Moroccan immigrants who arrived on the scene from the mid-1950s through the early 1960s. Aharon Lalouche was already in his own sixties when we arrived in town, making it hard for us to imagine that he had not always been a diminutive, wizened Moroccan, dispensing provender to his fellow immigrants. Among the real old-timers in town, his store was still known as *makolet ha'ma'abara*.

Although the *ma'abara* had been leveled, although nearly all Aharon's neighborhood customers had relocated, although the nearby kindergarten had been closed for lack of nearby clientele, Aharon, remnant of an earlier era, held to his post. In those years between the demolition of the *ma'abara* and the construction of Ben-Gurion, customers must have been exceedingly scarce. But the *makolet* was all that Aharon had, and so hold out he did.

Whatever the season, whatever the weather, Aharon opened for business never later than 6:00 A.M. so as to catch those few faithful regulars who would come to shop a distance from home. Throughout that lean period, his earliest, steadiest customers were construction workers—mainly Arabs from Gaza—who bought cheese, salami, bread, and drinks on credit against their weekly pay. Sometimes Aharon would mutter when one failed to appear at the end of the week. The store's busiest stretch came between 9:45 and 10:15 when students on break between classes at the nearby high school crowded in, buying or filching rolls, ice cream, and candy. Taking off only for lunch and a brief nap, when he would be spelled by one of his sons, Aharon remained open until 8:00 or 9:00 at night. To us he was Morris Bober, Malamud's Polish grocer, in Moroccan guise: *makolet* was his fate.

Hard times ended abruptly in 1977 when a flood of us new arrivals—new customers—brought justification and unaccustomed prosperity for the old grocer.

Aharon's cramped domain was illuminated by the unsteady glow of a single fluorescent fixture. Entering the premises was something like lowering oneself into a cavern. In winter, the old man warmed himself with innumerable drafts of tea, insufficient to permit him to doff his heavy coat. In summer, a single ceiling fan twirled lackadaisically, and the acrid smell of spoiled milk permeated the air. Still, Aharon made no improvements on his store, and from behind the scarred counter, a picture of dour Moroccan "wonder rabbi" Baba Sali, cowled in gabardine, perpetually peered down from the wall.

Aharon had little patience with cash register or calculator. Figuring each transaction on a strip of brown paper, he kept track of credit customers on slips deposited in an unsorted pile in a cigar box. Not an hour passed without either an irate housewife challenging his account of her debt or a supplier cajoling him to stock a new product or demanding payment for the old. These entertainments could last for twenty minutes or more, in the course of which both Aharon and the aggrieved party would periodically submit their briefs to waiting customers. Sometimes the jury was amused, other times just exasperated.

"My Tami couldn't have bought ice cream three weeks ago. We forbid her to buy things like that."

"But look; here I've marked 'sixty *lirot*, 3/1, Bouskila.' And look, here are her initials. Tell her," Aharon would exclaim histrionically, turning in my direction, "doesn't this say sixty *lirot*, 3/1, Bouskila?"

In truth, I couldn't decipher Aharon's hand and certainly not Tami's initials, but seeking resolution—and above all closure—usually I would nod vigorously. In my experience, both Aharon's arithmetic and his integrity were impeccable.

"Should I stop giving things to your daughter?" Aharon would finally inquire craftily. This was his trump. Most residents of the Ben-Gurion Quarter could not manage without credit.

"I didn't say that," Mrs. Bouskila replied in more measured tones. "But give her only what I write on my list. This time I'll pay what you say. Part now, part tomorrow."

Aharon would never leave his store unattended. One day, however, Shai, when he was three years old, wandered from the house without our knowledge. The next thing we knew Aharon, visibly shaken, deposited him at our front door. He'd seen our son heading for the street, in front of one of the delivery trucks that to this day periodically swivel illegal U's in front of the *makolet*. Aharon had scooped Shai out of the path of harm and returned him safely to our front door. Like the Lone Ranger, however, not even for a moment could he linger for a cold drink or to receive our expression of gratitude: his *makolet* was unattended.

Soon after taking over his father's store, Haim expanded into the adjoining premises, doubling the floor space. He bought a new refrigeration unit, improved the lighting, even used a calculator. Baba Sali still presides on the wall; it's impossible to tell whether he looks down more with sadness or with approbation. For a time "Haim's"—the only market servicing both Ben-Gurion and the newer Shaked neighborhood—was so crowded that I occasionally ventured further afield for the morning's milk, cheese, and baguettes. Two years ago, however, a minimarket opened in Shaked, so, boom years fizzling, it is young Haim who now wears the caged expression of Morris Bober.

Later in the day I returned to inspect the strange sign that now distinguished our local *makolet*. Crenulated at its corners, it bore a close resemblance to a rook on a chessboard. This, in fact, would have been no more astonishing than the fact that it was an historical marker, the standard sort that the Society for the Protection of Land and Nature authorizes for natural and historical sites. Said marker declared that this was the site of Yeroham's second *ma'abara*, from 1962 until its demolition inhabited by immigrants from Morocco.

Later I learned from Debbi Golan, an American friend active with a small local group engaged in historical research, that this organization had provided the bureaucratic push to raise historical Yeroham to recognition. Among Israel's several dozen "development towns" (urban entities founded since 1948), only Yeroham has so far demonstrated such marked interest in the preservation of its immigrant heritage. After three years of effort, Yeroham now boasted seven officially designated national historic landmarks. A map for a self-guided, historical tour of Old Yeroham was under preparation, even, in time, a visitor's center!

Now, I don't imagine that very many residents of Haifa, not to mention tourists from overseas, will go out of their way to take a self-guided walking tour of Old Yeroham (founded 1951). Still, on the scenic route to Eilat, in conjunction with our overbrimming lake and splendid canyon, for those with imagination and a sense of history, a half-hour around Yeroham of Yore just might prove . . . piquant. Perhaps even an eye-opener. By the numbers, it would go something like this:

In front of the columnar monuments at the entrance to town, a Sign One designates the site of Yeroham's first *ma'abara*, settled by Rumanian immigrants between 1952 and 1954. For many years it has served as an army base on which may be found five original wooden period buildings, the only ones of their kind surviving in any development town. A block away stands Number Two, a plaque at the site of the town's first "industrial zone." (The only remaining structure from the period is currently the town's premier parlor of snooker, deemed, perhaps on puritanical grounds, unsuitable for historical recognition.)

To the left, just up the street, marker Number Three is attached to a dilapidated structure at one time inhabited by Eli Muchnik. He was not the very first mayor of Yeroham, but he was the first one with enough commitment to move here together with his family. He served, and they remained, for more than a decade. A return to the main street brings one to Sign Four, Yeroham's first clinic, or *kupat holim*, and to Five, site of the town's first kindergarten. Now more aromatic than formerly, currently it is our town's bakery. Cutting across an old playground and down an embankment, one comes to Plaque Six which marks Yeroham's first schoolhouse, and is today . . . a schoolhouse. And then a final jog up the embankment, across yet another street and through a wadi brings the visitor to Number Seven.

Naturally, all cultures are selective about what they choose to cele- brate, what they remember, and what they forget. Across the street from Seven is a plaque of another hue; it expresses gratitude to the Jewish Community of Montreal for providing the library, the tennis courts, and a good deal more which have enhanced the lives of Yero- ham's citizens. The long filled-in wadi on which the tennis courts were constructed, on the other hand, survives only in the memories of older area residents, Jews and Bedouin alike.

Plaque Number Seven would inform the Hebrew-reading visitor that he was standing at the site of Yeroham's second *ma'abara*, founded in 1962. It tells about asbestos huts, none of which remain today, in which immigrants from Morocco were housed and about the founding of the Ben-Gurion neighborhood in 1977. There is, however, no mention of the man who occupied these premises for so many years, the man who for more than two decades, twelve hours a day, six days a week, provided exemplary service for nearby residents. Please note, please know and recall, then, that Number Seven is "Aharon's."

READING . . .

AND SOLITUDE

WHEN I plopped down in front of my Apple that autumnal morning, I had something else in mind to mess around with on the keys. Something witty, mildly upbeat. Like toothpaste from an old tube, a few paragraphs had squeezed smoothly through before the thunk of the downstairs mailbox signaled a mid-morning break. I never got back to my smooth start; not for the first time had the postman unwittingly functioned as abortionist . . . and midwife.

The letter seemed be from a friend in Los Angeles who goes back thirty years . . . but on second glance the hand on the envelope was not Bob's at all, so even before I had sedulously slitted the crease of the envelope, my interior weather had turned about. Sandi's letter confirmed what I already suspected. Three weeks before, Bob had succumbed to the cancer he had been holding at bay for three embattled years. He was fifty-three.

I must own that Death has been sparing with me. One year earlier my father was gravely ill. Also with cancer. Astonishingly, at eighty-eight Dad earned a reprieve. On this afternoon in September, how ever, I forgot gratitude. I had planned to fly to L.A., to see my old friend on my next visit to America. Instead, I would write a check to the American Cancer Society in memory of a good man dead one month, ten thousand miles away. Pale anodyne for rage.

Bob and I first met in a barracks at the U.S. Army Language School in Monterey, California, where we both were training to be Russian interpreters. The year was 1961. A lapsee from the faith, also from Back East, Bob came from a large, combustible French-Canadian, Catholic family. We shared a passion for literature and an animus toward officers. After a few months, he and I with two other soldier-students rented a place in Berkeley, seventy-five miles north, where we could escape the army for weekends. Bob was with me the night I met my wife-to-be; August 19th never passes without him present in my mind.

I have never known a more vivid, more natural storyteller. Bob himself generally served as the uproarious butt of his tales of comic maladroitness. My favorite was his account of his big date with the gorgeous Chinese sophomore he had picked up at Sproul Plaza outside Cal's Student Union Building. She was on the swimming team, and they were to meet pool-side the following week. For the five intervening days in Monterey Bob effused tirelessly over Clarene Goon: her charm, her manner, her exotic beauty—total antithesis to occidental crassness. As I indelicately reminded Bob, he couldn't swim. No matter. She would teach him.

Later my friend related how well met he was at the appointed time and place, but not by the antithetical Clarene, who could not make it. No, Bob was greeted instead by Mother Goon . . . and Father Goon . . . and two grade school sister Goons . . . and not least of all by wise old Uncle Goon, still a champion diver. As Bob stood tiptoe in the water or hung on the edge to practice his kicking, one Goon after another in turn expressed particular pleasure in meeting Clarene's "Russian" friend. They plied him with dampened sandwiches. As the lithe little Goon sisters swam playfully between his legs, it was Uncle G. who gave Bob his first lesson in the art of swimming.

Bob's self-deprecating rendition of "First Date with Clarene" never failed to leave me convulsed. It's real point was not the absurdity of his being stood-up, but rather how exuberant, how joyful a time he passed with her family. Since the one he had left back in Waterbury was so thorny, so debilitating, Bob, as he invariably did with all loving families, had fallen in love with the Goon clan. All of them, that is, save the dragon girl herself, who on Date Two turned out to be an embodiment of the gum-chewing, slang-wielding, All-American twits he abhorred.

We were stationed together in Japan. In December Bob gave Marcia and me a ceramic urn on whose packaging carton he had painted lively, nostalgic scenes from "A Child's Christmas in Wales." In Japan Bob learned to do carpentry with queer-looking traditional Japanese tools. He learned to play the koto. If only he could have written about his experiences with a fraction of the art with which he could relate them! Most of all, you see, Bob wanted to be a Dylan Thomas, a poet, but he could never begin to please himself. Until the very end, he was my most reliable source of works by promising young American writers that I may have overlooked from my Israeli redoubt. His taste was flawless. Occasionally I would send him something I'd written, something that I thought came off particularly well or that I thought Bob, in particular, might appreciate.

Several years after the army—it was 1969—Bob lived with us for six months in an isolated pocket of The Bronx called City Island: seven thousand white ethnics alongside a boating, artsy set. Whereas my own career, marriage, political commitments seemed to me on course, unresolved conflicts rendered Bob vulnerable to self-doubt. Unto despair. Out of synch with each other, after a time we grew out of patience. In the end, we both split: Marcia and I with our two toddlers for one end of California, Bob for the other. For several years, we saw each other relatively little.

Throughout the seventies my closest friend was an African-American English instructor named Lionel Williams. Married to a Jewish woman, Lionel taught, worked on a dissertation—(not the one he wanted to write on Chester Himes, but the one on Donne he could get approved). He also finished the manuscript of a first novel which I read and which seemed very good. Like Bob, Lionel was highly supportive of our decision to put America behind us, to make aliya. Unlike any of our Jewish circle, both really understood.

Robert Beaulieu is not my first close friend to die much out of season. One morning in 1976, while backing out of his driveway in Healdsburg, north of San Francisco, Lionel got rammed by a kid in a Ford blasting at top speed over the crest of the hill. Crushed, he was pinned to his steering wheel. What could be more stupid? Or banal! Just what sense can one make of a young, talented man, his mind perhaps on "A Valediction: Forbidding Mourning," getting squashed like an insect while backing out of a driveway?

For some reason I have never fathomed—or forgiven—I was not informed in time to drive north for Lionel's funeral. His wife, two children, and promising novel disappeared somewhere into Canada. To this day, few weeks pass when something does not jar me into viewing the world from Lionel's particular slant. How he would grin at the gray whiskery patch that spreads so insolently beneath my chin. It is, of course, irrational, but for me something has always implicated bicentennial America in the erasure of my friend. Like Bob, eighteen years later Lionel remains one of my select, my private audience of readers, one for whom I try to write the very best that I possibly can, one who would appreciate this or that touch, and chucklingly disparage this piece of coyness, that of pretension.

Before we left America, Bob had set up as a carpenter, "carpenter of the stars," as he used to savor. He did remodeling work for the likes of Burt Reynolds, and met and married Sandi, whom he greatly loved, and fathered Annika and Devon. A late starter, he had remodeled his own life with spectacular success. Two summers ago, when I had to be in Los Angeles to research a manuscript, they put up with me for six weeks.

Cancer, slyer than a souped-up Ford, had already taken its toll. My friend had visibly aged, and weakened. At the time, however, the disease seemed to be in check, perhaps, as Bob so powerfully hoped, even checkmated. In fact, his insidious opponent was just biding its time. The book I was researching, one Bob will never read, appeared in 1992. In retrospect, the deeper importance of working on it was the opportunity it afforded me to visit at length with Bob, Sandi, and their two sweet children. That closed a loop which had dangled ever since his stay with us at City Island; it wove a sort of a symmetry over our thirty-year connection.

I propitiate myself that no serious unfinished business between us was left untransacted. But that's small solace for never again reading his infrequent notes, of never again seeing him with his kids, of never, ever again hearing him recount his classic swimming party with the Goons.

And now Bob has joined Lionel, neither of whom I saw nor can I imagine dressed up for a final laying out, as a full member in a very exclusive club—the silent readership of my dead sleepers. Out of the solitude of my upstairs room, the blank sheet, and the green screen, it is for them that I distance, measure, labor, and compose whatever provisional sense I may have of my passing days here in Israel.

Several months later I was informed that Allen Afterman, father of four, had succumbed suddenly, without warning, to a stroke. I would never tell him in person just how fine I thought *Desire for White*, his book of poems. No; I would not aim next summer for Kfar Clil after all.

I hate Death for its raw pitiless plunder, for prematurely fixing fangs into both the friend I intuited but never made and the one I had known for most of my life. Bob labored so long to shape his life harmoniously, to get it right. In the end he succeeded in authoring the loving family he always craved, in whom he took such justifiable pride and who now have been despoiled. Yes, I hate Death for his wife's and children's sake, but also for my own, for entailing what Donne so precisely observed would be a dwindling of my own essential self. I am not all that rich in friends who go back thirty years, in those who know me so well.

So Bob's defunct . . .
he was a handsome man

                        and what i want to know is
how do you like your blue-eyed boy
Mister Death

For you, Bob, like the poets you read often and loved fiercely, I am and shall remain unreconciled. Funct, I shall not yield you up all that soon or all that quickly.

THE POND

NONE of my standard diversionary tactics had availed. Home during school vacation, my gung-ho aquarist son persisted in distracting me from dispatching a book review—my morning's assignment—with news of the latest lowdown on chichlids, algae eaters, and assorted aqueous matters he had garnered from his latest issue of *Tropical Fish Hobbyist*. Then Shai framed a more general question: "Dad, just how big is a *pond?*"

"Uhhh, not very large. Why don't you try reading *Walden?* It's *the* great pond yarn."

"But do you think we could build one? You know how I always have to clean algae from the walls of the tank, check the acidity, and restock. Well, it says here that because there are so many microorgasms in ponds, fish are practically self-sustaining. The critters just fall in."

In a single stroke, my son had earned my bemused but undivided attention.

"Micro-orgasms! You don't say. Lucky fish. Let's see: in relation to our back yard, a pond would be on the order of the Mediterranean. All in all, I don't think it'd be very practical."

Which, to my surprise, seemed to satisfy him, but for me it entailed a train of notions about fish aswim in our national pond—some doing reasonably well, the less lucky struggling for air—which drew me far from my reviewer's task.

Soprano Galina Malinskaya, suffering from a head cold, accompanied by a pianist, came down from Beersheba to appear at Yeroham's Cultural Center. Save for a scattering of Americans, a solidly Russian audience packed the airless room. Women of a certain age and matronly aunts dressed grandly for the occasion. Young boys perched on ample laps—opportunities for an evening of kultura *are not to be scanted. One grande dame conspicuously extracted a fan with a Japanese motif from its case and for almost an hour fanned herself furiously.*

Malinskaya, a strikingly pretty brunette in her mid-30's, had been a principal singer for eight years at the Tadzhikistan Opera. Her repertoire—Russian schmaltz save for two arias from Carmen—wowed the locals. Mopping her brow, even occasionally dabbing her runny nose, Malinskaya was . . . merely . . . glorious.

More than a year after they had first registered, Dima and Natayla finally received an invitation to appear at the religious court in Beersheba. Marcia and I volunteered to accompany them. The appointment was for 11 A.M. Usually buoyant, Dima was somewhat subdued; Natalya, quietly nervous. We sat four to a bench in the narrow, crowded corridor on the second floor of the building. Every few minutes, one of the two doors at the end of the hallway opened and a dark-garbed, self-important clerk, cigarette dangling from his lips, a sheaf of papers in his hand, would scamper past us; moments later he would scurry back. Periodically, a name would be announced, and an individual or couple would rise and pass through one of the two doors. Fifteen or twenty minutes later, they would reappear.

Dima was Jewish; Natalya, Russian. She had studied Judaism for almost a year with a young, American-born rabbi in our town. We knew that she was committed, sincere, knowledgeable. More, she knew her stuff. There were former marriages; between them they had three children. She wanted very much to be Jewish.

"Don't worry," I assured silent Natalya. "It'll go well."

At 11:30 a handcuffed, foot-manacled prisoner escorted by an armed guard entered a door together with a woman wearing a shawl.

"A divorce," I commented. "Conversions have lower priority than divorces."

We laughed skittishly at every trifle. By noon, the four of us were the only ones still seated in the gloom-filled, smoky hallway.

Finally, a querulous clerk appeared, checked his list, drew Dima close and nodded. Our two friends entered. We were astonished to see the door reopen just ninety seconds later. Afterward, at a restaurant, Dima recounted what had occurred.

"They asked me if I was Jewish and whether I kept commandments, *mitzvot*. I answered that we sent our sons to religious schools, and that I tried my best. They asked, so I told him that we still slept together. For some reason, there wasn't a Russian interpreter on the premises. One rabbi nodded at the other two. Then the clerk said we could expect a letter. They didn't ask Natalya anything at all," he gasped. "They wouldn't even look at her."

Natalya knows that the court is not disposed to encourage her application to become Jewish. Eighteen months later, she awaits another letter from the religious court to fix an appointment for her next "interview."

Exercising remarkable control over his deep voice, powerful frame, and audience was silver-haired Georgi Yashunsky. His stage presence at our cultural center was compelling. His voice declamatory, then plummeting to a whisper, his Russian measures flowed like the Dneiper at full flood. His text: the poems of Bialik in the eighty-year Russian translation by Vladimir Jabotinsky. Performing Shakespeare, Checkhov, and Saroyan, the Leningrad-born actor played repertory in Chelyabinsk, Omsk, Tashkent, and back in his home city. His first career was capped by elevation to People's Artist of the Soviet Union. And now, a second career for the People's Artist who declares that "for many immigrants, Russian culture remains nourishment for the soul."

Without the leavening of our 450,000 newest *olim*, how depleted, how paltry, how stripped of color and vitality, how impoverished Israel's streets, classrooms, and landscape would seem! Like Frost's oven bird, what could we possibly make now of such a barren, diminished thing? Yet such was Israel in 1990, barely four years ago. So rapidly have these energetic, energizing newcomers become "absorbed"; so soon has that become a corollary flipside of taken-for-granted.

In 1993 we invited just a single Russian family to join our Passover seder: Dahvid, an engineer who now supervises a construction project in Beersheba, *his* Natalya, who works as a psychologist, their seventeen-year-old son and six-year-old daughter. So, in 1993 only a dozen of us leaned on our cushions like free men and women and raised four cups of wine. This was in marked contrast to the banner Passovers of '91 and '92 when, Russian-speakers to the left of me, Russian-speakers to the right, we numbered twenty or more participants. This meant that for the occasion we had to requisition our Ping-Pong table—fortunately, still dry as a bone from its immersion in our un–self-sustainable back yard.

At seders ten, five, even three years earlier I had pointedly appended a prayer for the release of Jews of bondage, especially from the Soviet Union. This past year—*voilà*—no Soviet Union! More to the point, except for several hundred leftover refuseniks, who can doubt that most of the millions still there remain by choice? On the other hand, every blessed month up to five thousand Russian Jews continue to arrive in Israel. That's one-third of the figure that Whitehall, disingenuously doubting "the absorptive capacity of Palestine," allotted for Jewish immigration in the late 1930s *for a year*. Under our very noses, most of that surge of new *olim* who arrived by the hundreds of thousands in the Big Bang of '90–'91 now seems far along the process of becoming simply friends, neighbors, and fellow Israelis.

Two years or more down the line, how are some of our seder guests of the early nineties doing? Dima works part-time and has entered a retraining course for sports teachers; Natalya is midway through a retraining course for drafts(wo)men. Vadim, Natan, and Oleg—my university students—are now all seniors, all doing nicely. Although her husband, Yevgeny, doesn't find much work as a dancer, Ludmila works full-time as subeditor on a Russian newspaper. Then there are Slava and *his* Ludmila. Both doctors, they have passed the test enabling them to practice medicine. After nearly a year of trying, Slava succeeded in landing a job at a clinic in Tel Aviv where they and their six-year-old daughter have moved. Ludmila, a gynecologist who worked for a while cleaning houses, has yet to meet with any job-hunting success.

The others? Misha, by training a geographer, works double shifts at a Yeroham factory; his wife, Elena, has started a six-month program consisting of half-day preparatory courses that will lead to job retraining programs. They have sometimes spoken about moving with their two little boys to Canada. Vitaly, an engineer who spent several months looking for work in Europe, has returned to factory work in Yeroham. His eleven-year-old son Avi, a straight-A student, refuses to consider leaving Israel. As for bald, taciturn Yuri, a turbo-engineer *there*, "here" just a factory hand, eight months ago he returned to his wife and son in Russia. He still maintains a local apartment, but no one knows when he will return . . . or if.

Spreading over the only back yard we've got, this pond of ours now sustains ten times the number of Jewish souls the British had argued it could possibly bear. Upon checking the acidity and monitoring the interactivity, it would seem that its micro-orgasmic capacity is truly prodigious. Practically self-sustaining? Only arguably and after a fashion, but, by increments—a little bang here, a little bang there—most of the newcomers we have come to know, to like, and to admire are making their way, slowly finding a niche. I propose that this too is food for the soul, and ample grounds even for plaintive oven birds to voice a celebratory note and to recall these extraordinary years of our augmentation. Things could always be better, but most of us fish have been damned lucky.

After Dima and Natalya had eaten five or six Friday nights at our house, one week after services we walked over to their building and mounted three flights to their functional, tidy apartment. Natalya greeted us shyly at the door, and, a bit self-consciously, we took our places at the table. Unlike most of our other Russian-born friends, they did not bring many knickknacks from their old home. Two candles glowed on the table in the corner—a tradition-laden, sentimental tableau recalling Moritz Oppenheim. Natalya's blonde hair was covered by a scarf. She keeps, we know, a kosher home. Dima raised his cup, opened to a marked page, and recited.

Dien shestov, ee zaverschenuy bwuili nevo ee zemlya ee fseo voinistbix. . . .

In this fashion, as deftly, as magically as Coleridge, did Dima transform the habitual into the strange, and tongue the extraordinary into the familiar . . . the shockingly familiar.

JACKET FARM

I N THE HEAT of the summer of 1992 my wife and I left Yeroham
to spend a Shabbat at Sa'ad (i.e., "Well-Being"), a kibbutz in the
western Negev. Founded in 1947 by observant Jews from Ger-
many and Austria, the fledgling settlement had been leveled by the
Egyptian army and rebuilt nearby immediately after the close of hostilities. Our hosts were Dahvid and Natalya. Through a connection at
Sa'ad, we had been instrumental in getting them accepted as provisional members of the kibbutz even though they were over thirty-five,
the technical age limit. Although in their first months they had been
enthusiastic about kibbutz life, in the end it did not suit them. Not
long after our visit, they returned to live in Yeroham.

Since the early eighties, palmy days for kibbutzim have gotten
frosty. Most are financially strapped and experience difficulty in attracting enough newcomers to compensate for defections among their
own young. Nevertheless, in a world gone ga-ga over gadgets, greed,
and ego, there are those for whom kibbutz values—simplicity, egalitarianism, equality of opportunity for women (even if often honored
in the breach)—retain much of their romantic appeal. In truth, had
Marcia and I arrived in Israel while still in our twenties, we would
surely have given kibbutz life very serious consideration.

However much veteran kibbutzniks might scoff, notwithstanding
many "reforms" over the past decade, it strikes me that the kibbutz
shares many salient features with the monastery: inward-looking, communal, disciplined, doctrinaire, self-sustaining (at least in principle),
rural, cashless, incurious, hospitable. That last in particular: both
monastery and kibbutz set aside a place where the wayfarer may be
received and few questions pressed. If he or she wishes to remain, the
currency is labor; conformity, the dues. For many an alien spirit, just
as the monastery emblematizes a quintessential Christian path, the
kibbutz embodies its Jewish counterpart. The maximal fulfillment of
the individual, whether socialist or religiously observant, runs through

145

the betterment of the whole. The result is not, perhaps, the exceptional life, but surely a good one. No small thing.

As might be expected for a long-established settlement, Kibbutz Sa'ad displayed an attractive façade. A closer look revealed significant discriminations. The dining halls were commodious but, in fact, little more than functional. For the synagogue, however, no expense had been spared. It was a balanced, well-proportioned structure whose upper half from a frontal perspective lent an impression of levitation. The overall effect—surely unintentional—was less Middle than Far Eastern. Interior decor was tasteful . . . and pricey. What struck me most, however, was an adventitious find: at my seat an unfamiliar edition of the prayer book. "Wien I, Sertstettang 15; Budapest VII, Urlag 1" read the publication data. The year—ominous 1936.

My impression of the synagogue at the following morning's service altered radically. The interior focus now seemed less on the elevated podium in the center of the spacious room than on the front. The cause: a large, really quite stunning stained glass window elevated high over the ornately covered ark where the Torah scrolls were deposited. Crosshatched by two sets of intersecting supports, its opulent panes at the touch of sunlight seemed to absorb, then bleed forth predominantly deep-blue hues. Illuminated was a forceful abstract pattern evoking what I took to be Moses receiving the tablets on which the Ten Commandments were engraved. What really compelled homage, however, was the window itself as a powerful, independent aesthetic statement.

Kibbutz regulars, tired after a week of labor, dispatched Saturday morning service in a breezy fashion. It almost certainly never occurred to any of them that their beautiful window, set off by its deep-set, cruciform frames, might be distracting, might even trigger alienating sensations of being seated in a church.

After intoning Kiddush over the wine, after the lunch, after some chat, the afternoon turned very hot, and, after so many years of living in an unhumid town at the end of the Oil Road, we were unused to the heavy air of the coastal region. The entire settlement lay at rest. Neither mad dog nor Englishman, not even a wandering child cast a shadow on the sultry paths of the recumbent settlement. Yet a solitary, curious visitor was abroad: across the green, lovingly tended lawns; along the paths of the remarkable, spiky garden of cacti collected from every arid quarter of the globe; around to the musty-scented dairy to yet another lush, tree-sheltered grassy expanse.

Not more than minutes from the painful incongruities of Gaza, a peaceable kingdom was at its Sabbath rest. Close by the silent, sleep-deserted synagogue, I lolled on the grass beneath a tall shade-tree in full leaf and looked vacantly past a tidy, slumbering playground, now in repose. The green and pleasant prospect was no less decorous than an estate in Hertfordshire, and its resident toilers, its eggmen, dairy-men, and gardeners had, it seemed to me, ample claim as Israel's, perhaps the Jewish people's truest restored aristocrats of the soil: hundreds of yeomen of well-being, of dukes and duchesses de Sa'ad.

In spite of the squabbles, the pettiness, the ideological discord and discordances, who could gainsay the astonishing result? This rural seat was, in its fashion, a jewel, a place gorgeous to behold, a work of art. Recumbent beneath a large tree at the edge of lawn for thirty or more minutes, I thought of neither Housman nor Wordsworth—or even Edward Thomas—but priestly Manley Hopkins: "My heart in hiding stirred for . . . the achieve of, the mastery of the thing."

It was still, still, still hot at five in the afternoon when some older children, trailed after by mothers and infants, emerged on the curvy pathways of the kibbutz. No one ran, no one yelled, . . . and no one paused to admire their tidy, little principality. I sat pondering what our hosts had told us earlier: in the past year a dozen young families had left this place; the yield of newly approved member families—just one!

Caught up in the rituals of departure, missing the first post-Shabbat bus to Beersheba, we caught instead a ride to Beersheba with a doctor and his wife. Soon thereafter we were seated on the last bus that evening going from Beersheba to Yeroham.

Although it has distinctive qualities of its own, I don't know anyone who might confuse Yeroham with a scene by Corot or Constable. Yet, odd to contemplate, my slapdash little town enjoys a peculiar relation with this kibbutz not distant from Gaza. For a number of years Yeroham has been attracting a continuous flow of young persons who grew up on that settlement. Put otherwise: for several years the emerald-like realm, founded in 1947 by now-aging German and Austrian Jews, so-called *Yekkes* (after the German for "jackets") because of their adherence to Teutonic standards of formality, order, and discipline, has been steadily hemorrhaging. Kibbutz Sa'ad, where the *Yekkes* still set the general tone and at general meetings call the communal tune, seems incapable of stanching the wound at its breast.

It was sheer chance that the very next week painted glass windows covering much of its eastern wall were installed in our synagogue in Yeroham. Officially named Afikim Banegev—"Streams in the Negev"—it is still referred to either as the "American Synagogue" or by its former official name, Mashmia Shalom—"Proclaim Peace!" Not long ago I served for two years as its president, something that still amuses me because president of a synagogue was one role I never dreamed I would ever assume. Mashmia Shalom is the only congregation in town that employs liturgy and prayer-book elements from both Sephardi and Ashkenazi traditions. Young couples in their twenties, including not a few refugees from well-being at a certain kibbutz in the western Negev, compose the bulk of the membership . . . and run it.

Resources, as may be imagined, are meager. For over ten years we crowded into a tiny structure—now a *beit midrash*, or study hall— unable to accumulate the means to build a larger structure. Today, however, although we are no longer so cramped, a first entrance into the enlarged precincts of Mashmia Shalom would scarcely stir anyone's heart in hiding. An electrical wire dangles across the ceiling and others protrude like green serpents from the floor around the raised platform in the center of the structure. We sit on plastic chairs that were jettisoned by a synagogue in Rehovot. The last rain of winter is still dripping through the roof, puddling in odd spots on the floor a month after the weather bureau stopped taking notice.

Nevertheless, a living congregation is more than the sum of its partitions or partners, more a function of persons than premises. For me, worship at Afikim Banegev has been more generally satisfactory than anywhere else I've ever been.

One of Afikim Banegev's youngest members is Anna Andersch-Marcus, some forty-five years past the boundary line for admission to a kibbutz. She is a painter of international repute, known for her vorticist style and work in stained glass. Originally from Hamburg, she was active in the German underground during the war. Anna and her husband, Shlomo, moved to Yeroham from Jerusalem six years ago. In addition to her painting, Anna tends a garden that would be the pride of any member of the *yekke* farm her former countrymen and-women established in a new land thirty-five years ago. The central motif of her painted glass window is based upon Zechariah's prophetic vision of the restoration of Jerusalem at the end of days, symbolically embodied by streams flowing in the desert. They are Anna's special gift to her fellow worshipers.

No; the windows are not *real* stained glass, which our congregation could not begin to afford, but Anna, in the fashion of artists, turned her limitation to advantage. As if they were afloat along our eastern wall, liquid colors softly swirl. The rounded rooftops of Jerusalem—browns, oranges, yellows, blues above and below—are relieved by vertical planes that seem to stream from a single, unseen source above the level of the ceiling.

In the course of Shabbat morning services at Yeroham's "Streams in the Negev," emanations from Anne's windows graze in turn over more than one-third of the field of men in the downstairs section. Looking up at any particular moment, Gershon's face might be blue-tinged, Moshe's bald spot awash in orange and temporary pink, the prayer book in my hands yellow, my fingers swimming in Jerusalem purple. Twenty minutes later, Gershon's upper torso is speckled pink and red; Moshe's pate has turned native hue but his arm is still dyed in Jerusalem tones; my hands and arms are Prussian blue. To the women above, what an inconstant chameleonoid lot we men at prayer must appear!

Anna Marcus's achievement—at once engaging and participatory, apt and symbolically complex, Jewish—seems to me an elegant fusion of art and faith. Perhaps, ironically, once more it is Hopkins, poet-priest of pied, comes to mind:

O

Glory be to God for dappled things—
    For skies of couple-colour as a brinded cow;
        For rose-moles all in a stipple upon trout that swim;

For strict kibbutz, round town, Jerusalem,
    Hassid, Gazan, women bathers at Elat;
        For each and all who wash in the aching light of sun;

The achieve of the thing.

HIGHER LAWS

NOT for nothing does *Bemidbar*, or "In the Desert," translate into English as the Book of Numbers. In fact, it sometimes seems that Moses' favorite ruse for keeping the ancient Israelites otherwise occupied was to order yet another census. Like my favorite among Sesame Street's more fantastical denizens, we Jews are also avid enumerators: "603, 548; 603, 549; 603, 550 Children of Israel. Heh! Heh! Heh! I *luv* to count."

I have an artist friend who is fascinated by gematria. Even though he is aware that I don't share his enthusiasm, he can never resist sharing his latest insights derived from the putative digital equivalencies that underlie the nature of all reality. What I *can* appreciate, of course, is the impetus: a drive to perceive order or pattern through the veil of seeming chaos that generally shades our lives. In April of '92, however, even I could not gainsay a powerful feeling that life—*my* life—had become enmeshed in a mysterious numbers game entailing numinous meanings, one in which I was less a player than another colored bead on the abacus.

It happened during the weeks of the counting of the days of omer, an enumerative binge partaken of by a significant proportion of Jews. Starting with the offering of the barley harvest on the second night of Passover—Number One—the figure mounts steadily toward Number Forty-Nine and convergence with its fixed omega point—the festival of the wheat harvest at Shavuot. The closest acquaintance most Americans have with such sustained annual reckoning flows in the opposite direction: starting at whichever point the priests of accountancy at Wal-Mart, K-Mart, and Wards decree, a countdown of shopping opportunities to Day One until Santa blasts off.

My computations in 1992 were more taxing than usual. Not only did my nonlinear faculties stretch to the usual limit merely keeping track of the nightly tally, but embedded like gyres within the omer's farther borders ran two contrary-tending, interior enumerations whose

150

higher meaning would come to pose as much an emotional burden as an interpretive conundrum.

It was still during *hol-hamoed*—the intermediate days of Passover week and the very start of the omer count—that our daughter-in-law's term of 270 days ran their course. Delivered unto us was a grandson, our von, too, zree, fourz grandchild. Heh! Heh! Heh! Permit a new grandfather some latitude: for the record, our newcomer happened to arrive on the birthday of Buddha. It was also the day on which Rav Joseph Soloveitchik, perhaps America's most respected Torah voice, drew his last breath.

A grandson meant the need to switch enumerative modes from a nine-month descent to zero hour to an eight-day ascent toward *brit milah*, the ritual circumcision celebration at which my newest descendant would get named.

The day after delivery, I phoned the new great-grandparents in far-off North Miami Beach.

"Mazel tov! Mazel tov! So what's his name?"

"He hasn't been officially named yet."

"So tell us unofficially."

"I really don't know what name Ted and Ilana have chosen. In fact, I don't even know whether they've decided yet on a name."

"What do you mean you don't know? Try to find out!"

"Well, it's not quite proper to ask yet."

"If you don't ask, how will you ever know what to call him? That's why we're asking."

"Touché. When Ted names him, I'll listen very closely. It'll happen during the ceremony itself, during the *brit*.

"The what?"

"The *bris*! The *bris*! Ilana's mother is coming two weeks from now to help out for a while but she'll miss the *bris*. I'll be the *sandek*. My first time in such a role. A rite of passage for me too."

"Well, hold tight. [Pause.] Are you sure you don't know his name?"

"Mom, believe me; I haven't a clue."

Next morning Marcia departed Yeroham for the scene of the cut—Yeshivat Har Etzion of Alon Shvut of Gush Etzion in Judea on the West Bank—to assist mother and father during the intervening week. And so on Day-the-Seventh, I left to join her and the rest of the young cast to prepare for the big event of the morrow. Chariots of cheese, sidecars of salads, flatbeds of fruit, quarts of quiche, carloads of cakes, Cokes, and ale startlingly materialized, awaiting deployment. Then there was Netanel, Anon's older sibling to consider: attention must be paid the forgotten fellow.

"So," I said to my son as together on the eve of the *brit* we arranged tables and chairs in the social hall. I pointed toward the Big Chair, the Hot Seat. "Does the *sandek* have anything special to pronounce?"

"Actually, no. Nothing at all. Nervous?"

"Me, nervous? What a notion!"

Thursday, Day-the-Eighth dawned. By 9:30, young, yeshiva-ish couples harmoniously mixing with Ilana's Jerusalem kin had filled the hall, noshing, sloshing, awaiting the please of the ritual surgeon, or *mohel*. (Not to mention his accomplice, the *sandek*.) At a subtle signal, Anon, gravely sleeping, got passed from hand to hand to hand to clenching hands.

"Just hold his legs firmly back out the way," the *mohel* ordered.

"Roger."

Though the little tadpole fought like a mighty tuna, I hung fast to the line like the fisherman follower of the great DiMaggio. My reward was soon forthcoming: a jet of piss, a high-pitched yowl, a glass of wine to celebrate the entrance into the Covenant of Abraham of Tuvia Elyahu ben Shlomo.

"Yes, Mother, TUVia, Tee-You-Vee-Eye-Eh, like Tevya-the-Milkman in *Fiddler*."

"DAIRY-man," whispered Marcia at my elbow, mildly guffawing away from the phone. "Tell her Tevya-the-DAIRYman. Not the MILK-man. Whoever heard of a Tevya-the-Milkman? And repeat the Tuvia, *not* the Tevya."

And then, two days later back in Yeroham on the Shabbat, with jarring suddenness, the laughter got eclipsed. Instead of the dairyman, cometh his silent stand-in, the iceman. A car overturned at three in the morning on the twisting Oil Road connecting Yeroham to Beer-sheba. The nineteen-year-old son of an old friend. Massive injuries. Hours later, on the operating table at Soroka Hospital in Beersheba, his young life drained away.

Sunday, just beyond the industrial zone, at Yeroham's new cemetery. My Holland-born friend, by instinct skeptical, son of Holocaust survivors, in his own right a survivor, was escorted by his Moroccan business partner—the town's ex-mayor—and an entourage of ex-pols. Then the arrival of the new mayor and *his* entourage. The dead boy's mother, also Dutch but turned true believer, obdurate, incompatible with the grieving father, wrench-hearted, divorced, supported by a circle of local ultra-Orthodox *haredim*. An older sister quietly sobbed. From two younger brothers, gravity; from two younger sisters, intermittent smiles.

Unremittingly wailing *her* grief, a Moroccan girlfriend, survivor of the crash. Two to three hundred—no one thought to take an accurate census—gaping, jostling, numbed townspeople stood about. Army buddies. Bouquets were laid at graveside. *Flowers*: a secular or a Christian but not a traditional Jewish custom. Suddenly, on command, an army honor guard—both young men and sobbing young women—marched toward the graveside. The young man had been in the army; he was entitled to a military funeral. Everyone, even the stalwarts of the *hevra kaddisha* burial society, gave way, stepped aside. Upstaged.

BLAM! BLAM! BLAM! Three shots, then sustained shrieks from the women. Centerpiece of the ceremony, the twenty-one grotesque shots punctured the disinterested sky of late afternoon. After some moments, the young soldiers marched off dispiritedly. Edging off singly, in pairs, disoriented mourners filled cars and waiting buses. After the strange shots, like strange fire at a biblical altar, amid alien flowers, smooth-faced stones placed on the fresh-dug earth reasserted the Jewishness of the scene.

Not now the eight-day countdown to the ritual cut but a seven-day ascent from the graveside—the grieving period known as shiva, or seven. The divorced couple grieved in separate rooms. Shai and I joined my old Dutch friend; my wife joined his wife for sitting. Talking. Praying. Drinking. Silence. Morning. Mourning. Evening. Sit-pray-talk-sip-silence-talktalktalk. The old days. Kitchens—his new business. Kitsch. *Olim*. The Golan. The Golem. Prague. Amsterdam. Anything and everything. Everything and anything. But one thing. The one thing. The only real thing. Until, after seven morns and nights of it, until the strain of a communal meal, until the count ran down. Except for my old friend, the survivor, who, whenever in the future he counts to six will always come up one short.

Events and emotions had deployed, positioned themselves as if a master sonneteer had designed their fluid form. My eight days down had been balanced—nearly balanced—by seven up and out. A hobbled chiasmus. And yet what yield of meaning could I extract from it all?

One possibility was outrageous, insupportable: a new bottom line for our Book of Numbers. Credit one Tuvia Elyahu-ben-Shlomo; debit one Asher-ben-Shlomo Ha-Levi. Dared I countenance such order, pattern, or theodicy? Would my gematrial friend, the artist, perceive it? Would my survivor friend, the kitchen-maker? Aii, and should not the order have been reversed: first the count down toward death, then the upward count to life? Moreover, there was the aesthetic flaw. In the end, it seemed to me that it all would make some kind of sense if only, if somehow or other, the missing eighth day out, the final, still unvoiced note of the chiasmic scale would somehow be fulfilled. Until then, I too would be obdurate.

And then, unexpectedly, all so simply, came the milkman. Exactly one week after the end of the shiva, yet another Yeroham friend, a fellow ex-American, rang our doorbell. Alan bore glad tidings: his wife had given birth to a boy. We were invited to Beersheba on the morrow to help them to celebrate the *brit milah* of their son.

BRUTE
NEIGHBORS

ONE of the wry pleasures America retains for its protean, hyper-mobile Jews is a sentimental return to the old neighborhood. Not, to be sure, is this for Jews alone. While nosing around Washington Square after years as an expatriate, waspish Henry James reveled in recollections of his formative years. At the nearer end of our century, waspish John Updike drives fifty-six-year-old Rabbit past his adolescent haunts in Brewer, Pennsylvania. But the scythe cuts closer to the quick for America's urban Jews. Cautiously afoot on once-familiar streets after the absence of decades, in silence we descry Congregation B'nai Jacob transmogrified into Nation of Islam's Mosque No. 15. Where once the sweet River Eggcream shlooped gently to the sea, now stands a bowling alley, bar, or bodega.

The pace of change in Israel rivals that of the land I left behind. Things, processes, life itself at times seem to accelerate in fast-forward. The effect is not necessarily tonic.

Two glossy, colorful brochures issued by the Yeroham Histadrut Workers' Council appeared in my mailbox during the same week. Together they constituted an invitation to attend official opening ceremonies of our town's spanking new *Hechal Hatarbut* (Temple of Culture). Even through days of intifada and crimp it was been evident that the Histadrut had spared little expense to erect in less than a year the country's newest pleasure dome. The largest building on the town's main street, the edifice resembles a student's exercise in cubism, as though a pile of outsized children's blocks had been set one upon the other: exterior walls are light-colored squares; a mouth-like entrance is composed of smaller, dark-contrasted cubes. Glancing past text and mug-shots of national and local Histadrut functionaries, the eye rests on Kodachromes of a spacious multi-tiered theater, of recessed overhead lighting, of actors' dressing-rooms, of marble (marble-ized?) floors.

Such pretentiousness brings to mind the anomaly of, say, the ornate opera house in Manaos, one thousand miles up the Amazon. La Scala de la Negev! Heaven knows what manner of Culture my little oasis may now anticipate. Deciding to skip the official opening of our local Temple, I recalled an earlier local opening ceremony that I did not bypass. From a cabinet I retrieved a faded clipping headlined WEL-LAND COUPLE SEES DEDICATION OF CENTRE, an article I myself had filed for *The Canadian Jewish News* of May 24, 1984. Because they believed in contributing to the welfare of Israelis living in marginal areas, Bernard and Edith Ennis had donated $500,000 (in Canadian dollars) to transform a dilapidated Yeroham gymnasium into the Ennis Arts Centre of Ramat Hanegev College. A photo veri-fies that among the luminaries gracing the occasion were U.S. Ambas-sador Samuel and Mrs. Lewis and Canadian Ambassador Vernon and Mrs. Tucker.

One minor but delicate matter that was withheld from the good couple from Ontario, as well as their ambassador, was that the conso-nants that compose their name in Hebrew signifies "rape." What, after all, would have been served by distressing the Canadians with the tidings that for much of Yeroham's citizenry, a Center for Rape Arts seemed to have been established in their midst?

Yes, from 1980 to 1985 Yeroham was the unlikely site of an arts college, an institution which simultaneously employed various of my own dubious services as English instructor, director of public relations, and director of overseas students. An eight-minute stroll down the block, across a *wadi*, then left along a street that twisted like a salted pretzel, past Ha-Nasi Elementary School and a homestead that boasted sheep, horses, goats, and chickens brought me to a neat, fence-sheaved, tree-shaded compound.

Ramat Hanegev College had been the inspiration of an American named Menahem Alexenberg. Equal parts educator, artist, and pro-moter, Alexenberg came to Yeroham in 1978. One Shabbat, while ambling on the road that scoops a figure-eight into the desert, he halted at the head of the loop at the sight of a handsome, newly completed, unoccupied building. Inquiry revealed that the Ministry of Education had authorized construction of the edifice as a school for disadvantaged students . . . in Ofakim!

Ofakim is a town west of Beersheba, on the other side of the Negev! So what was it doing in Yeroham? Nobody could say. Snafu. An administrative goof. Yeroham's disadvantaged students were already adequately served. But what—heh! heh! heh!—a good joke on Ofakim, eh?

Perhaps my quick-witted friend merely recalled Our Founder's hortative "If you will it, it is no dream." Or it may have been those Mickey Rooney—Judy Garland road shows tap dancing along the Great White Way. In any event, the fact was that Alexenberg knew how to get things moving. Here was Yeroham, newly equipped with a group of underemployed American academics and artists. There stood a spanking new building with no purpose.

"Hey, gang, let's start a college!"

A college in Yeroham? To be sure, Yeroham's Mayor Peres, not having munched popcorn at Saturday matinees back in Casablanca, had never imbibed subliminal lessons in American know-how and initiative. But perhaps he saw a way to dispose of what had become a white elephant? Or perhaps Alexenberg's antic enthusiasm was infectious. Whatever the cause, hizzonor tossed Alexenberg the keys to the kingdom.

One year later, basing itself on an eccentric curriculum that combined Jewish studies, desert studies, and conceptual art, Ramat Hanegev College opened its doors. For some a loony notion, for others an inspired one, over a period of five years this haphazard college was nurtured, attracted students (never quite enough), expanded, declined, grew again, and from time to time even seemed to have a future. I vividly recall an architect's drawing of the "campus of the future": dormitories, studios, classrooms, trees, lawns, statues, and stick drawings of students, students, students.

In 1985 Yeroham elected a mayor from a different party, one with an autocratic bent and a flair for demagoguery. Unable to control an institution of higher learning endowed with an independent board of trustees, he determined that none of this should ever come to pass. For the original building, a strikingly original alternate purpose was declared: a center for Yeroham's expanding population of the mentally disabled. For the Ennis Art Centre—a heavy padlock. For Ramat Hanegev College itself, limbo, not even a proper funeral. One can only conjecture what Mr. and Mrs. Bernard Ennis were informed . . . if anything. As for me, having neither cause nor desire to turn left past Ha-Nasi School in the direction of the old college, months passed into years.

In 1991 I learned from my younger daughter that the keys to the twelve hundred square meters of floor space of what once briefly served as the Ennis Art Centre had been consigned to the counselors of Yeroham's chapter of B'nai Akiva, a religious youth group. Since, my Miri informed me, only about fifteen kids turned up for Shabbat activities, that provided each youngster with eighty square meters in which to romp. Not bad.

After six years of avoiding these old precincts, the following morning my curious feet decided, as if on their own, to take a roundabout, long-abandoned route to the town center. Crossing the wadi, turning left past the elementary school (renamed Kol Ya'akov), I noted the selfsame livestock (their descendants, I reminded myself) grazing close to the object of my nostalgic trek. The ravages of time had exacted their inevitable toll: it took me exactly eight minutes and thirty seconds.

In both English and Hebrew, the bold sign on the outside wall proclaiming ENNIS ART CENTRE, RAMAT HANEGEV COLLEGE still hung high. Spiraling above was the college emblem, designed by Alexenberg himself, a great one for symbolic detail. It was now dirt-encrusted, barely discernible, surely a mysterious cipher to all but exceedingly few.

Tentatively, I descended the cement steps which had been cut into the desert floor on the approach to the vast building. Not a soul lurked in any direction. The large, metal front door was barred by a heavy padlock. The last time I had entered this cavernous place was for an opening night after its brief transformation into a gallery for Negev artists. It must have been about a year after the college had closed. Paintings and sculpture by Alan Rosenberg, formerly a Ramat Hanegev instructor, were on display. Alexenberg himself had returned to live in America.

Now most of the high windows were broken. Splinters of broken glass lay scattered over the grounds. Circling counterclockwise to the longer, desert side of the spectral building, I noted that here too most windows had been smashed. Pushing through weeds, I peered through barred windows. Inside was a former office, three abandoned desks stood in a row but their chairs were on end. Strewn over the floor was a jungle of paper clutter. Most of the other rooms, however, seemed barren of furnishings. Where were the college files, the library of hundreds of expensive art books, journals, religious commentaries, volumes of poetry? Had the place been vandalized?

Thinking back, I could not deny that the college never quite did get its academic act together. That it stayed afloat as long as it did may be attributed to equal parts of talent, magic, and will. Nevertheless, in Yeroham, a locale where educational performance has always been anemic, for a certain, brief period there had been college-level lectures, there had been students, there had been graduates, there had been . . . yes, . . . hope. Was not all that worthy of even a passing recollection?

Across from the window in another desolated chamber, once-upon-a-time a classroom, a plaque still hung askew on the wall. At an oblique angle through the window I could make out that the donors were the SOLOMON FAMILY, In Memory of ANNE C. RAVITZ. Whoever she is . . . or was. Whoever they are.

One day two years later I once again passed this way. B'nai Akiva youngsters no longer met here. There was no lock on the large metal door; it stood ajar. Inside, the vision of neglect, decay, and wanton destruction was appalling. Scattered papers from old files, art supplies, pieces of pottery and ceramic equipment, everything was higgledy-piggledy and knee-deep. Yet more ominous, from within filtered the stench of smoke and ashes into the hallway. Pushing farther within, where once the college's library had been stored in mounds of cartons, I stepped over blackened pages and charred piles. All was ash; all consumed. Some person or persons had indiscriminately, brutishly torched them all!

In the fall of 1993 both Ramat Hanegev buildings have been occupied by a new yeshiva. I must admit this is a far less disturbing prospect than a Killarney Rose or Mosque No. 15. Still, the choking off of funds to the college by its host organism, precipitating its slow, painful demise, had been a premeditated act of destruction, a thuggish violation which inerrantly prefigured what sooner or later would surely happen.

These days I once again try to avoid walking past Yeroham's Raped Art Center. If you don't think that Time can be a terrific joker, just ask the Ennises . . . or the Family Solomon.

HOUSE-COOLING

JUST as though I had never been favored with it before, every few
years Moshe-the-psychologist, my friend and next-door neighbor,
again tells me one of his favorite jokes. Since I never . . . well
hardly ever . . . remember punch lines, I don't much mind. Besides,
Moshe gets such pleasure out of the retelling, I wouldn't dream of
derailing him. It goes, I think, something like this.

Accompanied by a large, furry dog, a man sidles up to the bar.

"One glass of beer for me and another for my friend Willie."

"One for your dog!" said the astonished bartender. "Does Willie
drink beer?"

"He not only drinks, he talks."

"Who're you trying to kid?"

"If Willie answers three questions correctly, are the drinks on the
house?"

"A deal," replied the bartender.

So the man addressed his furry companion: "Willie, what do you
call the cross-weave of my jacket?"

"Woof, woof," responded the dog.

The bartender's jaw slackened; man and dog sipped their suds.

"The second question, how does my face feel before my morning
shave?"

"Rough, rough," responded the dog. Once again the pair quaffed.

"Now for the clincher. Willie, who is the greatest ballplayer of
all time?"

Without a moment's hesitation, the dog said "Ruuf, ruuf."

Man and dog downed their glasses and headed for the door. Had
the bartender *still* retained his skepticism, Moshe might have
prompted his dog-lover to pose a fourth puzzler: "If my friend Haim
doesn't answer the doorbell, where is he most likely to be found?"

"Roof, roof."

Bring that mutt a fresh tankard of brew! For the past ten years, ever since our second floor sprouted its majestic bulk over a portion of our modest downstairs dwelling, I have spent an inordinate amount of time dancing on the ceiling of the untampered-with original roof. Retainer of warmth, deflector of moisture, our dwelling's tough outer skin had formerly been to all intents and purposes inaccessible. Now, with a door at the top of the newly built stairs, it was metamorphosed into an "upstairs terrace," not to mention a palace of valuable junk. There are even times, my friends, when the seductive call of the chaise beneath the Negev sun can be downright compelling.

For my part, I direct the same diligence to keeping my roof dry as others in more dire circumstances have applied to their gunpowder. This zeal may be traced to my father-in-law, a taciturn sort who rarely offers advice. A homebuilder by trade, he was overheard one day to utter the following apothegm to a client: "Be good to your roof, and your roof'll be good to you."

As it happens, the surface of our current roof suffers from a notable defect: no, not a leak but a shallow basin that has successfully resisted the patchwork of three teams of local experts. The upshot: had you chanced to be looking upward between storms during Israel's lightly mourned wintry season of rain, you might have noted a certain rubber-booted figure, lightly armed with a squeegee-on-a-stick, slishing, sloshing, slooshing water from said basin to the opening of a drain on the front of the roof. Depending upon the elements, some days more than once. The fact is that keeping my roof dry has become something of a personal compulsion.

Now, it must be confessed that there are seasons when it's been known to get . . . ugh . . . hot down here in the north Negev. No; we hardly ever get the postnoon unbearables of the ardent Arava to the south, the humidity of Tel Aviv, or the desiccation of the Dead Sea shore. Our summers, in fact, are milder than well-remembered scorchers of the blazing San Joaquin Valley and a touch pleasanter than those I endured in my boyhood Bronx.

Still, it gets hot enough to notice, and so, since bleached surfaces deflect the sun's rays, a few summers ago for the first time in a decade I mortgaged two successive mornings to whitewash the tarred, bubbly black surface of our upstairs moonscape. At the end of my labors, the ivory surface beneath my feet was so bright it pained my eyes. To my bare soles, however, it was arctic cool and smooth as marble. What is more, the downstairs temperature had fallen five-to-eight Fahrendepths.

No question about it: I had been remiss. I knew well enough that tarred Negev roofs should be whitewashed every year or two. Moreover, actually mixing the white powder into a frothy brew, slopping the milky stuff over the pimply surface, stooping over corners, distended on hands and knees for application to the underhang—these bestow upon a householder that rare intimate relation with the uneven texture, the dimension, and the feel of what Thoreau called our outer garment.

The Prophet of Simplicity held that a house not purchased with the currency of sweat cannot truly be one's own. Yet even at the cost of discomfort, I had played roof truant. A psychological puzzler for Moshe my neighbor: had this dallying pointed toward an unacknowledged ambivalence about my dilly of an adopted homeland, one that whitewash had merely helped to disguise? Quashing these doubts, at the first opportunity I offered Moshe my leftover whitewash. Merely for the expenditure of two mornings, he might pursue, Ahab-like, the scorpions of repression not under the hot, black surfaces of id, but elegantly cruising through two coats of white, polar ice. I was as ebullient as Tom Sawyer over the glories of whitewash—*sid* in local parlance—but my post-Freudian friend would not bite.

In former years, I had applied far more time and effort to the pate of this house's predecessor: a California ranch-job with twice the floorspace and three times the overhang. That house had been centerpiece of an earlier, drier all-American dream. Even its city-bred occupant could tell, however, that the wooden shingles on its pitched roof were cracked and in dire need of lubrication. When my wife's father came to visit, he gazed overhead, reflectively rubbed his chin, and ultimately opined, "could use a little elbow grease up there."

So, much of that warm California summer vacation was spent plotting the lay of the terrain just overhead. For newcomers on the block, this was a display not merely of practicality but also of civic virtue. Shingle after everlovin' shingle inhaled its refreshing draft. Stretching a long-handled broom oozing with dark-green stain and oily slick-sop, continually replenished from precariously balanced pails, weight counterpoised against the tilt of the roof to check ignominious slip, the apartment-bred boy showed he could do the job! Many shingles were far too parched for cosmetic ministration; they needed replacement. A piece of cake for the fiddler on the roof, reveler in newfound self-sufficiency.

The task, which took up much of that summer, projected itself into the following one as well. One day, when the rest of the family had driven off to the coast, when the operation had become automatic, routine, I took a tumble.

"SH . . . . EET," I vividly recall silently screaming. "I'm going to FALL." I landed flat on my back, and for some minutes, before chancing inventory, just lay there. Winded. Then: no; no breaks. No; no blood. But freshly pomaded, roof and crown, from foot to toe I was the aboriginal Green Man, Queequeg fallen into great Heidelberg Tun, sticky-sleek as syrup.

Five years later we sold our well-oiled roof, not to mention the walls, floor, and miscellaneous remainder to the young couple who operated that town's Western Auto. Having fallen off of America and flown to the Negev, we have lived in Israel more than twice the seven good years of our California dream. Father-in-law's wisdom has become second nature, and like Tevya, I am an unacknowledged maestro of rooftops of the Ben-Gurion Quarter.

In mid-February of 1992, during a lull between the third and fourth rounds of storms of Israel's coldest, wettest winter on record, I stepped out onto my upper deck and, checking first to see that no one was looking, did something that once-upon-a-time I would have thought inconceivable. Then, leaving the evidence in full view, I promptly ducked back inside.

As a Concerned Citizen—Sometime Activist, in a previous incarnation I had been something of a political creature. New immigrants are richly blessed with grittier distractions. I had no time for my former pursuits. But, after five years in our national homeland, and heeding the call of habit and duty, I let myself be persuaded to stand for a four-year term for a seat on Yeroham's Labor Party Council. To my surprise, I was elected. What clearer ratification could there be that my absorption into the fabric of Israeli society had come to successful completion!

There's nothing as fleeting as pleasure. My plummet into the intricacies, disorder, and blood feuds that compose the stuff of municipal politics put me of a mind of a voyage to Lilliput. Slumped in my seat, rendered comatose after a half-hour's enchamberment among chimney-puffing pols, incorrigibly bound to the archaism of recognition from the chair before blabbing my piece, I was, it must be admitted, far from an effective representative. Almost surely my prinicpal contribution to local democracy was to fashion a more speedy quorum.

To compound my discomfort, at my final meeting my associates nominated a mayoral candidate whom I had copious cause to distrust. So there I was, morally obligated to display his oversized mug from my innocent roof, persuaded that it would be unethical not to vote for him, and less than enthralled when he won. Worse, "my man" was virtually alone among Labor candidates to emerge victorious that year in the predominantly Moroccan hinterland. Might this equivocal chap eventually parlay local success into a national role? What disagreeable genie had I helped to uncork!

When my term expired I stoutly proclaimed (to my wife at dinner) the Chertok Doctrine: no more posters staring out from our masthead; total withdrawal from local political entanglements. For almost seven years, in the course of which My Former Man—this time running as an Independent—was elected to a second term, did I hold firm to this resolve.

Three months before Israel's 1992 national elections, far from the madding whirl of Rabin placards and posters, Shamir billboards and leaflets, barely noticed by the pundits, my little town was positioned on the very cutting edge of these developments. Thanks to the persistent reports of our mayor's misdoings—most of which were related to his long-time dalliance with those malfeasant sharpies from Shas, the party of ultra-Orthodox Sephardi Jews—Yeroham was precipitated into the pleasures of a special election in March. Yes, for weeks on end many a Yeroham window, balcony, and roof displayed portraits proclaiming their inhabitants' allegiance either to incumbent Baruch or challenger Moti. (Contenders hereabouts are familiarly referred to by their given names—in Hebrew, their *privates*. Oh, how I do love our graphic tongue!)

Now, Moshe-next-door and I have ever been in close accord on issues of national importance. Unlike me, however, he had always been punctilious about avoiding local politics. Imagine my chagrin when I spotted his photo prominently displayed on the incumbent's brochures. My good friend was Number Six on Baruch's list for our election to our local council: too low for any chance of electoral success but high enough for general notice. The next day I spotted a placard laid across the back seat of Moshe's car. Who could doubt that that very placard, touting my bête noir, would soon be flying on an adjoining rooftop?

Resolve. What was happening to my firm resolve? What did I know about the challenger, Moti: an engineer, capable of running Yeroham's civil defense, Moroccan, personable, and (gulp) right-wing Likud. LIKUD. Briefly but manfully did I struggle—do not doubt it— but, faced by the imminent prospect of *that* visage hanging so close to home and darker visions of yet another baruchial term, the Chertok Doctrine came unglued.

"I'm going for a walk," I called offhandedly to my wife that very evening, and off I went to what banners unmistakably proclaimed to be the basement headquarters of Yeroham's Likud. Slinking inside, I was at once confronted by a former student, an inveterate troublemaker, from my very early days in town when I taught English in the local high school. His name had blissfully flown, but it was though he'd been expecting me for years.

"Haim. My teacher. I am fine. How are you? What is the time? Hch, hch!"

Marvelous. He still remembered all the English he ever knew. Like conspirators, we shook hands. Five minutes later I emerged with a large placard of my own: twin images of Moti affixed on side-by-side posters. Its message: Moti—Yeroham Needs Him. Probably because the incumbent was again running on an independent slate (though actively supported by Labor and Shas), party identification was blessedly discreet: *Mahal*, a minuscule Likud slip protruding from an envelope pictured on the poster's lower corner. Under cover of darkness, I made my way home. Wisely, Marcia smiled but said nothing.

The next day the world too discovered my dereliction. In the gloom of sunless dawn, beating my pal to the punch, I raised on my roofbalcony blazoned evidence of my adherence to the forces of Moti (and, squeaked Jimminy Cricket, to Li-kud, Li-kud, Li-kud). As if the very heavens were astonished—dismayed? offended!—two hours later lightning flashed, thunder bellowed, and a veritable deluge was delivered on poor Yeroham. Occasional snow and hail, intermittent heavy rain would follow. Like Jonah in the bowels of my home, I alone knew the cause. But the die had been cast; there was no turning back. Rescuing my dual Motis from the furies, when three days later the elements abated, I rehoisted them. Unrepentant, once again had I waded out into the great messy, ambiguous, fuzzy, hullabalooning public life of my adoptive country.

Until election day, although signs and placards abounded throughout the town, in our immediate eight-household complex only two banners—one for Baruch; the other for Moti—would be displayed. Oddly enough, these flew from the ramparts of the longstanding American friends. Alas, the ever-crucial Jewish-American bloc had splintered. To what end? Had we influenced any of the voters in the four Moroccan households immediately facing us to cast a ballot for Baruch instead of Moti, for Moti in place of Baruch? How droll! So in that blessed interim before glossies of Israel's superstar Yitzhaks superseded our local calendar boys, what truly did our signs signify?

Well, I recall something from Emerson, my mother-in-law's favorite philosopher. In one of his essays—which probably means somewhere in all of his essays—he conjures a tidal pattern for the spiritual life of Man: for a variable period, does Man ebb out to engage life's social and communal concerns until, surfeited, he withdraws to attend to personal or spiritual concerns. These are not, of course, wholly exclusive domains, and the phases are not absolutely distinct. Nevertheless, over fairly regular intervals, different for each, in and out, back and forth like a squeegee over the roof of our disposition, such was Emerson's dance of the healthy Soul. Reb Ralph Waldo may not be very trendy, but it does seem to me that he got it essentially right.

On March 4th, the day after our special election, two "American" households from Yeroham that for weeks had studiously, coolly avoided talking politics traveled to Beersheba for a warm night out on the town.

Usually my dreams are as retrievable as punch lines to jokes, but this gave me a chance to consult a captive professional about the meaning of a strange scene I had recently dreamed more than once. It seems that a man walked into a bar accompanied by a horse.

"One beer for me and another for my friend," said he.

"That horse drinks!" exclaimed the tall bartender.

"Not only does he drink, my friend. He's a talking horse."

"If that creature talks, drinks are on the house," said the surly bartender.

"Okay, Rufus, tell the man how to say 'born' in French?"

"Né, née."

The bartender winced.

"Very good. And how, Rufus, do horses express themselves most of the time?"

"Neigh, neigh."

The bartender looked pained.

"Excellent. Excellent. And now, good Rufus, do you think it probable that that chap who spends so many hours on his roof will ever take another major tumble."

"Nay, nay."

The bartender, who suddenly resembled George Bush, glowered: "Get the hell out of here. If you two want drinks on the house, you can do your drinking on the roof."

Out in the street, the horse turned to the man: "Maybe I should have said Tevya Cobb?"

FORMER INHABITANTS; WINTER VISITORS

I N THEIR provincial heart of hearts, editors in Manhattan and in Tel Aviv sense that their reactions to events of the day are an unreliable index of public sentiment. This commodity is to be unearthed in alterity: prototypical Brooklyn cabbies or salt-of-the-earthniks along Main Street in Peoria. Since negotiating an authentic Passage to Peoria would entail confrontation with that ultimate menace—oneself—journalists worldwide often opt for the predigested cipher uttered by the prefabricated native.

At their risk. One of my favorite instances of backlash from the provinces appeared in Lawrance Thompson's multivolume biography of Robert Frost. When a reporter for *The Boston Post* turned up unannounced at Frost's farm in Franconia, the poet received him, wry tongue firmly frozen in cheek. As if he'd stumbled over David Livingstone, the reporter filed his interview under the caption, "Finds Famous American Poet in White Mountain Village." Franconia was a place "forgotten by the whole world . . . buried in the snow, with more snow and more snow, nobody comes here. Once a day an old man in a pung drives over with a few bundles, and leaves them, and drives off again." The fortunate correspondent was directed to Frost's secluded homestead by "an old woman in the deserted general store."

Just some innocent nuggets of local color. But the old biddy, who Lawrance notes was "relatively young," was miffed enough by the gilding to file some colorful comments of her own in a letter to the editor: ". . . Had there been 'anybody home' your reporter would have known better than to have undertaken a five-or six-mile ride in

168

northern New Hampshire on February eleventh with nothing on but a summer overcoat. No wonder his appearance caused Mr. Frost's hens and roosters to cackle and crow. . . .

"Again, had there been 'anybody home,' . . . [your reporter] would have known by the way their sleigh-runners grated . . . that Franconia could not boast of snow enough for even decent sleighing. Here we have been praying for snow for the past four weeks so we could enjoy a good sleigh ride, to say nothing of business lying idle for the want of it, and your reporter reports to the world that we are literally buried in snow and then more snow. . . . Does he expect to find a crowd in a country store at nine o'clock in the morning? If he had only sent his card ahead, what a scramble there would have been to have gotten to that deserted place so the poor snow-bound country folks could have seen a real smarty chap from the city. . . ." [Signed] "The Old Woman in the Deserted Store."

Realizing that a reputation for accuracy is the hardest currency a journal possesses, the editor of *The Boston Post* was smarty enough to publish "The Old Woman's" complaint. Nowadays, such scrupulousness is less standard practice. It just so happens that right up there with the stall-keepers at Jerusalem's Mahane Yehuda market, my little weather vane of a town in the Negev serves as Israel's closest equivalent to Peoria. This is how it goes every few months or so on the domestic journalistic circuit.

"Rafi, get your ass down to . . . to . . . Ye-roo-ham. Get a 'little people's,' real folks' perspective piece."

Rafi, of course, has little inclination to schlep his ass all the way to the Negev, especially when, parked at his favorite café on Tel Aviv's Rehov Sheinkin, he can produce a perfectly suitable substitute piece: "'The Labor Party bureaucrats—the Mapainiks—screwed us good,' sputtered prefabricated native Oofnik Ben-Lulu, local pundit, from his alcoholic perch on Yeroham's dusty, decrepit main plaza. 'Anyway, they should close up the town and throw away the key.'" Ben-Lulu has been Our Town's most accessible Spokesperson for decades.

It was around six years ago that the greater world began growing savvy to Yeroham's unique niche in the Israeli psyche. One afternoon in October the BBC's Paul Reynolds drove down for some local background. BBC to the marrow, Reynolds could never be cited for an excess of admiration for the Jewish State. He spent an afternoon with me in my backyard. Several weeks later I recognized the Etonic tones of "Our Own Correspondent" reporting from "Yeer-o-haam, Deep in the heart of Israel's Negev Desert." To his credit, Reynolds had neither overdosed nor overdozed on my briefing. Within limitations, his report was . . . decent.

The record of *The Jerusalem Post*, Israel's widely cited English-language paper, is mixed. In 1986 reporter Robert Rosenberg, of late a mystery novelist, thought the best way to get a handle on Yeroham was a few hours' confabulation with a covey of newly elected politicians. The result was a stylish but meretricious farrago bearing little relation to reality. Five years later, however, demonstrating that the deed can indeed be done, *The Post*'s Abraham Rabinovich filed a measured, notably accurate piece on how Yeroham's Russian immigrants were getting on.

In any event, you may well imagine my trepidation when, thumbing through my son Shai's *National Geographic* for February '92, I came across an account of Israel's latest wave of aliya by journalist Tad Szulc, formerly of *The New York Times*. His tone seemed in the main positive, but then fresh forebodings arose: after Russians in Jerusalem, no place drew quite as much attention as . . . you guessed it! . . . Russians in Yeroham. Either by pung or by Peugeot, Szulc apparently had braved treacherous elements to make his way down to the Big Y, for this is how my town's portion began: "Driving through the Negev not far from where the Jews wandered with Moses for forty years, I see some of [former Housing Minister Ariel] Sharon's houses. All brick and stone, they rise like a mirage among the rocks and sand dunes of Yeroham, an old Bedouin settlement."

Tadzooks! What a colorful crock Smarty Chap concocted this time around for the beguilement of *National Geographic*'s armchair minions. Could it be that he had actually mistaken the Negev for the Sinai? Except for an incursion into the domain of the Amelekites, who made damned well sure our unforbearing forebears didn't loiter near *their* watering holes for too lengthy a quaff, Moses and the Jews cut a swath well to the south of the North Negev. And what a lost opportunity, because an ever so modest investigation would have yielded up to Szulc just the splash of biblical color for which he had overreached. Tradition has it that hard by Yeroham is the very wilderness where Hagar, wandering with Ishmael, came upon a well that saved their lives.

And look where Smarty's pretty prose further mis-steers the armchair traveler. Unless his canteen was spiked with vodka, it is difficult to account for that "mirage" among the rocks and sand dunes. Yeroham sits in high desert country; one may journey for thirty miles in any direction and come up duneless. Stick a shovel in the ground, Tad, if you can. After it rains, it's not so easy: the soil hereabouts is clayey loess.

But then things get curiouser and curiouser with all that "brick and stone." Why, an unwary NG reader might just be lulled into cabling a down-payment on one of the Negev's Colonial Estates, A. Sharon, developer. Alas, nary a one of Yeroham's newest units is constructed either of stone or of brick. Even were Vladislav Practicheski Pigletnov to turn up as a newest arrival from Kiev, he too would have to settle for cement block or prefabricated concrete walls—an adobe abode.

Were it not for the generally upbeat tenor of the article, one might suspect Szulc's designation of Yeroham as an "old Bedouin settlement" as more insidious than jes' plain dumb. When it was founded in 1951, not too distant was a Bedouin encampment of twenty families; most of them may still be found just about where they resided then. My suspicion is that Old Smarty confounded Bedouin with Nabutean because close by the shore of Lake Yeroham there does indeed sit a partially excavated mound, site of a formerly substantial Nabutean settlement whose last inhabitants departed around a thousand years ago. Well, at least he didn't call it an old "Palestinian" encampment.

To the good, Szulc did mention what most Israeli news-hawks still have missed about Yeroham: ". . . a new vitality. Construction is booming. . . . factories are expanding to take on additional workers." Which makes it hard to explain his understating the town's population by fifteen hundred people—that's 20 per cent, or merely the entire increase occasioned by the arrival of the Jews from Russia, presumably the very point of his article!

What might be as nonsensical as a man in a pung searching for a crowd at a country store in New Hampshire at nine in the morning? Well, how about a strange journalist surprised by the vigilance of an Israeli school guard? Walking past a schoolyard, Szulc notes pointedly that the fenced-in kids are "watched over by a white-haired gentleman with an automatic weapon. When I ask to talk with the kids, the guard eyes me suspiciously and blocks my way."

Aiming to make a jaunt to the Negev sound like a precarious mission, Smarty blurs the obvious: fear of child molesters in Des Moines or gang violence in Detroit is far more pervasive—and justifiably—than apprehension in Yeroham. I can assure Szulc that back in the late forties the schoolyard at P.S. 86 in The Bronx was also fence-enclosed, and as we played our tag and punchball, we were watched closely by two on-duty teachers who were at least as fearsome as the "white-haired gentleman." No, they did not bear rifles, but I do believe they would not have cottoned to a stranger, particularly one unable to speak English, desiring converse with any of us kids.

Incidentally, that guard's weapon probably also hearkens back to the late forties: it's about as automatic as a pea shooter. Ah, but compared to reporter Clyde Haberman, whose "Yeroham Journal" was featured in the Sunday *New York Times* two months later, Tad Szulc, whose article contains enough circumstantial evidence to verify that he actually was here, can line up for his Pulitzer.

Studded with potted aspersions like "languid Yeroham," "sense of apartness and second-class status," and "cheerless outpost on the fringe of the Negev," Haberman's plate of hash reflects the very sort of puerility in which our home-grown journalists have been known to indulge. Haberman claimed to have cornered two locals for typical footage. The first, a mother of eleven children, was depicted as distraught that "not one of [them] stayed in Yeroham." The second, "a young man trying to shake a recurring drug problem," made one quotable citation: "You need a visa to go from Yeroham to Tel Aviv." It apparently never occurred to our star reporter that the putative remark of his matron rather undermines the plaint of his hypothetical druggie.

The occasion for this in-depth hokum was then-Foreign Minister David Levy's pre-electoral outburst against alleged Ashkenazi bigotry in the senior ranks of Likud, a charge which had precious little to do with Yeroham, where the candidate who was overwhelmingly elected mayor in 1992's special election studiously avoided the least hint of divisive ethnic rhetoric. In truth, Yeroham is one of the worst places in all Israel from which to hoist the theme of ethnic friction. North Tel Aviv versus South? Yes. The neighborhoods of Jerusalem at odds? To be sure. But Yeroham's every neighborhood is as integrated as the local Establishment is. Just about the only thing Haberman got right was our current population figure.

The Old Lady in the Deserted Store had it just about right. Even if *The Times* or *National Geographic* is too magisterial ever to take notice, for their nickels, Yankee readers damn well expect a nickel's worth of accuracy. Replying to the complaint of a certain Yeroham subscriber, two months farther down the line a missive arrived from *National Geographic*'s Washington citadel. A young woman who admitted responsibity for checking the facts as reported by Szulc responded that he was a respected journalist, that no one knows precisely where Moses led the Children of Israel, and the fact that, after all, the school guard did hold a weapon substantiated that Szulc really did come to Yeroham in person. *Now* was I satisfied?

A sad corollary of my starting premise, the darker, self-hating inverse of Peoria-in-the-Negev: as Israel-bashing has existed since 1967 in certain intellectual circles in London and New York, so Yeroham-bashing has existed in congruent circles in Tel Aviv and Jerusalem. What makes this Jew-trashing *jeu d'espirit* less than amusing is that intramural fun 'n' games has now attracted major international players.

THE POND
IN WINTER

WHEN it is not an opening night or a matter of life or death, daily life in Israel often feels like an amateur production. It is sometimes diverting, sometimes amusing . . . and sometimes decidedly not. Even seventeen years here has not disabused me of the illusion, shared by many other former Americans, that time, *our* time, has value. No matter how philosophical our posture, we simply do not relish seeing it wadded up like a stick of Wrigley's. True, one allows that the West does not have a lock on progressive notions. Nevertheless, even relativity must admit bounds.

During our first years in the country, when we were more in the rigid grip of a rigid bureaucracy, how many times did some clerk dispatch us to another queue and to another clerk across town for a document or signature that (*a*) could not be obtained at that location, (*b*) could not be released in the absence of some other document or signature that he had neglected to mention, or (*c*) was not really needed in the first place? Whenever we listen to the experiences of Russian newcomers, the wintry frustration of those early years returns unmitigated by the passage of time.

Typically, any of the foregoing could have been ascertained by a clerk-to-clerk phone call. Painfully, over time we learned to make our precious time sufficiently prickly to prod that clerk to lift his receiver; gradually we learned the ropes well enough to untie most knots ourselves or to make others do the jumping. But not always. The following incident took place in January of 1988; the intervening years make it seem funny . . . almost. It is never one's own but only the other fella's impotence that's so hilarious.

With an 11 o'clock class to teach at the university, I boarded the Beersheba-bound bus at my neighborhood stop at 9:32. At that hour, the trip normally should take forty minutes, so I would arrive on

174

campus around 10:40. The driver, Yisroel, was a particularly gregarious chap, his white hair cut very short. He had been plying Negev routes for many years and was well known for loudly discoursing on affairs of state and for chatting up his prettier passengers. After pickups in the Ben-Gurion, Shaked, and Eli Cohen neighborhoods, Yisroel swerved east to the ultra-Orthodox, Persian, and Giva quarters, then he finally turned back onto the Yeroham's main street. The bus was very nearly full.

The final stop in town stands directly across from an army base, but on this day only a young woman wearing a flowery skirt stood waiting. Upon boarding, she exchanged inaudible words with Yisroel. Then, surprisingly, she backed off the bus. Odder still, instead of heading west for the main road to Beersheba, our bus began slowly, oh so slowly backward up the main street of town. In reverse! Perplexed, we passengers looked askance, then at each other, then finally toward our uncharacteristically tightlipped driver. Unperturbed, Yisroel maneuvered the vehicle past a cross-street and continued to snail in reverse for yet another half-block. Finally he backed one-handed into a tight space in front of Bank Hapoalim.

By this time, many of us sleepsitters had found our voices; disgruntled puzzlement floated toward our driver. It was repaid with haughty silence, with not a hint of explanation. I glanced nervously at my watch. I had a class to teach. How could I have, so inexplicably, not taken this very sort of delay into account? Across the aisle Debbi, a children's nurse at the town clinic, held her own young, fidgeting daughter on her lap. It was she who first marched to the front of the bus to confront Yisroel. Exuding charm, he was unflappable.

"It'll only be a few more minutes," was all he would volunteer.

Chutzpah! By what right should a busload of fifty paying passengers be crated backward, and then left to languish and stall? Still, although now we murmurers seemed to constitute a majority, there was no outright mutiny. It was as if Yisroel enjoyed the superior wisdom or prerogatives of Moses in the desert. Was I wrong that some of my fellow passengers, surely ones with no Beersheba deadline to meet, seemed to be enjoying the unexpected incident?

Again I glared toward the front door, looked obsessively at my watch, searched uselessly for eye contact in the rearview mirror, again glanced toward my wrist. Each ten seconds felt like sixty, each passing minute more like five. The delay became insupportable. After jotting down #15222, the number stenciled on the front door, I melodramatically rose and strode purposefully toward the front of the bus. Feeling every eye grooving into the back of my head, like rebellious Korah, I gave in a measured voice my displeasure. Did Yisroel really want me to file an official complaint with the authorities?

Hardly. Nevertheless, Yisroel maintained an enviable calm. He would regret this imposition, I vaguely threatened, before limply returning to my seat.

Shortly thereafter the temptress in the flowery skirt reappeared accompanied by a tall man. He was not lame. He was not blind. Merely late—perhaps delayed by a bank clerk—the man had confidently sent his lady-accomplice to persuade the driver to wait for him! No matter the inconvenience for fifty other passengers. Astonishingly, wait the driver did, as did we for ten additional minutes. Mollified by forward motion, conscious that I probably would not be late to class after all, I breathed a sigh of relief.

To his credit, Yisroel did not speed to make up for lost time. We pulled into the station in Beersheba at 10:19. Upon debussing, I overheard two fellow passengers bestow upon him a *kol ha-koved*, a high compliment for being a really fine fellow, a *gever*.

Altogether, I had lost a mere ten minutes. Big deal! In a land of road blocks and occasional bomb scares, that was hardly earthshaking. I am reasonably certain that no student detected either deficiency in my delivery or anxiety occasioned by loss of preparation time. But then again, was it not worth the notice of anyone in authority that doing a good turn for two passengers had cost fifty other passengers almost six hours of cumulative time?

Several years earlier, having witnessed a driver display insulting behavior toward a Bedouin passenger, I had written a letter to the Egged Bus Cooperative's Complaint Department. It responded promptly and to my satisfaction. On this occasion, however, I did not bother. Soon over my pique, I have not brooded long hours over this relatively inconsequential incident. Like the *gever* who, double-parking near my front door to give my neighbor a lift to work, announces his presence by a prolonged depression of his horn, thereby roundly depressing me, Yisroel-the-bus-driver was merely doing someone a disinterested good turn. Backward up Main Street! That it might have unpleasant repercussions for others either factored in as negligible or never crossed his mind at all. Viewed from a value-free angle, isn't backward just another style of motion? Even if the rules do mandate that the proper way to pass GO is from the direction of Boardwalk, does it really matter whether some local folks down on Mediterranean Avenue have their own good and proper reasons for an occasional irregularity? To the best of my knowledge, Yisroel did not pocket two hundred illicit shekels or make it even to Oriental Ave. with that pretty young thing. Besides, in the end, backward can get a player around the board just as fast as forward, right?

Six years, make that seventeen years, have passed, and many things in Israel have altered for the better. Nevertheless, whenever similar incidents still occur . . . as indeed they do . . . the depth of my wintry discontent sometimes seems unfathomable. The reason is that to this very day, not all of us are playing by the same rules. As it happens, Yisroel was that driver's real name, and one may make whatever allegorical capital one likes out of it. There simply are times, my friends, when the Middle Eastern Kulturkampf of the Jews from the East vs. Jews from the West reminds me of little more than an old Bob Gibson tune that could be subtitled "The Yankee's Complaint":

> Eastbound train on a westbound track
> Westbound train on an eastbound track
> Both those trains are runnin' fine
> What a helluva way to run a railway line.

SPRING

MY WIFE and I met in Berkeley in the sixties, a good time and place to be young and in love. After classes, she worked as a cashier at the U.A. Theater on Shattuck, so there was a period when we got to see the middles of some movies and the endings of others, sometimes several times. Not the sort of fare that our friends were seeing—BrealB films like BJules and JimB, or BThe Four Hundred BlowsB—but free was free, and it didn't much matter to us. To this day, Audrey Hepburn goggled-eyed in front of the window of Tiffany's is a household icon redolent of angel dust.

While, as it were, our backs have been turned, the sixties have turned into the nineties, and our children's interest in what exercised our intellectual passions so intensely back then is strictly anecdotal. As for the rest, it's . . . well . . . history. Worse, History, which neither they nor most professional historians will ever get quite right simply because they were not there. Anyway, during that span of decades a lot of Moon River has flowed under the bridge, and our family has relocated, proliferated, gone multigenerational. In Israel, we have undergone our own second coming. For good reason. Here alone is the Jewish people a growth enterprise, do matres- and patresfamilias thrive. In short, we know that we have been lucky, for which we are thankful, but we also are conscious that our major life choices have been fortunate, so we have helped to make our luck.

But now a confession: from time to time, especially as the thickets of Thursday-night preparation for Shabbat dissolve into the frenzy of Friday, when in endless permutations the younger kids, the kids with spouses of their own, the grandkids, the kids returning from boarding school or with friends from the army, our own friends with BtheirB kids, newcomer immigrants (with their immigrant kids) do indeed BcomeB—yes, yes, I exaggerate, but in the cause of higher truth—it has been difficult, even perilous, for the arch of Shabbat to prop a sinking feeling, an inner depression of spirit.

Late one Saturday night in March, after guests had departed, as I was rinsing the last dish, drying a final spoon of the three less than tranquil Shabbat meals, I realized that it was the workaday week of toil and drudgery that loomed subversively before me as an oasis from the hot sands of Shabbat-past. Did I dare give voice to the heretical, ungracious, icy notion that, like a second piece of pecan pie, from time to time even those closest to our affections can sometimes become indigestible? That is not, of course, the way it is supposed to be. But . . . but there it was.

"You too?" my good wife whispered when I cautiously vented my incendiary thoughts. Hah! Our cabal laid, on Sunday we broke word of it to the endearing family we had hatched and loved. We needed a break from Shabbat Ben familleB in Yeroham. A time away, to be by ourselves.

"No problem," chimed sympathetic voices. "With whom will you stay?"

Everyone knows, after all, that Israel's Hiltons, Larommes, and Dans were erected not to service us second-worlders shackled to our shekels but for yen-yoked, dollar-doling camera-toters. The understood expedient for such as we was to do unto others as unto us has ofttimes been done: contrive to get ourselves invited for a Shabbat with Jerusalem pals, kibbutz cronies, no matter who or where . . . just away from our own kith, kin, and kitchen.

Ah, but this was different. Vee veally vonted to be BaloneB. An unshared Shabbat, a selfish Shabbat. Yes! Catered to. Yes! YES! Power to the Parents! And so it happened that the following Friday morning I threw checkbook and a change of clothes into an overnight case, and we flew the coop, leaving Yeroham and Shabbat preparations in the competent hands of the chickens and grandpoultry. If it suited our offspring to splatter food on floor and walls, tear beams from joints, let it all flow! For one of the rare occasions since when we first descended upon Israel as rank tourists scouting out the land, the two of us would simply check ourselves into a hotel.

Two hours later, the conspirators checked into a hospice on Tel Aviv's Hayarkon Street, just across from the blue, blue Mediterranean. It was called the Basel. According to an unimpeachable source, that afternoon the giggly couple from the Negev ordered a platter of cold cuts from room service. Several regulars at the imposing synagogue on Ben-Yehuda Street noticed a couple of out-of-season American tourists at Friday evening services. The maitre d' recalls that she ordered chicken; he, the beef. The rest is silence.

The following morning we once again descended to the dining room for Breakfast at Basel's. Before we could rise to fill our plates, a blonde-tasseled waitress (blouse-tagged Svetlana) filled our cups to the brim with coffee. The buffet was a cornucopia stuffed with smoked herring, pickled herring, jellied herring, soft cheeses, hard cheeses, cottage cheese; overflowing with yogurt plain and fruity, cold cereal, hot cereal, soft rolls, hard rolls, breads, Jell-O, and fresh fruit. As soon as one offering dwindled, it was swiftly replenished by a rubber-soled attendant.

I filled my plate. I ate. I drank. I drank. I ate.

"Another cup of coffee, sir?"

Why not? Another visit to the buffet. Juice. A cheese I hadn't noticed before. What's that fish? A different cereal, another roll, honey. Yet another visitation from solicitous Svetlana. Pace yourself. No rush. Yet another amble to the buttery bar. Just take. Eat. Sip. Take. Not a cup later to rinse, not a dish later to wash. Punctilious me, scrupuloso of the fast of Esther, the fast of the first-born, the fasts of Gedaliah, of Av, of Tammuz, Tevet, and Kippur, I did not bypass a cheese, insult a fish, overlook a salad, or leave a Jell-O mold undefiled.

"Another cup of coffee, sir?"

Dreamily nodding, I sipped very, very slowly. As it spiraled down, the steamy liquid seemed to melt, then utterly dissolve the accumulated store of disaffection which I had freighted inside the day before. I could not inhale another morsel, but I was mightily reluctant to do anything that might hasten lowering the curtain on Breakfast at Basel's. Oh, the ritual, the ambience, the plenitude, the . . . oh . . . BgemutlichkeitB. ("Exactly," my wife smiled in accord.) To be sure, food was the overt matter, but the subtext of this Temple Service was Endless Love. And Salvation. Surely we must deserve this taste of heaven. Like the chosen ones at other tables, we surely must be worthy.

In fact—give a cheese here, take a lox there—the Basel's buffet was much like the one we had enjoyed at the Plaza in '74. It suddenly struck me as remarkable that throughout all those years that I was getting kids off to school, preparing lectures, going off to reserve duty, and all the rest, on all those mornings Irit, Mimiko, Asnat, and Svetlana had been serving up seductive coffee at the interchangeable buffets of the Basel, the Dan, the Hilton, the Hyatt—all Israel's wondrous pleasure domes. What had I been missing? What had I not?

Then, like a sudden, restorative shaft of light, my Shabbat morning folded in upon itself, dissolving into "Sunday Morning," Wallace Stevens' verdant vision of perpetual Shabbat.

> Is there no change in death in paradise?
> Does ripe fruit never fall? Or do the boughs
> Hang always heavy in that perfect sky. . . ?

Had I taken snapshots of all the blessed ones dining at ease in all Israel's hostelries on all those mornings for all those years, and had I run them through on a primitive cinematograph, the sequence of images would have had less consequence than five minutes of Bugs Bunny's outwitting Elmer Fudd. Even in the eternal springtime of Jewish heaven, the richest imaginations of our sages have recoiled at the enormity of devising a plot equal in interest and vitality to a single weekly cycle of our ordinary lives.

The rest of the day? Oh, it was nice, very nice. A walk along the sea, back along the promenade, a visit to Bialik's House, even a promenade among the crowds of children, daddies, and balloonmen along Rehov Dizengoff. Toward its close, seabirds fluttered in the sky over the Mediterranean.

> We live in an old chaos of the sun. . . .
> Deer walk upon our mountains, and the quail
> Whistle about us their spontaneous cries,
> Sweet berries ripen in the wilderness;
> And, in the isolation of the sky,
> At evening, casual flocks of pigeons make
> Ambiguous undulations as they sink,
> Downward to darkness, on extended wings.

That evening, like Holly Golightlies, we nabobs of the Negev glided home to Yeroham. Restored, we could scarcely wait to re-enter the middle of the movie, to hear what ordinary wonders had occurred in our absence.

PART FOUR.
MY AMERICAN PROBLEM
. . . AND OURS

Shuki couldn't at first understand who I said was calling—when he did, he pretended to be stupified. "What's a nice Jewish boy like you doing in a place like this?"

"I come regularly every twenty years to be sure everything's okay."

Philip Roth
(*The Counterlife*)

MY AMERICAN PROBLEM

. . . AND OURS

VERY decade or so *Commentary* editor Norman Podhoretz produces an essay that generates considerable controversy. Most recently, reversing his longstanding refusal to criticize Israeli foreign or defense policies, he wrote "A Statement on the Peace Process" (April 1993). Way back in the early 1960s Podhoretz published his confessional "My Negro Problem—and Ours," an audacious revelation, then dissection, of his ambivalent feelings—he labeled them "twisted"—toward African Americans (still at the time "Negroes"). How I would have recoiled at the notion that thirty years later aliya would precipitate a parallel dilemma for me!

One spring morning in 1992 my friend Chaim Meirsdorf, formerly of Minneapolis, now a photographer in Jerusalem as well as an occasional guide to less familiar corners of the desert, stopped by Yeroham with some daytripping clients—one family from Los Angeles, the second from suburban Philadelphia. Tourists. Businessmen. Forty-something wives topped by babushkas, their husbands by colorful yarmulkehs. Six children were randomly distributed. Their objective: to taste—nay, to consume—a "real Negev experience."

Out of the heart of darkness I produced off-the-beaten-track coffee, Coke, cookies. Their spokesperson, the man of business from L. A., inquired, "So, what's it like to move from California to a small burg in the Negev? Do you really get along with these people here?"

The heavy spin on that final phrase insinuated a complicity from which I inwardly recoiled, but these were matters I had much pondered after all, so, overriding hesitation, I launched into what I thought an adequate response. It was soon apparent, however, that only the sixteen-year-old girl, who was participating in a one-year program in Jerusalem, could sustain even a semblance of interest. Abruptly, I cut myself short:

[To the women:] "But enough of that. I just got an idea. Would you like to tour the house? It's a typical Negev dwelling. For some reason, the natives quaintly label it a *patio.*"

With what relief they instantly rose to their feet! Off we went. Downstairs bedrooms (beds unmade). Garden: plum tree, grapes, flowers (scant interest). Upstairs terrace and, pearl of the *patio,* studiously untidy, my cherished study.

L. A. B-Man: You work on *that* thing [i.e., my antiquated Apple II]!

Ex-Yank: Yep.

L. A.: I brought a PC with our luggage to sell here. State of the art. I'm asking only $4,000.

Wily ex-Yank: You don't say?

L. A. [back downstairs]: Tacky [I overheard him remark to his wife]. Nice [to me]. Thanks a lot. Time we were off to see some ruins. [To my rabbinic friend:] Nabuteans, right?

Friendly guide: You got it!

From doorbell to departure, I had clocked only thirty minutes. For such American types, Jewishness is second, first, and final nature. Very different from the Jewishness of many Russian Jews, fractional Jews, or non-Jewish spouses of Russian Jews I've gotten to know. *Zhids* no more, they are still trying to get a handle on the implications of what being a Jew might mean, especially in a Jewish land. I admire their earnestness, and whenever they inquire about something, their attentiveness. But especially, their humor. Perhaps the clearest indication of the deepening chasm between us ex-U.S.ers and American Jews is that we laugh at different things; at the same things, we laugh differently.

Two months after displaying my home quaint home, it was a group of twelve American high school students, participants in a five-week summer program, who crowded into my living room one afternoon to listen to a "writer" ramble and grumble over facets of Israeli life as well as his former incarnation in K-Mart–land. Similar groups turn up every summer, so I generally know what and whom to expect.

Like Podhoretz in the sixties, I occupied autobiographical terrain, but higher than the adolescent bogs so bloodied in the guerilla campaigns of Chairman Mao Richler, Fidel Roth, or Wooly (Ho Ho) Allen: for me, a gradual affirmation of my Jewish identity, subversion of the ideal of America as destiny's chosen child, and then aliya. Attractive Alison, articulate Jeremy, nearly all the Stacys and Kims were better prepped, more genuinely attentive than many of their predecessors in summers past. Still it came to pass that, sipping iced water cocktails, they tossed off some of the same chunky old chestnuts that, more in sorrow than in anger, they have surely heard their parents utter in a noninterrogatory mode. Like these tough nuts:

(*a*) Do you really believe all Jews should live in Israel?

(*b*) But don't you think it's good that America has a strong Jewish community? Even for Israel's sake?

(*c*) How could Israel survive without the support of American Jews?

(*d*) What makes you so sure American Jewish life has no future?

(*e*) Should American Jews publicly criticize Israel?

(*f*) If you found Vietnam disillusioning when you lived in America, how about Sabra and Shatila?

(*g*) Don't you sometimes regret leaving America?

(*h*) Where's the bathroom?

After years of deploying a variety of strategies, I have despaired of penetrating the vinyl hearts of platonic Zionists of the diaspora. On this occasion, I settled for caustic snappiness: honest partial retorts, some brusque, even bullying.[1] The thing is, the real objective of such questions is to elicit assurance that the interlocutors are also okay. The desideratum? That they are absolved of culpability, blemish, or blame. Some rather more sensitive American Jews seem to require absolution with some frequency. Many others, of course, don't give a damn.

In some respects relations between Israelis and our voluntarily dispersed brethren resemble conciliatory gatherings of Jews and Germans or ecumenical encounters between Jews and Christians. Our very being entails profound ambivalence, a sense of guilt in the *other*. However pleasant the circumstances, good the will, mutual the understanding, or zingy the vibes, the one thing Israelis cannot truly bestow is absolution. Hence, the bafflement, the frustration, the disappointment that clouds even the more "positive" of these occasions.

In the end, Podhoretz admitted that the final solution for his and our Negro problem was—out with it!—miscegenation! Yes, Faulkner's worst nightmare was Podhoretz's grasped straw. Nothing programmatic, mind you, but still merely the most humane, most effective way Podhoretz could then conceive to resolve America's long-running racial melodrama.

The summer preceding these encounters with tourists and high schoolers on my home turf, a woman participant at an international conference of Jewish "progressives" came down from Jerusalem to spend a Shabbat with us in Yeroham. Call her Nitza. Our lives, it seemed, were shooting in opposing trajectories: raised in The Bronx, a decade-long Californian, I now wrote and taught at a university in Israel. Raised in Israel, Nitza taught at a college in New England.

We talked together passionately long after the Shabbat lights flipped off. Nitza had her mitigating circumstances, her *reasons*. Tough circumstances. Terrific reasons. Fiercely noncommittal, empathetically nonjudgmental, I sympathetically comprehended all. Until, that is, Nitza demanded a verdict. She insisted upon a full acquittal. Had Israel left her any choice? What did I really think?

Nitza could not warm to my answer.

Some years after airing his problem to general scrutiny, Podhoretz published *Making It* (Random House, 1967), an account of a promising young man from Brooklyn who scrambled to success in the nut-crunching literary jungles of Manhattan. It's scarcely accidental, then, that the ex-Brooklynite's resolution of his Negro problem and ours was an unscrubbed version of mating it, a strategy that has been vigorously pursued by every third generation of American Jewry from the very start of the Republic. In a Jewish mode, it is assimilation the easy way. Reasons for it have always been . . . well . . . terrific.

After my roomful of teenaged Erics and Melissas had gone their way, one was overheard fulminating, "Why the hell do we get pitches for aliya everywhere we go? I'm perfectly happy being Jewish in America. Why can't Israelis just show us around this postage stamp country and learn to live and let live? Like us Americans!"

Well, unlike Podhoretz and the Negroes, unlike Quentin Compson and the South, deep down I really do not fear or hate these visitors. No; not, I think, even a little. But I must confess that my forbearance has worn exceedingly thin, and I no longer look forward with pleasure to encountering typical Jewish-American visitors when they make my local scene, south of Beersheba. Increasingly, even with their charming kids, feelings twist again, like they did last summer.

Nowadays, when I go to America, aside from family or former colleagues, most of the people I anticipate seeing again bear names like Johnson, Frentz, MacDonald, Corcoran, Weales, Norris, Clarity, Lee. Not, it may be noted, Jewish-sounding names, simply because most of my remaining American friends are not Jews. The reason for this anomaly, I have concluded, is that miles but no stony barrier, no residue of mutual disappointment or recrimination, nothing unsayable separates us.

Yes, it seems to me that my chronic American problem is getting increasingly acute. Truth to tell, I don't much enjoy meeting up with many of them anymore. For the most part, they ask either far too little . . . or too damned much.

NOTE

1. (a) A similar concern was voiced in the Book of Numbers by the tribes of Reuben and Gad. Moses, that Zionist zealot, managed to come up with a decent compromise to salve their consciences. However reluctantly, I could swallow a reasonable equivalent for our fast-fading Robin and Gardner tribes, but I don't mean a tax write-off or two weeks in a five-star hostelry.

(b) In the last analysis, American support for Israel is like anti-Semitism. Both are not much affected by what Jews do or do not do.

(c) You could bet your sweet VISA that Israel surely would survive.

(d) Just raise a finger to the wind on any American university campus: disaffection and intermarriage are merely the rule. My hunch is that at any juncture the actual number of Jews in America is as many as a half-million fewer than official estimates.

(e) Sure, but what I usually read is ill-informed, tasteless, or both.

(f) The differences between Vietnam and Lebanon are far more salient than their spurious similarities.

(g) Nu? I also occasionally regret not having taken piano lessons. The real point is how much more I would have regretted not moving here.

SOMETHING OF A ZIONIST

F ROM RUBBLE wrought, Robert Frost concluded that Something there was that did not love a wall. Although not myself of notably mystical temperament, I too am persuaded of a Something—a force, a presence, a spirit of the place, the taxman who until last year used to surcharge each departing Israeli 250 shekels (around 100 dollars), a personal daemon—that does not wish to release me easily whenever occasion calls for me to fly westerly. Since I take wing annually, after nearly two decades one would think that by now I should have learned all the ropes. Indeed, before each departure, I *think* that I have uncrossed each stitch, untied every knot. In the end, it never, ever works. Always, always in unexpected guise, Something choreographs creative twists of plot, inventive bits of stage action to keep the blasé traveler alert, to make the journey . . . uhh . . . lively.

Consider a prototypical leave-taking. Before departing for a month in the States, I naturally endeavor to leave the family's finances in the least possible disorder. On the Thursday before my Sunday takeoff, in the back of the paper, I chanced to notice a small item stating that on that very Sunday employees at Bank Leumi might be striking. Hah! Little time to spare. On Friday morning, I journeyed twelve kilometers from my Negev home to distant Dimona, seat of the Leumi branch office where I then kept a foreign currency account. Some hours later I returned home, not with cash alone but with the inner glow that comes of having won a skirmish against the configuration of forces Something had begun to marshal against my flight.

My satisfaction was grossly premature; retaliation was swift. The Friday afternoon news report disclosed that Israel's public service employees, including its airport personnel, planned sporadic industrial action for the coming week. Machinations of grand conspiracy! Getting away this year would take all the endurance, craft, and luck I

190

could muster. On Sunday morning, I caught an Egged bus to the Beersheba terminal in ample time to board the Airport Special, only to be informed that the airport bus would not make its normal run.

"Why not?" I inquired of the pretty mouth behind the bars at the information booth, as if anything she said mattered a fig.

"Because it won't," she countered.

I called off hostilities and backed off. It was transparent that the Something truly did not want me to leave, and that was that. Weighing my options only momentarily, I boarded a waiting bus at the dock for Tel Aviv, and only ninety minutes later, schlepped my two suitcases six blocks through the crowded city streets—this was before the recent opening of the world's largest bus terminal in Tel Aviv—to the departure point for buses to Ben-Gurion Airport. Yes, there still remained time to spare . . . if I didn't have to leapfrog any new barriers.

Upon arriving at the airport, I apprehensively scanned the scene for signs of new trouble. Not a whiff of strikers. Confidence surging, I breezed through Security and, upon boarding the aircraft, found no one else occupying my seat. When we took off precisely on time, I foolhardily considered myself as good as in New York. Could Something wield its power beyond the border? Hardly likely. Ahead lay only an overnight stay in Brussels for which I had outfitted myself with Israeli-baked rolls in case the "continental breakfast" I would be served the following morning would prove scanty in kosher sustenance.

Somewhere on the outskirts of Brussels International Airport I slept a victor's sleep, confident that Something was vulnerable, and the following morning I deftly smuggled my kosher contraband with me into the hotel coffee shop. Those two rolls and a cup of coffee would compose my caloric intake until my early afternoon flight. Meanwhile, there was time enough for a stroll through a neighborhood shopping center in the Belgian capital, a city devoted to multinationals and the filling of the belly. Shop window after window displayed regiments of cakes and fruit tortes, gorgeous chunks of cheese, sumptuous cuts of meat. By the time a load of carefree travelers boarded the special bus from the hotel to the Brussels international airport for the final thrust toward New York, there was among them one hungry Israeli traveler.

Midday street traffic was surprisingly heavy; the bus barely crawled until, finally, congestion thickened into sheer stalemate. After ten minutes, a fellow sufferer accosted the driver.

"Oh, today the ground workers are mounting an industrial action, sir," the driver replied.

"A STRIKE!" groaned a chorus of Israelis.

"Yes," the driver blandly verified as if to a load of schoolchildren. "You know, an industrial action."

"How long will it take us to get moving?"

"Who knows? That's the picket line just ahead of us."

Indeed there was.

"How far is it to the airport from here?" one clear-headed passenger, not from Yeroham, thought to inquire ten minutes later.

"Not far," replied the driver jauntily. "Just two blocks ahead and then to a short distance to the right."

Several of us immediately fetched our bags and began to trudge to the airport. Perhaps the strikers would react violently? Not a bit. Without incident, we penetrated the double line of marching airport workers. Then, my two cases getting heavier by the step, we turned right and walked and walked and walked. Who would have guessed that having artfully threaded the needle of an Israeli airport strike I would fall victim to Something of the sort in Brussels!

Bearing and gallantly grinning, eventually even I arrived at the terminal and settled down to await the early afternoon flight to New York. Surely little more could happen, and the walk had sharpened my appetite. With only ninety minutes to flight time, however, I could await my airborne heated, tinfoiled victuals with tranquillity.

Just then I noticed that although the departure board still listed the New York flight "on time," it had been sandwiched by flights to Toulouse, Frankfurt, Zurich, Birmingham, each of which was menacingly preceded by a cute little asterisk. Meaning? A delay of two to three hours. Might somehow New York yet prove the golden exception?

Fat chance! Like lemons and cherries on a one-armed bandit, at four different times in the following hour, and then the hour after that, and then yet one hour more, the numbers adjacent to New York spun higher and higher. It was a weary three-and-a-half hours later that we New-York–bound passengers crowded at the window to watch white-shirted, cravatted front-office personnel clumsily load our luggage into the gut of the 747. It was yet an hour later, my gastric juices rumbling in competition with the airplane's engines, that I climbed the steps to the open door of our waiting jet.

Lightheaded from hunger, I summoned forth a terminal, tactless comment in the terminal for a fellow sufferer, a kibbutznik I had engaged in conversation. "My only consolation is that airlines always serve kosher meals first."

"Hmmph," was the sum of his ill-natured reply.

Twenty minutes later, belted in, restored by a slug of orange juice, I watched the team of fresh-faced Sabena flight attendants on the starboard side of the craft push and pull a meal cart from the front of the plane. Like a vaguely remembered dream, an ominous germ of concern registered in the lower layers of consciousness. Slapping it down as I would a mosquito, I refused to countenance its presence.

"Excuse me," I inquired with a gracious smile as two flight attendants finally reached abreast of my row. Something in me already knew the worst. "Have you forgotten that I ordered a kosher meal?"

"Oh, weren't you informed?" the taller one responded pertly. "Because of the industrial action, we could not receive the special meals at the airport."

My mouth fell open. No words issued from my throat, and there was no tidbit with which to fill it. It would not surprise me to learn from an eyewitness that my tongue was lolling.

"But," the young woman assured me enthusiasically, "we do have fresh fruit and nuts. Would they be all right?"

"Well, I suppose they must," I returned weakly. It was, after all, not her fault. It was not anybody's fault; it was just Something that always happens. And while I worked my way through an orange, an apple, four packets of assorted nuts, and a shapely kiwi, I spied my kibbutz companion two rows ahead impassively consuming his savory meal. Belgians are, after all, particularly noted for love of good food and drink. Three strikes. I was out. A small solace—the kiwi that sustained me was probably nurtured not far from my Negev home.

Looking back, I can discern reason to take some comfort in all this. Something there is, you see, that knows substantial cause for ensuring that a former American's departures from home to his former homeland not be straightforward, not be easy, not pleasant . . . or *normal*. Viewed in a reflective light—from my study in Yeroham, a town that prior to 1948 did not exist—there is something reassuring in that.

THIRSTY
IN FRESNO

W HENEVER Americans—the least accountable of Israel's immigrants—fly off for longer than a few weeks, no matter
how unimpeachable their motives, a vapor of suspicion lin-
gers behind. Grounds are ample. Item: in 1983, under the rubric
"From Kalinga [sic] to Yeroham," a photo of Marcia, our two
American-born children, my own grinning visage, and a three-
paragraph tale of Zionist fulfillment graced a Jewish Agency promo-
tional poster. It featured six other photos and similiar vignettes as well.
Even before that poster was issued, two of the other six life studies
had flown from the country for the greater world.

In November of 1986, exactly a decade after decamping from California for new lives in the Negev, Marcia and I returned to the States
for an open-ended American visit—a self-appointed "sabbatical" to
Fresno with Shai and Miriam, then nine and seven.

In the ten years since we had left, the only occasion when Fresno
had made the Israeli news was in 1983 when a major earthquake
shook up the southeast corner of Fresno County. (Seven years, exactly
one postearthquake decade later the town would hit the Israeli air-
waves again when two good ol' boys, tossed bodily out of a bar, returned a few hours later to gun down everyone in sight.) Nor in 1986
had things been going well for Fresno's good name back in the States.
In a much-publicized, computerized listing of U.S. metropolitan
areas ranked for "livability," its tight syndrome of grueling summers,
foggy winters, puce-tinted skies, and chronic unemployment had consigned Fresno a placement of dead last. Rubbing satiric salt into the
wound, *Fresno*, a feeble Carole Burnett spoof of *Dallas*, was being
aired weekly.

The city-limits sign on Highway 99 south of the city proclaimed
its population to stand at 250,000, about double what it had been in

194

1961 when first I had arrived here, apprehensively busing over the Coastal Range from my army base at Monterey. My objective? A first meeting with my future wife's parents. In any event, notwithstanding weather, welfare, and Burnett, the prognostication is that within fifty years Fresno will embrace 1 million souls. And despite its low viability rating, Fresno's tossed salad of Armenians, Oakies, Japanese, Chicanos, Italians, African Americans, Basques, and Southeast Asia Hmong has always seemed to me a zesty mix. Jews? Aiii, there was the rub. The estimate in 1986 still hovered around two thousand, the same figure folks had bandied about back in the sixties.

On the first Shabbat back in town, Friday evening's taste of treacly Manishewitz evoked a specifically American Jewish past. Come morning, I hiked two miles down Fruit to Shields and Congregation Beth Jacob to attend services. *Shachrit* was conducted by an old friend, the only member of the community who had ever visited us in Israel. He was assisted by a younger man, a refugee from the Tel Aviv suburb of B'nei Brak, bastion of Orthodoxy, who delivered a disconcertingly earnest sermon. Dispatched to Central California by a New York kosher winery, then fired and stranded on this interior shore, he clung like a vine to his newfound mission to bring *yiddishkeit* to Fresno.

"They are thirsty," he later insisted, "for the real thing."

The local Jewry he confronted that Shabbat morning comprised altogether twenty souls: fourteen vintage males; two boys (the son of the president and a prospective bar mitzvah), three women, and a young girl. The only regular distaff attendee turned out to be a Seventh Day Adventist in need of quenching. Wherever Fresno's other give-or-take 1,981 Jews might be found on a typical Saturday morning, it was surely not at the city's other synagogue—Congregation Beth Israel (Reform)—which long before had entirely dispensed with Saturday morning services. The yield? On a normal Shabbat morning, synagogue attendance in Fresno fluctuated between a heady 1-to-2 per cent of its potential.

Several days later we enrolled our children at the Powers School, a mile's walk from my mother-in-law's home. Their adjustment to secularism turned out to be bewilderingly rapid. Shai decided for the nonce to be "Jesse." A visitor from Israel, to be sure, but disburdened of yarmulke, he delighted in sharing his new tag with Messrs. Helms and Jackson, two frequent players on the six o'clock news. We did not quarrel with the logic of his decision. What more has America ever meant for newcomers than the possibility of a shiny new identity?

However, our arrival was inauspiciously timed for our son-the-assimilationist: the week before Christmas vacation, both second-and fourth-grade teachers issued urgent requests for classroom talks on "Hanukkah in Israel" for the series "Christmases Around the World." Noblesse oblige: my first public performance in America would be an afternoon talk about Hanukkah with a Menorah-lighting demonstration for second-graders. Ten minutes later, hands fluttered from every quarter.

"Where is Israel?"

"What do people do there?"

"Is it dangerous?"

"Do only Jewish people live there?"

"Why do you wear that little round beanie on your head?"

Overcoming reluctance, Jesse performed the same service for his new fourth grade classmates, and then was borrowed for an encore by an otherwise bereft fifth grade. Strange? Was this not, after all, a middle-class neighborhood? Surely there were plenty of Jews living here. Were they all lying low? Or simply lying.

Meanwhile, my own colorful, crocheted yarmulke doubled as a lightning rod; the charge was usually positive. While standing in line at the Department of Motor Vehicles, for example, I was approached by a vaguely familiar figure in his late forties.

"New in Fresno? I'm Don P."

"I *thought* I recognized you," I countered. "Not really new. I used to live in Coalinga. You and your wife visited us when you were contemplating moving to Israel. It must have been twelve years ago. We're here for a visit."

"I remember now. Well, in the end we decided to stay put here in Fresno. My wife couldn't possibly have adjusted to Israel."

"So how is Jewish life in Fresno?"

"Not bad at all," he assured me. "I don't go to any synagogue, but a small group of us do a lot of Jewish things together. Like last year we baked our own matzos and made our own wine for Passover. And every morning I *daven* while I'm out jogging."

"Come again?"

"I pray while I jog . . . at the same time."

By good fortune, just then my turn came round with the clerk.

"Good seeing you again, Don."

Unprepared for the change wrought by the passage of ten years, I had anticipated that our children would walk to and from school by themselves. Not a chance. Americans were now afraid to allow grade-schoolers to walk abroad unsupervised. Every child was either bused or met by a parent in the school parking lot. Some weeks later we heard Fresno's year-end homicide stats: the "All-American City" had notched nearly four hundred murders—more than one a day! Surely double-to-triple the annual toll in "dangerous Israel."

Most days I combined meeting the children with walking Patrick, my niece's Irish Setter. A number of householders along that mile stretch of Arthur Avenue, a thoroughfare of sprawling junipers, gnarled cypresses, and expansive lawns, greeted us. Although signs at every corner proclaimed NEIGHBORHOOD WATCH: Strangers Will Be Reported to the Police, to the best of my knowledge, no one ever reported the presence of a bearded stranger in his forties with the doily on his head. Perhaps I owe this to Patrick, my friendly guarantor.

With Jen and Ted managing by themselves back in Israel, the spirit of mercantilism in the air, we celebrated an arid little Hanukkah that year. To most passers-by, the nightly play of our candlelight in the neighborhood's sole Menorah likely signified zero. My friend at Beth Jacob invited the kids to a presentation of an animated film about Hanukkah; only Miriam could be cajoled. Perhaps twenty kids were on hand. The screen was small, the sound unsynchronized, the children squirmy: once again Sunday School had worked its old gray magic.

In a classroom lottery, Jesse drew Mission Dolores of San Francisco for his "project," a matter fraught with ambiguity. Whereas in Israel "missionary" carries a pejorative burden, in California padres were the heroic founding fathers. In order to help Jesse construct his scale model of the mission, we undertook an excursion to the Bay Area. At the Hillel House in Berkeley, where twenty-four years before we had been married, Marcia and I were informed that the entire East Bay could not boast a single kosher eatery. But over in San Francisco, we were assured, flourished a Chinese vegetarian palace that had received rabbinic approval. We took what nourishment we could from apples, crackers, and visions of the morrow's Oriental feast.

After a morning of wandering mossy paths in Muir Woods and around claustrophobic Mission Dolores, stomachs rumbling, we pointed our vehicle toward the succor of Chinatown. The circumnavigation of Union Square through the pre-Christmas crowd of shoppers took a full hour. Little matter for pilgrims! From two blocks away, I made out the large, beckoning sign—LOTUS GARDEN.

"Come on! Come on!" I intoned, feigning heartiness to my flagging family. "It's no mirage! There it stands."

Moments later we stood like wraiths before the locked glass door. Affixed was a neatly typed little card: "The Lotus Garden will be closed from December 23rd–26th. We appreciate your patronage." I was completely undone. Over a forty-eight–hour stretch, a light lunch at the Office of *Tikkun* in Oakland had been our only repast. Only to those still credulous about the "renaissance of Jewishness in America" could this have come to pass. Marcia captained us across Market Street and out, out, and away from the dolorous City of Gold.

At a New Year's Eve gathering at the home of old friends, several couples were *yordim*—Israelis who moved to the U.S. Agribusiness-capital Fresno is a magnet for the drip-irrigation crowd—an Israeli, that is, ex-Israeli, specialty. It wasn't until after midnight that I found myself conversing with an attractive *yoredet*, a mother of two, who taught folk dancing at the Jewish Community Center.

"Of *course* we're coming back to Israel," she replied with alacrity. "We've never really left. We speak only Hebrew with the children, and go back to Herzliya several times a year."

From the beginning of January, I settled into a comfortable regimen. Writing during the morning hours on a word processor at the home of old friends, I would bear intimate witness to the poignancy of Jewish parenting in America. Citing internecine warfare among Fresno's Jews, the couple had removed themselves from all synagogue affiliations, but, astonishingly, two of their children had committed themselves to an "observant lifestyle." Ingenuously, I congratulated them on having so successfully inculcated strong Jewish attachment in their children. Where so many others have failed, my friend and his wife had succeeded.

He would have none of it. The Jewish consciousness of two of his children pleased him little more than the hang-loosedess of the third or the conventionality of the fourth. Each in his or her own way seemed determined to reject a devoted father's best dreams. Had I remained in America, would I have done any better with Shai, a.k.a.

Jesse? Or with butterfly Miri, soon to be invited to her first slumber party?

We forwent the language instruction California mandates for children whose native tongue is not English, but I was uncomfortable that our kids actually *liked* going to school in America. Even ten years after the stringencies of the California tax rebellion, the plenitude of an ordinary California classroom, a sharp contrast to the spartan patchiness of its Israeli counterpart, was dazzling. Here they were bestowed not only books and pencils but crayons! America! After a few weeks Miriam was scoring hundreds on her weekly spelling tests, and Jesse would be first in his class to complete his mission model.

One afternoon Jesse, Patrick, and I found ourselves walking in tandem with an elderly man who had turned onto Arthur Avenue from a cross street. He sported a florid mustache, a peaked cap, and baggy walking shorts. Elbows pumping, fulsomely puffing, shoulders hunched, he was the duck-strutting reincarnation of Groucho.

"I don't do this for fun, you know," he muttered gravely, pointing at his chest. Was I imagining a trace of *Mittel-Europa* in his voice? "Doctor's orders. I had a bypass." Jesse eyed him stealthily. "Would you guess I was seventy-two?" I shook my head. "I own that house on the corner. Been trying to buy the empty lot across the street from the woman who owns it. People use it for a weed dump. But she won't sell."

"Maybe you should raise your offer?" I suggested, warming to the friendly codger. This was, after all, my ice-breaking conversation on Arthur Ave. Where might it lead?

"Nah! That's not what she wants." He hesitated for just a moment. "Let me tell you something you won't believe, and that no one will tell you, Sonny. It's a great day when the glands finally leave a man in peace. That's the day when he finally feels free."

Upon imparting this hard-won nugget, he turned at his own corner and marched past the very lot he had unsuccessfully tried to purchase from his glandular neighbor.

"That's right, young fella," he called, "and I aim to celebrate my one hundred and twentieth birthday."

"Bye!" Jesse yelled after him with a shrug of his young shoulders.

Later that week Marcia and I drove to visit another old friend, this time for brunch. The husband who once shared this house had long since left the scene; in his place was someone new, someone not Jewish. What of her son, the troubled adolescent?

"Oh, Niles is a physicist at Cal Tech."

"A physicist. Terrific!"

"But it wasn't easy," she hastened to add. "He used to wreck things. For a long time, he refused to study; then he dropped out of high school entirely. At eighteen, he left home to join a motorcyle gang. Postcards arrived from Denver, Chicago, all over."

"Well, at least he kept in touch." But she wasn't laughing.

"I never knew where he was or what he was doing. It turns out that for a while he was involved with the Nazis."

"Nazis!"

"Well, it was just a phase, but they were Nazis all right. After eighteen months, he came back and decided to go to the university. Today he's at Cal Tech, but we're not very close. It's all too much for me to understand."

Walking home after services that week, two blocks north of Shields I thought a Jew-hating thunderbolt had finally struck. Heavy footsteps tracked me from behind. Fists clenched, I warily pivoted and confronted a young man in an open white shirt. On his head sat a black satin yarmulke.

"Shabbat Shalom!"

"Shabbat Shalom! My wife told me that she saw a bearded man wearing a *kippa* pass earlier. I didn't think it was possible. We live in Los Angeles; we're visiting my in-laws for Shabbat."

"In-laws? Who are your in-laws?" I asked tactlessly.

"You wouldn't know them. My wife's a convert." Plainly, there was something on his mind. "The thing is, Fresno would be much cheaper than L.A., and we like it well enough. What's the situation here for raising a Jewish family?"

I was struck by the notion of how the two of us would look from afar, say on a satellite photo: two gesticulating figures conferring for twenty minutes on an unlikely street corner. Fresno. Saturday. Label it "Visitors." I could not not offer him much grounds for local Jewish hope. But why, I later wondered, did someone concerned about raising Jewish children confine himself to a choice between Los Angeles and Fresno?

That week we visited friends in Coalinga, sixty miles to the southwest. The sign at the town's edge still ominously announced JESUS

IS LORD OF COALINGA followed by a listing of twenty local churches. Before returning to Fresno, while Marcia disappeared into a fast food shop, I stopped to refuel at the Union 76 on Elm.

"Are you folks really Jews?" the young attendant inquired through the curve of the windshield.

I nodded.

"My wife wears the same sort of kerchief over her hair as yours. I think we're pretty much the same as you Jews. We're not Trinitarians. You from here?"

"Just visiting now. I used to teach at the community college. We moved to Israel . . . the Holy Land . . . ten years ago. What *are* you and your wife?"

"We're with the monotheist branch of Seventh Day Adventists. Lots of Adventists believe in three gods, but we believe in one. I'd love to visit Israel some day. Say, what do you Jews make of Jesus?"

I handed over a credit card. For a fleeting moment, I was tempted by honesty. In the nick of time, Marcia turned up bearing a box of crackers that had passed muster. "Well, we have a lot in common, it seems. Been nice talkin' to you. Good luck."

"Sure 'nough. Have a nice day."

The next afternoon, driving a block from Powers, Miriam at my side, I was signaled by steady honking from behind. What now? A young woman pulled up parallel. Beside her sat a little girl.

"I spotted your *kippa*. We'd heard that there were visitors from Israel at the school. My husband and I met in Jerusalem. Lived there for a year. Our daughter is a first-grader. Perhaps your . . ."

" . . . Miri . . ."

" . . . Miri would like to play with our Anat after school some time?"

For our few remaining weeks in Fresno, I regularly drove our daughter to play at Anat's rambling house. Although their street retained an air of gentility, the surrounding neighborhood suffered from the steady encroachment of rentals and multiple dwellings. Anat's father headed Fresno's chapter of B'nai Brith. On the second visit, I ventured the inevitable.

"We love Israel," she responded, "but you can see how we live here. . . ."

" . . . !"

Even with people I liked well enough, I was getting testy. The time had come to fix a date to return home. But first a chore. I had been snookered into speaking about Israel to the progressive ladies of the local chapter of the Women's International League for Peace and Freedom. "Israel's been drawing a lot of flak from some members, especially several of the Jewish ones," I was forewarned.

The only time WILPF could gather was on Saturday. Lacking Don P.'s versatility, after *davening* I walked two miles along tree-shaded streets to a home where twenty-five women had gathered to hear "an authentic spokesman of the Israeli peace community." Was I truly that? Feeling half an imposter, en route I fashioned my rhetorical strategy. Granting at the outset that Israel had an urgent need to talk directly to Palestinians and that the Palestinian cause was . . . umm . . . not without merit, what I actually spoke about were its manifest deficiencies.

Thirty minutes later, Question Time. My host had whispered that the *real* Israel-baiters had not come. Just as well. A young woman prefaced her remarks by noting that her first husband had been a Palestinian. Little to fear from *that* quarter. A college student asked what Progressives in America could do to promote peace between Israelis and Palestinians. How duplicitous dared I be?

What *about* the Israeli Left?

Finally, I was done. A woman in her fifties, blue-tinted coif swept into a beehive, approached with a beatific smile. She seemed more the canasta than the parlor-meeting type. Slyer than she appeared, she clasped both my hands in hers. "I loved your talk, Professor Chertok. You don't know how good it makes me feel to know that the likes of *you* are over *there*."

Touché.

Next day via Miri came a request to address Fresno's chapter of B'nai Brith. The city's per capita level of Jewish giving, I was informed, was dead last among all major American cities. More grist for Carol Burnett. But too late. I had transacted all of the Jewish-American business for which I had taste. Honda sold, five days later we were headed back *there*.

Over the Atlantic, at the back of the airplane, I joined a *minyan* predominantly composed of ultra-Orthodox Jews. For the occasion, we felt joined. At Brussels airport, however, where we had to confirm seats for the second leg of the flight, I chose the line of eight miscellaneous travelers rather than the one consisting of just three dark-garbed coreligionists. As I'd anticipated, I reached my clerk before even the second in the more disputatious line could be dealt with. The closer I got to Israel, the less I could afford sentimentality.

Yes, once again I had experienced how Jews live in America. In the course of five months, we had encountered only one person who had expressed a real thirst to visit Israel. It was my fellow monotheist, the high octane gunner of Coalinga.

RUBBER

JEWS

TWO SUMMERS later, needing to spend five weeks in Los Angeles, I stayed at the home of an old army friend and his family who lived one block from Venice Boulevard—a "transition" zone bordering middle class and proletarian terrains. On occasion, the better part of valor led me to resort to plopping his son's visored cap over my *kippa*. In a flash, the visiting Israeli Jew magically disappeared beneath the rubric WILLY NELSON AND HIS FRIENDS. Was I practicing concealment? No doubt. Deception? A somewhat knottier matter, but without question my petty internalization of the diaspora jeebees would soon converge with a larger duplicity.

I arranged to spend a Shabbat with members of a young and growing Orthodox congregation in Venice. Fronting the very edge of Pacific surf, Venice seemed an uncongenial locale for traditional Judaism to take root, and yet a well-known experiment in resurgent Orthodoxy had apparently been thriving there for more than a decade. Most of the members of the community were either converts or "returnees" to Judaism; many of them had built or purchased houses on contiguous plots. Others lived as close as possible.

On Friday afternoon, I was received cordially by a lawyer and his wife at their home. Joined by four other male congregants, conspicuously got up in ties and jackets, we briskly walked the half-mile stretch through posthippie, working-class streets, toward their oceanfront synagogue. At a street corner, a harsh voice called out from a passing car.

"STINKING Jews! Go back to Israel, you stinking JEWS."

No one responded. Indeed, no one gave the least sign that anything had been said, that anything had been heard. It was if nothing unusual at all had happened.

After services, I dined with three young, yuppish, joshy, allrightnik couples. The following day, another shock of confrontation: upon emerging at noon from the formality of the ornate, decorous, refurbished synagogue, we braved the glare, the bare, the dare of the beach!

I was one of five guests invited to eat at the sprawling home of a couple, both established writers. The man, a film critic, entertained us by prompting their two-year-old to display her prodigious musical memory. The table conversation evoked stability, solidity . . . yes, smugness. Nevertheless, something real was here; something to ponder as well about Jewish possibilities under the California sun.

Upon my return to the border zone after sundown, my eye was drawn to an article on the front page of the morning's *Los Angeles Times*: KEY FIGURE IN SLUM SUIT IN DEFAULT ON MAJOR LOANS. The subhead read "Hundreds of L. A. Investors Involved." The "key figure" was a seventy-year-old "respected figure in Los Angeles Jewish circles for thirty years." Reading on, I was startled to learn that the lawyer for two of the dummy corporations turned out to be my overnight host on Shabbat. An investor quoted at length by the reporter was none other than my luncheon host. The congregation's prominent rabbi's extenuating words for the accused were quoted at length. In fact, the article indicated that no fewer than *twenty-three families* of that beachfront congregation had made substantial investments and outrageous profits in furthering a complicated scam at the expense of the poverty-stricken.

Aside from the involvement of so many "good Jews" in something so unseemly, indeed repulsive, there was something else that was very queer. I had spent an entire day *davening*, dining, and talking in the company of members of this congregation. Table conversation had ranged from the characteristics of French Jewry, Tisha B'Av study sessions, and Kahaneism to divorce counseling, Mormons, and the filming of *Batman*. True, I had noted traces of self-consciousness and strained formality not common in Israel, but I was perfectly capable in Venice of doing as the Venetians.

Yes, inevitably, on several occasions pecuniary matters had been skirted, but they were quickly passed over. Although this scandal, which intimately touched the pillars of that community, had that very day exploded on the front page of the *L. A. Times*, as if by collective instinct, not a whisper of it passed the lips of the people I encountered. The only hint I could retrospectively retrieve had been what had seemed a cryptic allusion in the rabbi's Saturday morning sermon.

He had likened the Jewish people to rubber balls: the harder they were tossed to the ground, the higher they bounced back.

Well, wasn't this discretion in the presence of guests admirable, particularly on Shabbat? Perhaps, in a fashion, it was, and yet why then did I feel so conned? There was the scandal itself, to be sure, but equally noxious was the odor of cover-up, of hypocrisy. Certainly Israeli Jews are equally vulnerable to the temptation of sleazy, easy money. What I think almost inconceivable, however, is that under parallel circumstances a visitor to an Israeli household over a twenty-four–hour period—Orthodox or secular, on Shabbat or any other day of the week—would have heard or sensed nothing of what was foremost on most people's minds.

Perhaps it's just that we Israelis no longer feel the need to practice the sort of instinctive concealment still practiced by so many Willy Nelson American Jews, both those outside the "American Jewish community" and those positioned within. As for the good merchants of Venice, this rubber check may seem poor payment for their hospitality, but I am constrained to remark that they can scarcely fathom how abnormal their normality appeared to a casual visitor from Israel.

CODA.

WITLESS IN THE NEGEV

THE WEDDING hall in Beersheba was located just one block from the central bus station, so although we could not set out from Yeroham until sundown drew nigh, we were confident of arriving for the start of the ceremony. In fact, the darkness that heralded the eighteenth of Tammuz was just congealing as we entered the cavernous chamber.

Ranged around the crowded tables were dozens of broad, round East European faces. It was more like an aggregation of my resurrected great-uncles and -aunts attending one of their "affairs" than of leaner, angular faces with which I had grown familiar. The four-piece group, which all evening would alternate between Russian and Israeli tunes, was broadcasting a bouncy, Cossack melody. Too loud . . . yes, . . . but as these things go in Israel, not intolerable.

From across the festive ballroom Marcia spotted several of her co-workers from the Desert Research Center. As we inched our way between the tables and the roaming waiters, I scanned the room for Russian acquaintances from my army reserve unit. Not a one. We were famished. It had now passed 8:20; another year's fast of the seventeenth of Tammuz was closing out. Ay-men! Time for an ice-breaking olive and quick Cola quench, then a first pass at the food piled at the buffet.

At that precise moment, however, my momentum was frustrated by the approach of a young, dark-suited, bearded man, his head covered by a black satin yarmulke. The presiding rabbi was unmistakably headed straight for me! Should I have recognized him from a past function? Did he teach at my son's yeshiva? Would he offer an explanation, even an apology, for agreeing to officiate at a wedding on such an inauspicious date? Or perhaps the seventeenth still harbored a wisp of waning life. Would I be chided for dispatching it prematurely?

"Mazel tov!" he greeted me mechanically. "You will be my *e'd*—
the witness," he peremptorily ordered.

"I, the *e'd*!" I dumbly repeated. "I scarcely know a soul here. Also,
I've never been an *e'd* before. Are you sure it's me you want?"

Punctuating my demur, my stomach chose that moment to emulate
Vesuvius. The assignment seemed gratuitous, unfathomable. Under
the circumstances, it was a daunting prospect.

"Of course, I'm sure," the young rabbi insisted. "It's a mitzvah. I
was waiting for you to turn up. When I motion, come under the
wedding canopy. All you have to do is to hold the wine bottle and a
glass and follow instructions." Before I could lodge further protest,
he strode away. Marcia could scarcely contain her amusement. *I* was
the chosen one at the wedding feast. Why? Before I could spear another olive from the salads at our table, she had it figured out. "Look
around you!"

"I'm looking." Was I dense from lack of nourishment?

"How many bearded people do you see? How many men's heads
are covered?" In fact, there *was* one other aberration, an elderly scare-
crow at a distant corner table. But he, the rabbi, and I were the sum
total! Unlike secular Jewish academics at Chapel Hill or Berkeley,
secular Russian Jews were clean-shaven. The rabbi who had been
assigned to this wedding on a night following a day of fast must have
been close to despair awaiting the appearance of a suitable looking *e'd*
to appear. At the penultimate moment, I—his good spirit, his Ariel—
had been conjured.

I managed to consume yet one more spoonful of spicy olives, but
before I could temper it with even a single sip of suds, the imperious
summons to stand under the canopy was signaled, my second call to
distinction that day. I rose to my appointed mission and—man of
mystery—took my position at the very center of the ballroom.

This was the first time I had ever glimpsed dark-haired Varva; even
behind her veil it was obvious that she was a very pretty young woman.
I nodded solemnly at young Boris, the unassuming groom. Confus-
edly, he returned a subdued nod to the total stranger at his side who
bore a bottle of wine. If they had followed traditional Jewish nuptial
custom, the young couple would have fasted the day before their
wedding in any event, but I thought it unlikely. Thanks to the breach
in the walls of Jerusalem, the rabbi and I had in a fashion acted as their

symbolic stand-ins. Perhaps it would be propitious for their future? Or mine?

I had met Varva's mother just once before, at another wedding of a coworker's daughter. Was I a cousin of the groom? She clearly could not place this husband of her workmate. I, however, was privileged with superior knowledge: according to my wife, Mama was less than pleased that her daughter had chosen to marry so soon after completing her army service and before attending university.

The bride nibbled at her pretty lip. (Perhaps she had fasted after all?) Her mother glanced nervously at her watch. Was it late? Was I somehow at fault? Had I a free hand, I would have checked my fly. Too late. The rabbi began to intone. Mildly apprehensive of committing that day yet one more faux pas, I stood with a bottle of wine in one hand, a wineglass in the other, and avuncular if meandering thoughts. Video lights and every eye focused on the tableau at the center of the large hall. If a wild-haired creature pushing a stroller of menace should suddenly intrude upon the ceremony, if she should begin to rain imprecations down upon the young couple, it would surely fall to the *e'd* to blast the uninvited wedding guest with his bottle of red.

I began to ruminate on the potential of my official role as unlikely aide to the wedding party, to relish its subtle possibilities. Did the *e'd* have a ritual function that extended beyond this inauguratory evening? Did he appear at anniversaries and such just . . . oh . . . to offer a word or two of advice or to check on how the marriage was going? I thought not, but Judaism being Judaism, who could be entirely sure? Even the video camera recoiled at my errant thoughts.

If the marriage held—what American-bred demon issued *that* insurgent thought?—whenever Varva and Boris would play the video again, a fur-lined Russian voice would surely query, "Who the hell *is* that guy holding the wine and the cup, anyway?" And Varva's mother would recall, "He's the husband of Masha [sic]—she works at the lab—the official *e'd*." From the lower depths, my rebel stomach again made protest. I glanced sidewise; no one seemed to notice.

Roused from reverie by rabbinic grimace, I filled the cup and automatically but loudly responded to the benedictions. Was I really the only one in the hall saying *Ah-mayn*? It certainly seemed the case. Neither of the celebrants had any notion when to pass the cup, when to sip, or when just to abide. The real mystery was what stray or deep-seated impulse had brought so many of these Russian Jews to have chosen neither an American nor an Australian but an Israeli fate?

A ring materialized, words were repeated, and, although it took a second attempt, an innocent, cloth-wrapped cup splintered under the boot of the groom. Jewish custard pie in the face! Then cries of mazel tov filled the room. Like the fast of the seventeenth itself, this joyful shattering at weddings was supposed to evoke the fall of temples, sadness in the midst of celebration.

A final service rendered to the newly joined couple: attesting that the wedding had proceeded properly, I duly affixed my name to the official marriage agreement—the *ketuba*. There were spaces for two witnessing signatures, but only one *e'd* on hand to sign. And he was such a duplicitous, unreliable sort of witness whose brain had taken temporary refuge in his stomach. What good could it bode for the young couple? The rabbi would have to figure out how to deal with the blank space.

Then the ceremony was done, and in officious tones, following custom, the rabbi read the terms of the *ketuba* aloud. At the very end, the names of the wedding party were pronounced for the assembly. "Haim Chertok of Yeroham," supporting player, imperfect stranger to virtually everyone, had served as official *e'd* to the wedding party. Aside from gastric growls, he had acquitted himself without mishap. In the end, the fast of the seventeenth succumbed to kozatskys, sambas, schnapps, Russians, and the wedding feast of the eighteenth—elegy to redemptive Jewish comedy.